The Dictionary
of Useful Plants

The Dictionary

Nelson Coon

# of Useful Plants

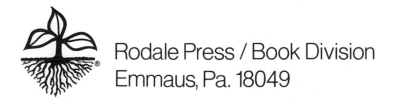

Rodale Press / Book Division
Emmaus, Pa. 18049

Library of Congress Cataloging in Publication Data

Coon, Nelson.
    The dictionary of useful plants.

    Includes bibliographies.
    1. Plants, Useful. I. Title.
Qk 98. 4. C66   581. 6 ' 1 ' 03   74-14947
ISBN 0-87857-090-X

Contents

Preface

*"And God said, Behold, I have given
you every herb bearing seed, which is
upon the face of all the earth, and every
tree, in the which is the fruit of a tree
yielding seed; to you it shall be for
meat."*
Genesis 1:29

In introducing this book to the reader, there may be two questions that come to the reader's mind—Why such a book? With what background does the author write it? My reasons roughly are these:

When, out of personal experience, I wrote *Using Wayside Plants,* in 1956–57, it was written with the Northeastern United States in mind, as that was what I knew. From that book grew my book on *Using Plants For Healing* and later, from experiences in working with blind people, my book on the importance of the sense of smell and of fragrant plants. But as the sales of *Wayside Plants* have reached an audience from coast to coast, I have realized that, although many of the plants were indeed found on the Pacific Coast, and far north and south, my books did not provide a compendious knowledge of the useful and edible plants of various areas such as the Rockies, the Southwest, the Northwest, and the like, all of which had a flora in part peculiar to its soils and climate.

Thus I came to feel that a more comprehensive reference work was needed, one which would pick out the most valuable useful plants of all parts of the United States, calling attention to the special merits of the plants. From my years as a professional librarian, I realized that libraries especially might want to have such a book on their shelves, as well as the many people presently much interested in conservation, ecology, health foods, etc.

I know that I have been asked often if I myself have a knowledge of, and myself use, the plants which are mentioned in this book, and here I can only refer to my original interest in the subject, which began in my childhood when I had to help my grandfather gather and boil down maple sap; when I had to pick sweet wild black cherries for my mother to dry or can; when I had to gather wild dock to use as greens instead of spinach or wild asparagus instead of buying it; or gather, in summer, all the black or red raspberries which grew in the Hudson Valley fields.

In later life living in an area populated largely by southern Europeans, I noted their great use of dandelion and chicory as a spring health measure, and I came to know mushroom experts, who told of their values. Living now on Martha's Vineyard, I have gathered many of the plants for home use that this book discusses. Elderberries, chokecherries, bayberries, blueberries, cranberries, rosehips, and many another natural bounty are gathered and gladly used.

Again as to medicinal values, last night being sleepless, I was eased into sleep by a pill made of a passion flower; this morning I ate rosehip jam; and tonight I may entertain my guests with a glass of chokecherry brandy. I use often an herbal salve made of oak bark, sumac berries, marshmallow root, and other herbs. We, all of us, in the United States use aspirin, which, although now synthesized, was introduced to the world by our American Indians, who chewed the bark of willows as an alleviant of pain.

On this subject of Indians, it may be noted in reading this book that much mention is made of the special use by one or another tribe of this or that plant, and here it should be pointed out that we owe a great debt to the Indian squaws who helped the colonial families to survive in our early days, and whose knowledge of the values of herbal medicines has given us much of present day value. To the extent possible, many important medicinal plants of Indian tribes from East to West are mentioned in the pages which follow.

As to the values of many of the native herbs as medicine, I can simply quote an article in the *Saturday Review* (Dec. 18, 1971) in which a doctor visiting in China (E. G. Diamond) says: "Numerous trained physicians went out of their way to tell me that initially they had not believed in Chinese traditional medicine [of which the knowledge goes back at least 5,000 years], and that it was only now that, as they were forced to practice it, together with western medicine, they were convinced that among the myriad of herbs there were new therapeutic agents. . . . Uniformly they said that many of the Chinese herbs were not effective, but . . . men of significant medical science achievement uniformly urged me to keep an open mind." Such an admonition is, then, the attitude that we moderns, dosed with synthetic drugs of often questionable reactions, should keep in mind, as we explore the medicine of the first Americans. Such a point of view is confirmed by discussions with a recently graduated pharmacist, who says that the pharmaceutical field is taking a second look at plant medicines, in view of the all-too-often side effects which synthetic drugs have been found to have.

In all of this work, the author makes no claims of knowing all there is to know about every plant discussed. In the mention of dye plants, dependence has been on a number of books on the subject, plus my possession of notes taken in the Appalachian Mountains among country women by an expert craft teacher some years ago.

In addition to the introductory chapters that now follow, there are bibliographies of the special books applying to various subjects, but the reader of this work living in any special section of the United States may well wish to find auxiliary material about the plants of the home region. Yearly, specialists in every field are giving us new books which detail plant uses far beyond the possibilities in this work, and thus a visit to your local library or book dealer is recommended.

In closing these few words, I would be remiss if I did not give credit to people of the present and the past who have helped me assemble, as best I could, this list of the useful plants of our great country.

First a word of thanks should go to a fine young chap, now in college, who in high school days did much botanical digging for me in assembling facts and pictures, Dana Bangs; to my charming typist Nancy Morris who, before and after acquiring a fine family, has done three books for me; and to M.C. Goldman and William Hylton of Rodale Press, who have pushed me into some fields of writing beyond previous efforts. And lastly, but by no means least, appreciation to my wife of more than half a century, Vesta, who has corrected my notable grammatical failings and cooked all the wild foods we have used.

Outside the work of these immediate helpers, a word of appreciation to the botanists in the New England Botanical Club, who have helped with their writings and advice; to a host of members of the Garden Writers Association and of the American Horticultural Society, who have encouraged me in many ways; and beyond these known folks, to all the writers of the more than 100 reference books, mentioned in the bibliography, on whose knowledge I have drawn, and, as well, to the botanical artists, whose illustrations have been used to give the reader simple likenesses of many of the useful plants.

The famous saying that "no man is an island" is a great truth for anyone writing a reference book, and to all these helpers above, my full appreciation.

Nelson Coon

Introduction

American Indians and Their Use of Plant Life

The last decade has shown increasingly that the native Indians and their culture, which early was pushed aside and under, offers much knowledge that would help us in many ways if we would but study it more carefully. We *are* understanding more and more the Indian concept of a "free life," and today the well-dressed man may be wearing an Indian-inspired bolo tie instead of a wider tie, or the young set may be wearing a full complement of Indian beads, belts, and brooches, all cultural uses of Indian knowledge.

Secretly, indeed, we wish to emulate those qualities which gave the American Indian what we look on as "the good life" and, with a laziness which is inherent in all our lives, we think of our native Americans as those (as Shakespeare says in *As You Like It*):

> Who doth ambition shun
> And loves to live i' the sun,
>   Seeking the food he eats,
>   And pleased with what he gets.

We think of the Indian as seeking the food he ate from the pure bounties of nature, his work (except the hunting) done by the hard-working squaws—the ancient counterpart of the thrifty, diligent housewife of today.

But actually what did the Indians eat? And can we learn something from a knowledge of their diet, as most certainly did the Colonists of the earlier days? Is there any knowledge that we can appropriate for our own use and satisfaction? There surely is.

As is obvious, the diet of various Indian tribes across the country would vary according to the plant and animal life native to each section. Nevertheless, it would not be hard to imagine some meals which Indians of the Northeast (for instance) might have had.

Thinking in the context of our own "proper" meals one could start with a soup (though in an Indian household this would be quite unlikely), but we do know that the Indians did gather and use such wild plants as watercress, sorrel, nettles, and wild onions which might be cooked, strained, and flavored with sassafras leaves, for it is such a dish that would be called Gumbo File in the South.

Perhaps we all know, but give little thought to the fact that our traditional Thanksgiving dinner menu is essentially an Indian menu, based on (then) wild turkey, deer, caribou, elk, or buffalo (on the plains). The vegetables would be corn that had been dried and stored, and dried shell beans, with cooked wild rice in areas where it grows. Cranberries from the swamplands in various areas were as popular then as now. For the Indians of Martha's Vineyard, for instance, the only exclusive rights which are theirs are the rights to gather cranberries from the open lands.

One could think of other meals that the Indians might have had if their customs were like those of today. One menu might have started with soup made from dried beans, a "main dish" of fried eels (than which there is nothing more succulent), a simply concocted corn bread—thin, brown, and tasty, squash baked in the embers of the fire, all rounded off with that favorite of New England tables that still bears the name of Indian Pudding, a sweetened baked mixture of cornmeal and honey (or molasses), and such wild fruits as the season could offer. These "authentic" Indian meals are not difficult to assemble from the shelves of your supermarket or be supplemented by gathering the materials yourself on some foray into the countryside, or on a camping trip.

In the case of the staples of the Indian diet, we know that basic foods were cultivated as well as gathered from the wild. Corn in the five basic types—flint, flour, dent, sweet, and pop—plus many Indian hybridized species and innumerable varieties, especially in colors, spread out across our continent from its homeland in Mexico, whence it came as many as two, three or four thousand years ago. Also there was the culture of beans, pumpkins and squash, of which Omaha tribes were known to have grown 48 varieties. Sunflowers were native to the Mississippi Valley, and other plants were indigenous to various geologic and climatic areas. Widely used, as well as the countless green herbs, were tubers of the groundnut (the so-called Jerusalem artichoke) and of the swampgrowing wapatoo, which we call arrowhead, *Sagittaria.*

Naturally, what the Indian used in his home would depend greatly on the climatic zone in which he lived and the natural growth of the area, but there seem to have been many additions to the cultivated vegetables that were so universally the staple of American Indian diets—things such as corn, and great varieties of beans, pumpkins, and squash. In summer, there were varieties of berries, rhizomes and roots of waterplants, nuts of many sorts from North to South, grapes, honey, (or maple sugar in some areas), sunflowers in the mid-country, rice in the northern lakes, or the fruits of cacti in the south. All these plants, and many more, are listed in this book, and, to the extent possible, recipes are given for a healthful use in our modern homes.

It should hardly be necessary to note that not all Indian food was from products of the plant world, for from East to West there were wild animals that could be taken with bow and arrow or, where there was water, fish might be had, often by poisoning schools of fishes with extracts of poisonous plants.

In my own vegetable garden, the ancient shell heaps give evidence that my beach area was used as a gathering spot for clams, quahogs, scallops, oysters, and crabs, since in the old days the changing tides and seasons brought in fish of many kinds. In the days before the coming of the white man there was honey or maple syrup to sweeten the unchlorinated water and for flavor the flowerheads of sumach were gathered, dried, and used to make a native cola.

It is quite possible that this picture of Indian food is a rather rosy one, for much of the time the food might well have been a dish which was part of this writer's diet when young, called then by the Indian appellation of supawn, this being nothing more nor less than "mush" or boiled cornmeal. A cookbook issued in Virginia in 1812 tells how to prepare "mush" and "Indian Pudding," as well as how to dry (as did the Indians) corn and beans and fruits such as cherries, blueberries, and other natural bounties that gave the Indians the vitamins they could not get from corn and beans. From their general use of these two vegetables, which are never part of any natural growth—they must be cultivated—we have that dish still called by the Indian name, succotash.

As suggested, there was a considerable variation of this wild food. In the South, it might have been varied with acorns and pecans, and in the spring, tender healthful pokeberry shoots; while in the Southwest, it was varied with pinon nuts and nopal or cactus-fruit. Again for the Indians of the Rocky Mountain area it would have been blue camass or any one of a number of roots and fruits which are found only in that area. In the bibliography, there are listings of the books covering specific parts of our country, which describe the edible plants of a region, the knowledge of the use of which has come down to us mostly from the long experience of our Indians.

In our search for healthful food today, one must remember that the empiric knowledge of the Indians is well worth studying, for in every way—from using seeds and feathers for ornament, fur and hide for clothing, wild and often poisonous plants for medicine, to using tobacco and mescal buttons as soporifics and hallucinogenic drugs— the Indian showed a knowledge of (and often a worship of) nature that should teach us much. One recent research on such uses tells us, for instance, that among the Great Lakes Indians, some 130 species of wild plants were used for food, 275 species for medicinal purposes, and some 27 for smoking.

Again, and often important in dry dusty Southwest areas, plants were used as chewing gum to allay thirst. Also important was the need for birth control medicines, and the different tribes found a variety of plants that would serve such a purpose. In some cases the plant was used as a male contraceptive.

Thus, although today "wild" drugs have been replaced by a dependence on synthetic drugs, a great deal of the empirical knowledge of Indians is still being used; and, in fact, there is a new trend of "taking a second look" at the medicines of primitive man which may again turn us to medicines just as effective and possibly less reactionary than chemical compounds. It is quite probable, of course, that of the above quoted 275 species of medicinal plants, many were administered by a tribal "medicine man" who depended as much on what today we would call "faith-healing" as on the properties of the plants. These medicine men were probably experts in the effective use of magical spells and incantations on those with mental disorders, while leaving the treatments of common complaints to the very knowledgeable squaws who really knew the properties of the plants which they searched and grubbed for every day. It was the squaw who administered potions and bound up wounds, and she, too, who taught our pioneer women much practical knowledge which gave credence to a whole school of Indian medicinal treatments widely acceptable in the early nineteenth century. A number of recent works on medicinal plants give such names of common plants as squawberry, -flower, -root, -huckleberry, -vine, -bush; all of these names indicate that our knowledge of their medicinal uses came to us via the humble squaws. This fact is further supported by a survey which shows that 30 percent of all the drugs of the American settlers were medicines of the Indians, while it was likely that the remaining 70 percent of drugs were herbal remedies brought from England or Europe where medicine was based on the "folk-medicine" knowledge of the thousand year old text of Dioscorides.

In indicating the kind of simple medicines that the squaws found in plants, mention might be made of the wide use of the dry powdered spores of puffballs as an effective styptic, the use of the leaves of the sweet fern as an astringent application to relieve ivy poisoning, and the juice of jewelweed—a plant described by Josselyn (1672) as being a "sovereign remedy for bruises of what kind soever"—for similar purposes and for general healing. The exudations of willow bark were used for sciatica, a knowledge that gave us aspirin, used for the same purpose today. In Maine, Indians combined the ash of maple with acorn oil to ease sore muscles, a practice which would surely differ greatly from that of the Indians of the Northwest, the South, or the Great Lakes district—and yet it would always be from the produce of some wild plant.

But, until the last decade, the use of such plant medicines was passing from our knowledge rapidly. In the early seventeenth century, the English herbalist Parkinson listed 3800 plants useful medicinally, a number that by 1820 had dropped in our country to only 223, and more recently to about 100. And of this 100, it is said that about 60 came from American Indian knowledge, including lobelia, puccoon, cohosh, pipsissewa, and others, and it is certainly likely, as one writer notes, that the medical status of our Indians was in many ways on a par with that of the Assyrians, Hebrews, and Greeks.

A good example of the importance of the appreciation of native remedies is to be found in the discovery and presently important use of rauwolfia, long used in India for high blood pressure, for the discovery of this has impelled drug companies to explore more widely the native drugs of many countries. Hence, today, exploration teams are going into the jungles of South America, to the South Pacific, to the tribal cultures of Africa, seeking drug plants that might extend the pharmacopoeia of our modern world.

One of the most experienced of these explorers, who has spent twelve years among the Indians on the Upper Amazon in Colombia, is Dr. Richard E. Schultes, curator of the botanical museum at Harvard University, who, in a recent talk on the widening panorama in medical botany, reported that while 75 to 80 percent of our drugs today are recent additions to the pharmacopoeia, and while medical research has accelerated, "the frontiers for discovery" have hardly been touched.

As one example of the possibilities still open to medical discovery, Dr. Schultes mentioned the lichens from which a number of antibiotic salves have been derived. There is good reason to suggest that this group of some 20,000 species may offer many more valuable medicines. This is a possibility which is presently being actively explored by Japanese chemists.

Recent articles and personal correspondence that I have had indicate that our American laboratories are working especially hard on the possibility of finding cancer-arresting drugs among the plants of the world. In a bulletin issued by the Public Health Service, Dr. Jonathan L. Hartwell said that: "If there is any hope in a chemical treatment for cancer, it is reasonable to believe that such an agent is as likely to originate from a plant as from pure synthesis."

From these comments it may be seen that perhaps the Indians with their empirical knowledge of medicine, gained over untold centuries, really "knew a thing or two," and while no one would recommend that we pull ourselves back into the age of either Indian cooking or Indian medicine, we can learn to appreciate more deeply our debt to the true American native.

Of course, today one finds our principal interest and "social concern" fastened on a range of plant products which carry the name of "hallucinogenic drugs," most of them (except possibly LSD) pure plant products. The widest used is, of course, tobacco, which in the sense of the scientist is a "narcotic"—a substance to benumb, and not necessarily what the name has come to imply—an addictive drug. Yet the failure of millions to abandon cigarettes in the light of medical research would indicate that the seemingly harmless tobacco of the Indians *is* an addictive drug with ultimate damage.

The Indian uses of tobacco and mescal, or among various Latin American tribes, the hallucinogenic mushrooms or a number of other plant narcotics, all seem to have been used, in Dr. Schultes' words, "in some way for escape from reality." Tobacco was used ceremonially by the Indians, a treasured necessity for ritual occasions. Schultes points out that "all narcotics, sometime in their history, have been linked to religion and magic. . . ." and that ". . . when problems do arise from the employment of narcotics, they arise after the narcotics

have passed from ceremonial to purely hedonic or recreational use."
He further points out that peyote (mescal) is used by primitive peoples *only* in a religious context.

In connection with today's "rites" of marijuana and such other of
the narcotics or hallucinogens (including tobacco and alcohol), it is
an obvious statement that few, if any of them, are conducted in any
atmosphere of organized or traditional religion, and thus such values
as they probably do possess fail to produce the inspirational and
releasing effects that were accomplished under the discipline of native religions.

All of this would not be to recommend that the use of these drugs
be accepted as a form of religious observance in our present culture,
but, again to quote Schultes:

> We can no longer afford to ignore reports of any aboriginal
> use of a plant merely because they seem to fall beyond the
> limit of our credence. To do so would be tantamount to the
> closing of a door, forever to entomb a peculiar kind of
> native knowledge which might lead us along the path of
> immeasurable progress.

In light of this background of the uses of the wild plants by the
Indians, should we not perhaps, in at least a courtesy gesture to the
Indian culture, learn to use and appreciate the knowledge and values
of the flora of our great land?

Bibliography

Agriculture, U.S. Dept. of. *Foods of the North American Indians.* Dept. of
Agric. Ann. Report, 1870.

American Ethnology, Bureau of. *American Indian Medicines.* Washington,
D.C.: Smithsonian Institution, 1957.

Carr, Luclen. "The Food of Certain American Indians and Their Method
of Preparing It." *Amer. Antiq. Soc., Proc.,* 1895.

Chamberlain, L.S. "Plants Used by the Indians of Eastern North America." *American Naturalist,* 1901.

Coville, F.V. *Notes on the Plants used by the Klamath Indians of Oregon.* Contrib.
U.S. National Herbarium, 1897.

Dodge, J.R., ed.   *Food Products of the North American Indians.* Report of Commissioner of Agri. for year 1870. Wash. D.C.: Government Printing Office, 1871.

Fenton, Wm.N.   *Contacts Between Iroquois Herbalism and Colonial Medicines.* Washington, D.C.: Smithsonian Institution, Smithsonian Report, 1941–1942.

Gilmore, Melvin R.   *Uses of Plants by the Indians of the Missouri River Region.* Washington, D.C.: Annual Report of Bureau of American Ethnology, Government Printing Office.

———.   *Some Native Nebraska Plants with Their Uses by the Dakotas.* Nebraska State Historical Society, 1913.

Hariot, Thomas.   *The First English Plantation of Virginia.* London, 1588.

Harris, George H.   "Root Foods of the Seneca Indians." *Rochester Acad. of Sci. Proc.,* 1891.

Harvard, V.   "Drink Plants of the North American Indians." *Torrey Bot. Club Bul.,* 1895.

———.   "Food Plants of the North American Indians." *Torrey Bot. Club Bul.,* 1896.

Heiser, C.B., Jr.   "The Sunflower Among the North American Indians." *American Philosophical Soc.* Vol. 95, No. 4 (Aug. 1951).

Iroquois Uses of Maize and Other Food Plants. New York State Museum, 1910.

Josselyn, John.   *New England Rarities Discovered.* London, 1672.

Kimbal, Yeffe and Anderson, Jean.   *The Art of American Indian Cooking.* New York: Doubleday, 1965.

Murphey, Edith Van Allen.   *Indian Uses of Native Plants.* Palm Desert, California: Desert Printers, 1959.

Palmer, Edward.   *Food Products of the North American Indians.* Dept. of Agric. Common Report, 1870.

Parker, Arthur C.   "Iroquois Uses of Maize and Other Food Plants." *New York State Museum,* Bul. #144, 1910.

Romero, John B.   *Botanical Lore of California Indians.* New York: Vantage Press, 1954.

Smith, Harlan I.   "Materia Medica of the Bella Coola and Neighboring Tribes of British Columbia." Ottawa: Bul. #56, 1927.

Stone, Eric.   *Medicine Among the American Indians.* Clio Medica vii. Darien, Conn.: Hafner Publ. Co., 1962.

Svoboda, Maria. *Plants that the American Indians Used.* Chicago Natural History Museum, 1964.

Tantaquidgeon, Gladys. *Notes on Gay Head Indians of Massachusetts,* 1930.

Train, Percy with Hendrick, Archer, and Andrews. *Medicinal Uses of Plants by Indian Tribes in Nevada.* Beltsville, Md., 1957.

Weiner, Michael A. *Earth Medicine, Earth Foods of North American Indians.* New York: Macmillan, 1972.

Wilson, T. *The Use of Wild Plants as a Food by Indians.* The Ottawa Naturalist, 1916.

Wittrock, M.A. and G.L. "Food Plants of the Indians." *Journ. of N.Y. Bot. Gardens,* Bul. #507, 1942.

Wyman, L.C. and Harris, Stuart K. "Navajo Indian Medicinal Ethnobotany." *U. of New Mexico,* Bul. #366, 1941.

Yanovsky, E. and Kingsbury, R.M. "Analyses of Some Indian Food Plants." *Journal of the Association of Official Agricultural Chemists* (Nov. 1938).

Yanovsky, E. *Food Plants of the North American Indians.* U.S.D.A. Misc. Publications, 1936.

American Plants Useful for Food

In considering the native, as well as the introduced roadside plants of our country which have been (or are) useful as a source for food, it should be remembered that basically *all* food comes from wild or once-wild plants. Primarily this is true, whether one gathers and uses the foliage, roots, seeds, and nuts from the wild, or whether one is considering the fact that wheat, soybeans, rice, corn, and other grains, which are "staples," are really improved and hybridized forms of quite primitive plants. Even our Indians of several thousand years ago were dependent on corn, beans, squash, and potatoes, which, although crudely cultivated, were much improved forms of wayside plants. Secondly, plants produce the important source of protein food which we call meat and fish, for both animals and fish survive on the plants of land and sea.

To a great extent the basic knowledge of the values and uses of wild and unimproved plants was somewhat forgotten in the days of the great advances in food production, and of prosperity, around the turn of this century. One didn't need to go out and pick fruits and nuts when grocery shelves were bulging with a great variety of foods. When the living is easy and even blackberries can be bought in supermarkets, who is going to bother scrambling amongst the thorns for misshapen fruits of small size? But today, as common knowledge of the potentially dangerous chemicals used in growing and processing food and of the known health values in eating raw or unprocessed foods is much better understood, many of the understanding oldsters and inquiring younger people, want to go "back to nature" in at least small ways.

Without question, it is true that some of our wild plants aren't eaten any more, for the very good reason that their cultivated descendants are better in every respect. No one who has ever tried them could prefer wild celery, parsnips, or cabbage to their commercial varieties. But what about wild roadside strawberries or raspberries for flavor, against the kinds in the market which are offered to us because "they ship well"? And is there any food with as much valuable vitamin C as the rose hips, which can often and easily be gathered from the wild?

This book contains many uses of plants of the wild, other than for food, but essentially it is food that is basic and widely available. Naturally, not all the plants of one species are found in every state because of the great climatic and geological zones of which our country is made. As the reader of this book may be encouraged to explore the wealth of wild offerings in his own little chunk of America, he will come to appreciate the wealth that wild America has to offer. A growing interest in the interrelationship of man and nature (ecology) has come to make us all think twice about how we can appreciate the vast web of those interrelationships that make plants, animals and man so dependent, one on the other.

The fact of the matter is, that a little weekend edible plant hunting can give some salutary ecological lessons. Next time, for instance, if you are out weeding the chickweed from the flower beds, try keeping it in the food chain instead of making it into compost or burning it. Used as salad or boiled for a few minutes with butter, this common winter-growing weed has a delicious and delicate spinachy taste, while the seeds are fine for the canary or parakeet.

Actually there is something quite satisfying about learning about the availability of our wild foods, and it could well help to satisfy that innate, atavistic hunting urge. With the proliferation of motor homes and the increase of camping of one kind or another, wild foods may provide pleasing additions to the lives of those families "on-the-road" as well as provide children a strong beginning in nature education—something that has been too much lost in the movement of folks from the farm to urban life.

In searching for foods here and there across the country, one begins to learn, firsthand, the complete and delicate relationships that plants have with their environment: their dependence on birds to carry their seeds, animals to crop the grass that shuts out their light, on wind and sunshine and the balance of chemicals in the soil, and ultimately on our own good grace, as to whether they survive at all. It is on the products, wild or cultivated, of this intricate network of forces, that our very sustenance depends. So it is that a little more living off the wild could be a big boost to a respectful attitude toward the earth.

Beyond all this there is the fact that one enjoys better health from the wild food, which is free from all the pollutions that come from the many hands through which food passes, from cultivator to sales counter. Also there is probably greater value food-wise in wild things in that the growing plant has been nourished by the natural environment rather than through what some think of as the "pollution of chemical fertilizers."

Finally there are the satisfaction and knowledge that come from foraging in the wild for one's own food stuffs, beyond any food values it might have. As Euell Gibbons, my fellow-writer on this subject, says in one of his books:

> I know of no outdoor sport which can furnish me with as
> much pleasure as foraging for wild food which can be made
> into exquisite dishes to share with family and friends.

As to methods of preparing the gatherings of the wild for serving on the table, this will be shown to the extent possible. Certainly the ordinarily skilled housewife will know in general how to make simple salads, to "stew up some greens," to make jelly and jam as well from wild fruits as from cultivated, to make soups from root and other vegetables, to make pies from various fruits, or to concoct tasty drinks both fresh or alcoholic. The same imagination is required in preparing wild foods as for preparing any meal.

I can say that while writing this book, I found, just a few hundred feet up the street, a wild chokecherry tree masquerading as a street tree, and with permission from the owner, I gathered great buckets of the finest tasty cherries I have ever seen. They went into a most beautiful jelly and into chokecherry cordial to serve to my guests alongside the winter fire. A little effort and fun for me, a little work for my wife (in which she took pleasure), and food and drink for later pleasure with our friends.

Of course there are many recipe books and guides beyond the pages of this book, and these are detailed in the following bibliography.

Bibliography

Allegro, John M.   *The Sacred Mushroom and the Cross.* London: Hodder and
         Stoughton, 1970.

Anderson, E.   *White Oak Acorns as Food.* Missouri Bot. Garden, Bul. #12,
         1924.

Angier, Bradford.   *Free for the Eating*. Harrisburg, Pa.: Stackpole Co., 1966.

———.   *Living off the Country*. Harrisburg, Pa.: Stackpole Co., 1961.

———.   *More Free for the Eating Wild Foods*. Harrisburg, Pa.: Stackpole, 1969.

———.   *How to Live in the Woods for $10 a Month*. Harrisburg, Pa.: Stackpole Co., 1956.

———.   *Wilderness Cookery*. Harrisburg, Pa.: Stackpole Co., 1961.

Berglund, Berndt.   *The Edible Wild*. New York: Scribners, 1971.

Burt, Calvin and Heyl, Franl.   *Edible Poisonous Plants of the Western States.*

Charles, V.K.   *Some Common Mushrooms and How to Know Them*. U.S. Dept. of Agric. Bul.

Cheney, R.H.   "Tea Substitutes in the United States." *Journal of N.Y. Bot. Garden*, May 1942.

Christensen, Clyde M.   *Common Edible Mushrooms*, Newton Centre, Mass.: Branford Co., undated.

Classen, P.W.   "A Possible New Source of Food Supply." *Scientific Monthly* (1919).

Coffin, George S.   "Vermont's Native Mushrooms." *Vermont Life*, 1956.

Compain, Michel.   *Guide de l'Herboriste-Droguiste*. Limoges: Ed. Compain, 1939.

Coon, Nelson.   *Using Wayside Plants*. 4th Ed. Revised. New York: Hearthside Press, 1970.

Crowhurst, Adrian.   *The Weed Cookbook*. New York: Lancer Books, 1971.

———.   *The Flower Cookbook*. New York: Lancer Books, 1970.

Dennis, R.G.   *Common British Fungi*. London: Hawthorn, 1950.

Fernald, M.L. and Kinsey, A.C.   *Edible Wild Plants of Eastern North America*. Revised. New York: Harper & Bros., 1958.

Findlay, W.P.K.   *Wayside and Woodland Fungi*. London: Frederick Warne, 1967.

Gibbons, Euell.   *Stalking the Wild Asparagus*. New York: David McKay, 1962.

Graham, V. Ovid.   *Mushrooms of the Great Lakes Area*. 1944. Reprint. New York; Dover, 1973.

Harris, Chas. B.   *Eat the Weeds*. Barre, Mass.: Barre Pub., 1969.

Hatfield, Audrey W.   *Pleasures of Wild Plants*. London: Taplinger, 1967.

———.   *How to Enjoy Your Weeds*. London: Taplinger, 1969.

Hopkins, M. "Wild Plants Used in Cookery," *N.Y. Bot. Gardens Journal,* 1942.

Ipswich Sanctuary. *Eating Wild.* Mass. Audubon Soc., 1971.

Johnson, J.R. *Anyone Can Live Off the Land.* New York: Longmans, Green & Co., 1961.

Kaufman, C.H. *Gilled Mushrooms.* 1918. Reprint. New York: Dover, 1973.

Krieger, Louis C.C. *The Mushroom Handbook.* 1936. Reprint. New York: Dover, 1973.

McIlvaine, Chas. *One Thousand American Fungi.* New York: Dover, 1972.

McNicol, Mary. *Flower Cookery.* New York: Fleet Pub. Corp., 1967.

Martin, Geo. W. *Food in the Wilderness.* Bremerton, Wash., 1963.

Medsger, Oliver P. *Edible Wild Plants.* New York: MacMillan, 1945.

Morton, J.F. "Principal Wild Food Plants of the United States." *Economic Botany,* (Oct-Dec. 1963).

Muenscher, W.C. and Rice, Myron A. *Garden Spice and Wild Pot-Herbs.* Ithaca, N.Y.: Cornell Univ. Press, 1955.

Perez-Llano, G.A. "Lichens, Their Biological and Economic Significance; Lichens Used as Food by Man." *The Botanical Review,* (Jan. 1944).

Schultes, R. Evans. *New World Indians and Their Hallucinogenic Plants.* Barnes Arboretum, 1968.

Smith, Alexander H. *The Mushroom Hunter's Field Guide.* Ann Arbor: Univ. of Mich. Press, 1963.

Snell, Walter and Dick, E.A. *A Glossary of Mycology.* Cambridge, Mass.: Harvard Univ. Press, 1971.

Sturtevant, E.L. *Edible Plants of the World.* 1919. Reprint. New York: Dover, 1973.

Thomas, Wm. Sturgis, M.D. *Field Book of Common Mushrooms.* New York: G.P. Putnam's Sons, 1948.

Vliet, R. *A Manual of Woodslore Survival as Developed at Philmont on How to Eat Weeds and Like Them.* Springer, New Mexico: Tribune Press, n.d.

Wakefield, E.M. *Common British Fungi.* London: Hawthorn, 1950.

Wasson, R. Gordon. *Soma, the Divine Mushroom.* New York: Harcourt, Brace, 1965.

Wilder, Walter Beebe. *Bounty of the Wayside.* New York: Doubleday, 1946.

Medicinal Plants and Their Uses

Why include plants of possible medicinal value in a book such as this when modern medicine knows so much and the drug stores are loaded with medicines based on the most scientific research? The answer to that question is that quite a number of medicines found in a modern pharmacy are derived in whole or in part from plants, and there is more than a little evidence to suggest that modern science is presently taking a second look at the possibility of using newly discovered or freshly appraised old plant medicines. Since some of the synthesized drugs have side-effects in given conditions that plant drugs do not seem to have, there is a tendency to go back to nature —at least in part.

One comes also to the fact that the best doctors are understanding that, either in its normal workings of body or mind, or with the things that nature has to offer, nature should be understood. That this is not a new thought was suggested in a discussion by Dr. Herbert Ratner (a professor at Loyola University) in which he said, in part:

> The tradition of medicine, which began with Hippocrates, recognizes that the prime physician on any case is nature, and that the doctor's role is to work with nature, to assist, support and minister to her. As a matter of fact, the very word physician is derived from the Greek *Phusis*, which means nature. . . . The physician cooperates with nature's forces, which are ordered to health.

Thus it is the contention of this author that one should not do less than explore the medicinal values of the wild plants that are everywhere to be found and with such knowledge, perhaps to be able to help out in some emergency situation, or perhaps help to appreciate another one of the many values of our wild life. Certainly, as explored in another chapter, the Indians knew a lot about such plant values, a knowledge which in some cases, they passed on to the early colonists.

By the time of the American Revolution, there seems to have been a sort of dichotomy about the use of drugs, with the soldiers depending largely on medicines (patent and otherwise, but mostly of plant origin) from England, yet with native drug plants (the knowledge of which came from the Indians) readily available. An advertisement in the *New York Gazette* of July 29, 1776 suggested (in part): "The good people of the neighboring towns . . . by carefully collecting and curing quantities of useful herbs will greatly promote the good of the Army, and considerably benefit themselves." And there is further evidence to suggest that quite a number of botanical drugs indigenous to the colonies and often grown in family herb gardens were widely employed, but our army did not have the knowledge and the system to gather, prepare, and make use of them.

After the Revolution, the values of our native drug plants grew widely from help supplied by the squaws; and it was somewhere around 1820 that the members of the communities which came to be known as Shakers, found that the growing and selling of medicinal herbs was just one of their ways of making a livelihood. This industry was of course helped by the dislike after the wars of 1776 and 1812 of buying material of any kind from England. So, in the communes on the east side of the Hudson River, grew up a large (for that time) industry selling herbal medicines. Actually, a catalog of the Shakers' offerings was issued in 1833, which on its title page suggested:

> Why send to Europe's distant shores
> For plants which grow at our own doors?

This whole story is too long to detail here, but from this Shaker industry grew, in the late nineteenth century, the patent medicine craze centered around plant drugs, this producing a revulsion as synthetics appeared in the early twentieth century.

All through these years the American housewife was simply using the knowledge passed on to her by ancestor, neighbor, or the more knowledgeable Indians, enclaves of whom lived (as even a few do today) near many country communities. It was true in this case that the kinds of plant knowledge passed along would vary greatly according to the region concerned. Those in the Southwest were basing their medicines on information passed along from the tremendous medicinal knowledge of the great Mexican culture of which they were a part, as we know from the great treatise on Mexican medicines produced (under Spanish auspices) as the *Badianus Manuscript*, as early as 1552. But medicinal plant knowledge was present in all Indian communities and much of this has come down to us today. Here in this book some medicinal uses of plants are presented simply as statements of possible uses, as found in the various books in the bibliography.

In making the listing of the hundreds of plants of medicinally useful value it has not been found possible to indicate comparative values or to detail methods of preparation or dosages. This can only be done after extensive study by the reader. The part of the plants to be used, the method of extraction, and the form in which the medicine is to be taken are all a part of home pharmaceutical knowledge. For internal use a plant medicine may be a conserve, a decoction, an electuary prepared with honey, an infusion, or just an expression of juices. Or, perhaps it will be an ointment, a poultice of plaster, pills, or a syrup.

Thus, there is little the author can do here except to suggest that, as with other uses of plants, the reader go a-walking in the woods and fields, and study plants, read a little botany, and possibly experiment at home with simple plant medicines, with vitamin-rich foods, and with all the other values of our native plant life. In concluding these general remarks I quote from the Shaker catalog of 1833:

> A blade of grass, a simple flower,
> Cull'd from the dewy lea:
> These, these shall speak, with touching power,
> Of change and health to thee.

One must descend from the historical and poetic view of plants and thus, in discussing medicinal values along with the plants themselves, in this section, it may be helpful to add a few words as to the kinds of preparations which can be made from plant material, calling them under their quite common names, such as infusions, decoctions, tinctures, etc. Certainly any reader wishing to concoct and use medicine from wild plants should do as much research as possible, as to known values, doses, and possible after or side effects. For this purpose, a number of valuable books with more information may be found in the bibliography.

INFUSIONS   An infusion is prepared by pouring boiling water over bruised roots, bark, herbs, seeds at a rate of about one pint of water to an ounce of material. Doses to be taken would be from a tablespoonful to a small wineglassful.

DECOCTIONS   Here cold water is added to plant parts, and then the mixture is boiled for about a half hour, cooled, and strained. As some water always boils away, it is suggested to use 1½ pints to the ounce of material.

LIQUID EXTRACTS   Perhaps not easy for the "home doctor," extracts are concentrations of plant values derived by evaporating moisture by heat, or more technical methods. Storing of such extracts, later to be taken in water, makes the keeping of medicines simpler.

TINCTURES   Spirits of wine can be used for drugs containing gummy or resinous material or in any situation where extraction by alcohol, rather than water, is needed.

PILLS   The most widely used method of drug administration, pills are made from concentrated extracts. They are not easily made under home conditions.

CAPSULES   Gelatine containers into which oils or balsams or drugs of nauseating taste are put to make the taking easier.

SUPPOSITORIES   Medicines are added to material of a solid but soluble base, to be used for treating diseases of the rectum.

TEAS, TISANES, BEVERAGES, AND AMBROSIALS   Teas are made of herbs of various kinds and have been used for a long time as a common method for supplying the medicinal values of all sorts of plants, some important, some pleasant.

Medicinal Uses of Common Plants and Their Products

In offering some simple selected medicinal uses of wild plants, the reader (or possible user) should note carefully that all these listings are suggestions rather than doctor's prescriptions. Actually some of the plants listed might be poisonous in nature, if wrong doses were taken, and thus in many cases more detailed research on them should be done. The names given are the most accepted common names of the plant, and for more details, the use of the index is suggested, to find the page on which the plants are scientifically named, described, and their locale noted.

Also in this list, some useful materials are mentioned that are not wild plants but material or produce from our gardens, but the attempt was to make the list below as useful as possible.

It will be noted that some plants are starred (*) and here the plant may be especially dangerous, unless used under medical supervision, or with more than ordinary knowledge.

ABRASIVES
  Horsetails
    (*Equisetum*)
ABSORBENTS
  Sphagnum moss,
    "wool" of
    cinnamon fern
ALCOHOLISM
  Gold thread
ANTHELMINTIC
  (for worms)
  Tansy
  Male fern
ANTISCORBUTIC
  Citrus fruit
  Grapes
ANTISEPTIC
  Garlic
  Dogwood
  Witchhazel
  Oak bark
  Sphagnum moss
ASTRINGENT
  Tea
  Oak bark
  Sumac
  Blackberry
  Witchhazel
  Dogwood
  Prunella

BRONCHIAL
  ASTHMA
  Garlic
  Pleurisy root
  Mountain balm
  Gum plant
  Red clover
BURNS
  Bread and hot
    milk poultice
  Wash with strong
    tea
  Salve of Irish moss
    and cucumber
  Juice around
    quince seeds
  Leaves of *Aloe vera*
BEE STINGS (to
  ease)
  Vinegar
  Honeysuckle vine
    juice
  Rue
  Chamomile
  Aloe vera

CATHARTIC
  Rhubarb
  Buckthorn*
  Mayapple*
  Castor oil

COLDS
  Yarrow tea
  Hot lemonade
  Tea of Irish moss,
    lemon,
    goldenrod and
    honey
COLIC
  Infusion of
    pennyroyal
CONSTIPATION
  Yeast
  Irish moss
CORD (for
  emergency use)
  Fibers of Spanish
    bayonet,
    milkweed,
    marshmallow, or
    linden tree bark
COUGH AND SORE
  THROAT
  Irish moss
  Honey
  White pine bark
  Gold thread
  Black currant jam
  Coltsfoot

DIARRHEA
  Blackberry brandy
  Strong tea
  Grape juice
  Oatmeal
  "An Apple a day"
  Infusion of
    hemlock bark,
    blackberry
    leaves, white oak
    bark, or judas
    tree
DIET FOOD (low
  starch)
  Jerusalem
    artichokes
DIGESTION
  Sweet flag
  Angelica
  Gum-plant
  Hop seed
  Papaya extract
  Yerba buena
DIURETICS
  Asparagus
  Juniper berries
  Bearberry
  Grapes
  Moonseed
  Wintergreen

ENERGY (Quick)
  Honey
  Grape juice
  Brandy
ENZYMES
  Papayas
EYES
  Sagebrush

EXPECTORANT
  Black currant
  White pine
  Poplar buds
  Horehound
  Sunflower seed
  Yerba santa
EMETICS
  Holly foliage*
  Western cliffrose
  Elkweed
  Wake-robin roots

FEVERS
  Lemonade, hot
FLATULENCE
  Mint
  Ginger
  Nutmeg
  Sage
  Angostura bitters

HEART
  Digitalis*
  Lily-of-the-valley*
HEMOSTATIC
  Puffball spores

INSECT
  REPELLANT
  Onion and garlic
    juice
  Chamomile
  Lemon verbena
  Garlic juice (ticks)
ITCH
  Narrow dock
  Gum-plant
  Celandine
  Cornstarch

LAXATIVES-
  PURGATIVES
  Agave juice
  Figs, pears, prunes
  Olive oil
  Bunchberry bark
  Chaparral tea
  Wahoo berries
  Walnuts
  Horehound
  Mulberry fruit
  Buckthorn fruit*
  Rhubarb
LOTION (hair set)
  Juice around
    quince seeds
LOTION (Skin)
  Juice of cucumber
  Irish moss
LUBRICANT
  (Intestinal)
  Irish moss

POISON IVY
  (Antidotes)
  Rub areas with
    crushed
    jewelweed and
    sweet fern leaves
  Gum-plant
POULTICES
  Mustard seed

RHEUMATISM
  Birch bark
  Black snakeroot*
  Rheumatism weed
  Boneset
  Bean trefoil
  Pokeweed*
  Elderberry
  Bittersweet

SEDATIVES AND
  SOPORIFICS
  Chamomile tea
  Valerian
  Pine bark tea
  Hot lemonade
  Horse balm
SHAMPOO
  Soapwort
  Amole
  Yucca
  Clethra flowers
SORES
  Gold thread
  Healing herb
  Flaxseed
  Plantain
STIMULANT
  Coffee, tea, brandy

STOMACHIC
  (Digestant)
  Angostura bitters
  Mint
  Parsley
  Horseradish
  Cayenne pepper
  Barley and barley
    broth

TEAS (Healthful)
  Sassafras
  Goldenrod
  Dogwood, yarrow
  Red sumach
TEETH
  Strawberries
  Clove oil
  Bayberry

TONICS
  Native gingers
  Chamomile
  Watercress
  Boneset
TOOTHBRUSH
  (Indian)
  Crushed dogwood
    stems

VITAMIN C
  Rose hips
  Watercress
  Parsley

WAX (Ironing pads
  and candles)
  Bayberry seeds

Bibliography

Altschul, Siri von Ries. *Drugs and Foods From Little Known Plants.* Cambridge, Mass.. Harvard Univ. Press, 1973.

Andrews, E.D. and F. *Shaker Herbs and Herbalists.* Berkshire Garden Center, 1959.

Barton, Benj. Smith. *Collections for an Essay Towards a Materia Medica of the U.S.* Philadelphia: 1798 and 1804.

Blair, Thos. S. *Botanic Drugs.* Cincinnati: Therapeutic Digest Publ. Co., 1917.

Boericke and Runyon. *Homeopathic Materia Medica.* Philadelphia: 1922.

Brown, O. Phelps. *The Complete Herbalist.* Jersey City, N.J.: 1856.

Buchman, Dian D. *Complete Herbal Guide to Natural Health and Beauty.* New York: Doubleday, 1973.

Budge, Sir E. A. Wallis. *The Divine Origin of the Craft of the Herbalist.* London: Culpepper House, 1928.

Burn, Harold. *Drugs, Medicine and Man.* New York: Charles Scribner's Sons, 1962.

Carter, Kate B. *Pioneer Home Cures of Common Diseases.* Salt Lake City: Daughters of Utah Pioneers, 1958.

_____. *Pioneer Medicines.* Salt Lake City: Daughters of Utah Pioneers, 1958.

Clarkson, Rosetta E. *Golden Age of Herbs and Herbalists.* New York: Dover, 1973.

Coon, Nelson. *Using Plants for Healing.* New York: Hearthside, 1963.

de Bairacli Levy, Juliette. *Herbal Handbook for Farm and Stable.* New York: Faber and Faber, 1963.

_____. *Herbal Handbook for Everyone.* Newton Centre, Mass: Branford, 1966.

_____. *Nature's Children.* New York: Schocken Books, 1971.

_____. *Complete Herbal Book for the Dog.* New York: Arco Publ. Co., 1972.

de Lazlo, Henry G. *Library of Medicinal Plants.* Cambridge, England: Heffer and Sons, 1958.

Dioscorides. *The Greek Herbal.* London: Oxford University Press, 1934.

Evelyn, John. *Acetaria, a Discourse of Salletts.* 1699. Reprint. Brooklyn Botanic Garden, 1937.

Fernie, W.T. *Herbal Simples.* London: J. Wright Pub., 1914.

Fox, Wm. *Family Botanic Guide.* Sheffield, Fox & Sons, 1916.

Gerard, John. *The Herbal.* Ed. by T. Johnson, London, 1636.

Gibbons, Euell. *Stalking the Healthful Herbs.* New York: David McKay Co., 1966.

Gosselin, Raymond. "The Status of Natural Products in the American Pharmaceutical Market." *Lloydia* 24 (4) (1962): 241–243.

Grieve, Mrs. M. *A Modern Herbal.* Darien, Conn.: Hafner Pub. Co., Inc., 1967.

Hardacre, Val. *Woodland Nuggets of Gold-Ginseng.* New York: Vantage Press, 1968.

Harper-Shove, F. *The Prescriber and Clinical Repertory of Medicinal Herbs.* 2nd ed. Bognor Regis: Health Press, 1938.

Harris, Ben Charles. *Kitchen Medicines.* Barre, Mass.: Barre Pub., 1968.

_____. *Eat the Weeds.* Barre, Mass.: Barre Pub., 1968.

Henkel, Alice. *American Medicinal Leaves and Herbs.* U.S.D.A. Bul. #219, 1911.

Jarvis, D.C. *Folk Medicine.* New York: Henry Holt & Co., 1958.

Kadans, Joseph M.   *Encyclopedia of Medicinal Herbs.* New York: Arc Books, 1972.

Kirschner, H.E.   *Nature's Healing Grasses.* Yucaipa, Calif.: H.C. White, 1960.

Law, Donald.   *Herb Growing for Health.* New York: Arc Books, 1971.

Leyel, Mrs. C.F.   *Green Medicine.* London: Faber and Faber, 1952.

_____.   *Elixirs of Life.* London: Faber and Faber, 1958.

Lloyd, J.U. and C.G.   *Origin and History of the Pharmacopoeia Vegetable Drugs.* Caxton, 1929.

Lloyd, J.U.   *Drugs and Medicines of North America.* Lloyd Library Bulletin #31, 1931.

Lucas, Richard.   *Nature's Medicines.* Englewood Cliffs, N.J.: Prentice Hall, 1966.

_____.   *Common and Uncommon Uses of Herbs for Healthful Living.* Englewood Cliffs, N.J.: Prentice-Hall, 1969.

Marks, Geoffrey.   *The Medical Garden.* New York: Scribner, 1971.

Martinez, Maximino.   *Plantas Medicinales De Mexico.* Editiones Botas, 1954.

Massey, A.B.   *Medicinal Plants.* Virginia: Polytech Inst. Bul. #30, 1942.

Meyer, James F.   *The Herbalist.* Hammond, Ind. Bot. Gardens, 1939.

Mességué, Maurice.   *Of Men and Plants* New York: Macmillan, 1972.

Millspaugh, Chas. F.   *Medicinal Plants.* Philadelphia: John C. Yorston & Co., 1892.

National Research Council.   *A Survey of Wild Medicinal Plants of the United States: Their Distribution and Abundance.* Com. on Pharmacognosy, circa 1940.

Quelch, Mary Thorne.   *The Herb Garden.* London: Faber & Faber, 1941.

_____.   *Herbs for Daily Use.* London: Faber & Faber, 1946.

Schafer, Violet.   *Herbcraft.* California: Yerba Buena Press, 1971.

Shelton, Ferne.   *Pioneer Comforts and Kitchen Remedies.* High Point, N.C.: Hutcraft, 1965.

Sievers, A.F.   *American Medicinal Plants of Commercial Importance.* U.S.D.A. Publ. #77, 1930.

Simmonite, W.J.   *The Simmonite-Culpepper Remedies.* London: Foulsham & Co., 1957.

Simmons, Adelma S.   *Herb Growing in Four Seasons.* Princeton: D. Van Nostrand Co., Inc., 1964.

Step, Edward. *Herbs of Healing.* London: Hutchinson, 1926.

Taylor, Lyda A. *Plants Used as Curatives.* Bot. Museum, 1940.

Tobe, John H. *Proven Herbal Remedies.* Tobe, 1969.

Verrill, A.H. *Foods America Gave the World.* LC. Page & Co.

Webster, Helen N. *Herbs, How to Grow Them and Use Them.* Boston, Mass.: Hale, Cushman & Flint.

Weiner, Michael A. *Earth Medicines, Earth Foods.* New York: Macmillan, 1972.

Williams, Louis O. *Drug and Condiment Plants.* U.S.D.A. Handbook, 1960.

Wren, R.C. *Potters Encyclopedia of Botanical Drugs and Preparations.* London: Pitman, 1956.

Youngken, Heber W. *Textbook of Pharmacognosy.* 6th ed. New York: Blakiston (O.P.), 1948.

Poison Plants of the United States

Any discussion of the flora in our country must, in all fairness, make some mention of the plants which are not in the useful list, or which, indeed, may be definitely harmful.

However, here a problem begins, for some plants which are harmful when eaten or touched may be beautiful and useful in the landscape, or some plants when eaten may offer gustatory delights, while parts of the same plant may be highly poisonous. Or again, what is good at one season of the year may be poisonous at another. Examples of these three would be poison ivy, chokecherries, and pokeweed. The bright Christmas flower—the poinsettia—has a number of quite poisonous relatives, but is itself comparatively harmless. One of the florists' primroses is no longer grown because it is quite possible to get a bad rash from the foliage. Beyond this, one comes to "poisonous" qualities which may not even exist, as in the case of a myth that has grown around one of the bright Christmas peppers. Its foliage *is* rated as poisonous, but by legend it was said that if the plant appeared in the home a death would occur.

The fact remains that there are in this great land of ours many plants, even things of beauty and utility, which are poisonous in one way or another. Such plants are found among all native botanical types: algae, fungi, ferns, herbs, vines, shrubs, and trees.

And as hinted, the term "poisonous plants" may designate not only kinds of plants, but also a wide range of poisonous or disturbing effects. Such effects may be classified as *allergies,* coming from wind-blown spores or pollen, *dermatitis* or skin irritation due to direct contact, *internal poisoning* caused by eating, or *mechanical injury* due to scratching by prickles or thorns. As a sample of the poisons in several categories, a few important ones are these:

DERMATITIS		INTERNAL
Poison ivy and oak	Wild parsnip	POISONS
Spotted spurge	Manchineel	Apple-of-Peru
Spurge nettle		Baneberry
Stinging nettle		Beech

Black cherry   Ground cherry   Mushrooms
Black locust   Holly   Nightshade
Black snakeroot   Horse nettle   Oak (acorns)
Bloodroot   Hydrangea   Poison hemlock
Blue cohosh   Jack-in-the-pulpit   Pokeweed
Buckeye   Jequirity pea   Prickly poppy
Buckthorn   Jimsonweed   Rattlebox
Burning bush   Kentucky coffee   Rayless goldenrod
Buttercup   tree   Rhododendron
Castor bean   Larkspur   Rock poppy
Chinaberry   Lobelia   Spurge
Coontie   Mayapple   Star-of-Bethlehem
Corn cockle   Mescal bean   Strawberry bush
Coyotillo   Mexican   Virginia creeper
Cycads   pricklepoppy   Water hemlock
Dicentra   Mistletoe   White snakeroot
Dogbane   Monkshood   Wild balsam apple
Elderberry   Moonseed   Yellow jessamine
Elephant ear   Mountain laurel   Yellow nightshade
False hellebore   Mulberry   Yew
Golden seal

Allowing that there are many plants to avoid on the above list, how does someone interested in the uses of the great wild bounty of our country keep away from the dangers that exist? As a beginning it would be well to have on hand a good reference book, for which the new work by Hardin and Arena, *Human Poisoning,* would be ideal. Further, it should be known that there are in many states, to be found through your local doctor, Poison Control Centers which can give advice if certain plants are ingested. And, as *Human Poisoning* suggests, there are the following basic ways to avoid plant poisoning.

1. Become familiar with the dangerous plants in your own neighborhood.

2. Do not eat wild plants, including mushrooms, unless *positive* of identification.

3. Keep plants, seeds, fruits, and bulbs away from infants.

4. Teach children at an early age to keep unknown plants and plant parts out of their mouths.

5. Teach children to recognize poison ivy or other causes of dermatitis in your area.

6. Be certain you know the plants used by children as playthings (seeds, fruits, stems, etc.) or as skewers for meat.

7. Do not allow children to suck nectar from flowers or make "tea" from leaves of any plants.

8. Avoid smoke from burning plants, unless you know exactly what they are.

9. Remember that heating and cooking do not always destroy the toxic substance.

10. Store labeled bulbs and seeds safely away from children and pets.

11. Do not make homemade medicines from native or cultivated plants without careful research. Beyond all this discussion of the dangers in the poisonous plants of our country, the reader should remember that in addition to medicinal values in a number of otherwise poisonous plants, some of the poisons have somewhat hidden values. Here one can especially remember the uses made by our native Indians of plants for poisoning fishes of which three species are notable: *Eremocarpus setigerus, Aesculus californica,* and *Chlorogalum pomeridianum.*

A native California botanist wrote to me that these plants were important to the Poma and other Indians. The first named plant is called the turkey mullein and belongs to the often poisonous *Euphorbia* family. The weed was beaten on rocks at the inlet of a large waterhole, and the catch of poisoned fish often ran to hundreds of pounds, the poison taken by the fish not being harmful when the fish were eaten.

Much more might be written about this matter of poison plants, and to the extent possible, comments are made in the discussion of plants in the Dictionary section, but it simply should be remembered by all who explore our bounties that, with plants, as with people, there are the bad as well as the good.

Bibliography

Arnold, Harry L. *Poisonous Plants of Hawaii.* Rutland, Vt.: Chas. E. Tuttle, 1968.

Creekmore, Hubert. *Daffodils Are Dangerous.* New York: Walker & Co., 1966.

Hardin, James W. and Arena, Jay M. *Human Poisoning From Native and Cultivated Plants.* North Carolina: Duke Univ. Press, 1969.

Hunter, Beatrice T.   *Gardening Without Poisons.* Boston, Mass.: Houghton-Mifflin, 1964.

Kingsbury, John M.   *Deadly Harvest.* New York: Holt, Rinehart & Winston, 1965.

Kingsbury, John M.   *Poisonous Plants of the U.S. and Canada.* Englewood Cliffs, N.J.: Prentice-Hall, Inc., 1964.

Muenscher, W.C.   *Poisonous Plants of the U.S.* New York: Macmillan, 1964.

————.   *Garden Spice and Wild Pot Herbs.* Ithaca, N.Y.: Comstock, 1955.

Spencer, E.R.   *Just Weeds.* New York: Scribners, 1957.

Youngken, Heber W.   *Common Poisonous Plants of New England.* Publ. Health Service Publication 1220, 1964.

Plants Useful for Crafts

Although the use of plants and their parts as food and medicine has been primary in every stage of civilization, it is not hard to establish through the findings of archeology and the readings of early books, such as those of China and of our own background civilizations (including the Bible), that there are many uses for plant products that every nature-lover should know about.

It is not possible within a relatively few paragraphs to define every minor plant use, but only to point out the various categories of uses of the trees, bushes, and plants which grow everywhere in our country, from mountain to desert. The names given here will be those of most common uses, and for more identification the reader is directed to the index since with some of these plants, such as bearberry (*Arctostaphylos uvaursi*), it would take nearly this whole page to list the regional appellations.

The first useful category would be plants which have or do provide a variety of fibers, either for the making of clothes or ropes. Obviously the kind of plant so used will vary from the widely spread common cattails, to the mesquite bush of the Southwest, or some palms in Florida. A common-name list of plants so used would be:

Century plant	Milkweed	Marijuana plant
Redbud	Bedstraw	Flax
Reeds	Bullrushes	Cattails
Nettles	Mesquite	Adam's needle
Turkey beard	Indian hemp	Basswood
Grasses	Cowania	Hickory (splints)

Plant material has long been used in the tanning of leather, and here the chemicals in the bark (especially) and other parts of trees have provided uses for hemlock, ocotillo, bearberry, and common dock, to name a few. Additional uses of plants are as follows.

ABRASIVES—Widely spread horsetails (*Equisetum*).

ABSORBENTS—Sphagnum moss (this is the source of peat moss); the "wool" of the cinnamon fern.

BROOMS AND BRUSHES—Various plants have tough flexible wood

for making brooms. A variety of corn known as broom corn is still a commercial crop, grown for the purpose its name suggests.

CANDLES—Bayberries principally give wax for good candles.

GARDEN HELPS—Simple tools may be made from hard wood, plants stakes, and other things. Fresh sphagnum moss ground fine makes the finest of seed beds. And the best mulch is plant matter—straw, leaves, and the like.

IMPLEMENTS—Any hard woods, such as the ironwood of the West or the ultra-hard beetlebung trees of the East are still used to make tools of many sorts.

INK—Elderberry fruits or gall nuts from oak trees both make permanent inks.

MOTH PREVENTIVE—Shavings of red cedar and similar fragrant woods will keep out the moths.

"RUBBER" PLANTS—The viscous exudations of such plants as milkweed, goldenrod, and yellow bells are possible mild substitutes for the real (also plant-derived) rubber.

RUSH SEATING—There is nothing that excels the comfort, long life, and natural beauty of leaves of rushes or cattails, when properly woven in a chair frame.

SCOURING BRUSHES—Of old, country people in need of a good scouring material for dirty pans used the crushed stems of horsetails which actually contain a sort of iron-like substance in their heads.

SOAP—The roots of the soapwort plant when crushed and the juice used, give a good soap-like substance which actually is much used in museums for the washing of rare silk items. Another plant which can be used as a quick soap in the fall when the shrub is in bloom, are the flower heads of sweet pepper bush.

TOYS—Who does not remember when, as a small child, some simple doll-like things were made for them out in the woods or fields? The possibilities of such uses are wonderful, and go back through the earliest civilizations about which we know.

Bibliography

Beauchamp, W.M.   *Aboriginal Uses of Wood.* N.Y. State Museum Bul. #76, 1906.

Coon, Nelson.   *Using Wayside Plants.* New York: Hearthside Press, 1957.

Creekmore, Betsey B.   *Traditional American Crafts.* New York: Hearthside Press, 1968.

Jaeger, Ellsworth.   *Easy Crafts and Nature Crafts.* New York: MacMillan, n.d.

Kephart, H.   *The Book of Camping and Woodcraft.* Century Co., 1909.

Ormond, C.   *Complete Book of Outdoor Lore.* New York: Harper & Row, 1964.

Oswald, Fred W.   *Beginners Guide to Useful Plants.* Washington, D.C.: Anderson-Kramer, 1956.

Schaffer, Florence M.   *Driftwood Miniatures.* New York: Hearthside Press, 1967.

Squires, Mabel.   *New Trends in Dried Arrangements.*

Tenenbaum, Frances.   *Gardening with Wild Flowers.* New York: Scribners, 1973.

Thompson, Dorothea S.   *Creative Decorations with Dried Flowers.* New York: Hearthside Press, 1967.

Von Miklos, Josephine.   *Wild Flowers in Your Home.* New York: Doubleday, 1968.

Whitlock and Rankin.   *New Techniques with Dried Flowers.* New York: Hearthside Press, 1967.

Dye Plants of the United States

The uses of wild (as well as cultivated) plants are manifold, and some principal suggestions have been made as to culinary, medicinal and craft uses. All such are, indeed, of great value, but among other uses, none represents the kind of combined beauty and utility that is found in the use of wild plants for dyeing. Presently, with the increased interest in ecology, conservation, and the like, there are many who want to see just what are the more natural values that are found in things of the wild, and dyes are one of them.

In the case of dyes made from plants we have a product simply and relatively easily made from plant parts, which give colors quite unduplicatable in the world of chemistry. There is a softness of color (and often unexpected variableness) in wools and silk dyed with plant dyes, making the colors "easy on the eyes," as differentiated from the gaudy hues of the synthetic materials.

This introduction cannot in any way attempt to give detailed methods of pursuing the actions of dyeing, and happily, for the interested person, there are a number of very excellent modern (and short) books, all listed in the bibliography.

Taking a quick look at the story of dyeing as discussed in such books, it is very interesting to note how mankind seems to hanker for color—color in his clothing, in his home, and in the utilitarian objects which surround him. Art works without color may well be appealing in certain forms, but with color added they are so much more so.

A review of the history of using plants for their extractable colors takes us back, as do so many other subjects, to the ancient Chinese civilization where, in their literature, are noted dye workshops as existing around 3000 B.C. The Egyptians were great lovers of colored clothing and almost everyone knows about how the Phoenicians were making a big business out of Tyrian purple, a dye color made from shells from the ocean, some fifteen centuries before Christ. Again, Marco Polo told us some 700 years ago about the manufacture of indigo from plant material, over in the Indus Valley.

Here in America, in the relics of the very ancient civilizations of

Peru and Chile, it has been found that the peoples there knew more about kinds of weaving than any civilization we know about, and that the dye colors used in that fabulous weaving were bright from natural dyes, having remained so for over 2000 years. The Indians of our United States also had some of this knowledge, and as with so much other understanding of plant uses, turned their skills over to the early colonists for them to add to their European knowledge. Especially does this seem to have been true in the then remote areas, such as Appalachia. But then in the early twentieth century there came a lull in the interest in plant dyes, when people were dazzled by the brightnesses of chemistry. But today more and more we are understanding that there is nothing like the soft beauty and permanence of plant dyes.

As just a suggestion of the various kinds of colors, some of which can be had from the plants listed in this book, and to perhaps intrigue the uninitiated reader, here are some simple listings.

BLUE DYES—indigo is perhaps the most widely-known blue dye, obtained from a widely spread and tropical plant *Indigofera tinctoria*. Woad *(Isatis tinctoria)* is a European dye plant, which yields a blue color.

RED DYES—Unfortunately, as with blues, most of the good reds are made from plants which are not native, though some have been imported and grown. About the only wild plant which yields a true red dye is the pokeberry, the fruit of which is a lovely bright red. Several lichens (rock and white crottle) provide soft reds, while both the sundew *(Drosera)* and the spindle tree *(Euonymus)* give a purple color.

YELLOW—Here again some of the best yellows are from imported species, but hobby-dyers use these from our land:
Quercus Velutina—Black oak, yielding "quercitron."
Polygonum persicaria—Smartweed.
Fraxinus americana—White ash.
Rumex (various species)—Common docks in a number of varieties.
Malus—Apple bark provides yellow.
Solidago (various species)—Goldenrod flowers are rated as excellent.
Pteridium (various species)—Bracken root.
Sassafras albidum—The bark produces a good orange yellow.
BROWNS—*Heather* (with alum).
Juglans (various species)—Durable browns from walnut roots and nuts.
Tsuga canadensis—Hemlock bark gives good reddish-brown. Several

lichens give brown, mostly the parmelias.

The above plants are, properly used, among those able to give the most permanent dye colors, but a few of the plants giving sometimes fugitive colors would be these:

RED—Barberry berries, Cranberry fruit, and pink flowers of the shore rose.

YELLOW—The bark of apple trees, and of barberry, any part of the plant called great celandine, and the roots and stems of gold thread, as well as some lichens.

BLUE—The fruits of blueberry, and of grapes, and the berries of horsebrier.

VIOLET—The fruits of elderberry and of some varieties of grapes.

BEIGE—Some fern leaves and the bark of sassafras.

TAN—Leaves and stems of pokeberry and the hulls of black walnuts.

BROWN—The bark of black cherry, of pokeberries and walnut hulls, and certain lichens.

GREEN—The leaves of the common ragweed.

Assuming now that one has collected one or more of the above plants for an experiment in dyeing, and hopefully also read more about it than in this short chapter, how does one go about some basic dyeing?

First, and assuming that we are talking here about the dyeing of wool, which unlike cotton and synthetics, is much easier to work with for good results, how much material would one collect?

BARK—one peck finely chopped.

LEAVES—¾ peck, dried.

HULLS—one peck.

FLOWERS—1½ quarts of dried or 1½ pecks fresh flower heads.

ROOTS—highly variable.

How to Extract the Dye

Whatever part of the plant is used, it should be pounded or cut small if necessary, and covered with water, then brought to just below the boiling point and simmered gently until the color has been extracted. Some dyes, bark for instance, will require longer simmering before they will yield a good color. Other dyes are ruined by it.

Some dye plants, if cut or broken into small pieces, and then let stand over night in enough water to cover, will make a strongly colored solution by morning. If there is still some color left in the dye plant, it may be simmered in water for a while until the color comes out, and then this color added to the rest of the solution.

The dye plant may be put in a cheesecloth bag, tied loosely so that the water will come in contact with all of the plant material. This method will eliminate the necessity of straining the dye after the color has been extracted. If the plant is not tied in cheesecloth, the dye should be strained before the wool is introduced.

Here it may also be noted that after extraction, certain colors may be combined to produce various soft shades and colors, but the knowledge of what to combine would come only through long experimentation. This is especially true because the color of the extracted dye very often has but little relation to the final color of the finished product.

Dyeing would be an utterly simple process if one could count on all plant colors being "fast" and washable, but almost none are, and so something must be done to the wool to fix the color. This is the *mordanting* process which can be done either before, during, or after actual dyeing, the timing having considerable to do with the intensity and fastness of color. Here is another place for individual experimentation, and here again we shall, for simplification, discuss just one method, the pre-dyeing mordanting.

The materials used are alum, chrome (potassium dichromate), copperas (ferrous sulphate), and tannic acid (commercial or from a natural source of tannin such as oak galls or sumac leaves). By using different mordants, a variety of shades and sometimes even different colors may be obtained from the dye.

ALUM MORDANT   This is the most commonly used of all mordants, and, used in combination with ordinary cream of tartar, brightens the wool. For each pound of wool to be dyed (all recipes given here are based on one pound of wool) use: three or four ounces of potash alum to one ounce of cream of tartar. Dissolve these in about four gallons of cold soft water. Put on stove and as the water warms up, immerse the wool (after it has first been wet in water and squeezed dry). Now heat gradually to boiling, stirring and turning the wool all the time. Boil gently for one hour, adding more water to keep the proportion of liquid to wool always the same. Remove from the fire and let the wool stand in the water overnight. Next morning remove wool, squeeze dry, roll in a towel, and put in a cool place ready for actual dyeing.

CHROME MORDANT   Dissolve in 4½ gallons of soft water, ½ ounces of potassium dichromate and proceed as for alum mordant above.

DYEING   Now we come to the actual dyeing itself.

1. Dye the full amount of any possible yarn or cloth of each color needed for a piece of handicraft at one time, instead of trying to match the color by a second dyeing. Vegetable dye materials vary so much that it is almost impossible to duplicate colors exactly. Anyone who has tried to match a given yarn or cloth will realize that this same statement is true of commercial dyes also.

2. If work is done in the summer time, there will be less damage from spills if the work is done outdoors.

3. To obtain colors lighter or darker, vary the proportion of dye to water.

4. Wool should never be boiled hard or stirred around very much while being dyed as it may cause shrinkage and matting.

Exact details as to formulas for both color and kind of material should be obtained in one of the more exhaustive books noted in the bibliography, but basically these pages are suggestive as to modes of procedure.

The dye stuff, which has been prepared as above, is now put on the stove cold. The materials to be dyed are first rinsed well (to remove excess mordanting solution) and squeezed dry. If they are skeins of wool, they may be very loosely tied and dipped and removed on sticks or wooden forks. Keep dipping and dyeing or stirring gently in the now-boiling dye, until the material has reached the desired color. Then remove from the heat and allow the material to cool in the dye water. Lift it out, carefully squeezing out excess mixture and rinse in clean water until no color comes out with the rinse. Now dry in a suitable place, and the job is done.

Sometimes for certain colors (and this is for experimentation) a hot soap bath after dyeing will brighten and further set the colors.

ALTERNATIVE PROCEDURES   Beyond this somewhat standard method in dyeing there are other possible orders of procedure.

1. The wool may be boiled first with the dye, then the mordant can be added to the same dye bath.

2. The wool may be boiled with dye and the mordant in the same bath together.

3. The wool may be first mordanted, dyed, and then mordanted again to insure the maximum of fastness.

Each of these procedures will produce different color effects, and here is where experience based on study and experiment comes into the picture.

In summation it may be said that much of the success of the whole process depends on the care used in mordanting, while the character of the color depends upon the nature of the mordant. The chrome mordant mentioned tends to produce a golden hue with some materials; tin brightens the color and iron darkens the color. If one were interested in using entirely botanical material for both dyes and mordants, there are possibilities of using oak galls, wood ashes, sumac, hemlock, sorrel, and similar plants to provide the necessary chemical changes that will enable the dye to bite (Latin-mordere) into the wool, all of which and many other possibilities are suggested in some of the more detailed books on dyeing.

Bibliography

Adrosko, Rita J.   *Natural Dyes and Home Dyeing*. New York: Dover Press, 1971. (Published also under the title *Natural Dyes in the United States* as Bul. #281, National Museum from Supt. of Documents, Washington, D.C.)

Barkley, F.A.   *The Uses of the Sumacs by the American Indian*. Missouri Bot. Garden, Bul. #25, 1937.

Bemiss, Elijah.   *The Dyer's Companion.* 1815. Reprint. New York: Dover Press, 1973.

Davidson, Mary F.   *The Dye Pot.* Middleboro, Ky.: 1950.

Kierstead, Sallie P.   *Natural Dyes.* Somerville, Ma.: Bruce-Humphries, 1950.

Kramer, Jack.   *Natural Dyes, Plants and Processes.* New York: Scribners, 1972.

Leechman, Douglas.   *Vegetable Dyes From North American Plants.* Herb Society of America.

Lesch, Alma.   *Vegetable Dyeing.* New York: Watson-Guptill, 1970.

Sweet, H.R.   *The Uses of the Sumacs by the American Indian.* Missouri Bot. Garden, Bul. #25, 1937.

Bibliography of Botanical and Reference Books

Bailey, L.H. *Hortus Second*. New York: Macmillan, 1942.

Claus, Edw. P. and Tyler, Varro E., Jr. *Pharmacognosy*. 5th ed. Phila., Pa.: Lea & Febiger, 1965.

de Candolle, A.L.P. *Origin of Cultivated Plants*. 1855. Reprint. New York: Hafner Pub. Co., 1967.

Fernald, M.D. *Gray's Manual of Botany*. Boston: Amcr. Book Co., 1950.

Grigson, Geoffrey. *The Englishman's Flora*. London: Phoenix House, 1955.

Hall, Elizabeth. *List of Herb Literature*. Herb Society Annual Report, 1948.

Hedrick, U.P. *Sturtevant's Notes on Edible Plants*. N.Y. Dept. Agric. Annual Report XXVII. 1919. Reprint. New York: Dover Press, 1972.

Lindley, John. *Medical and Economical Botany*. London: Bradbury and Evans, 1856.

Marshall, Humphrey. *Arbustum Americanum*. The American Grove, 1785.

Meehan, Thomas. *The Native Wild Flowers and Ferns of the United States*. Boston: Prang, 1878.

Rexford, O. *101 Useful Weeds and Wildings*. 1942.

Rickett, Harold W. *Wild Flowers of the U.S.A.* New York: McGraw-Hill, Inc., 1966 *et. seq.*

Robbins, Wilfred W. and Ramaley, Francis. *Plants Useful to Man*. New York: Blakiston's Sons & Co., 1937.

Sargent, F.L. *Plants and Their Uses*. New York: Holt, 1913.

Saunders, Chas. F. *Useful Wild Plants of the U.S. and Canada*. New York: McBride, 1934.

Taylor, Kathryn S. *A Traveler's Guide to Roadside Wildflowers*. New York: Farrar, Straus & Giroux, Inc., 1949.

Theophrastus. *Enquiry Into Plants—250 B.C.* Sir Arthur Hort, trans. London: Heinemann, 1916.

Uphof, J.C.T.   *Dictionary of Economic Plants.* New York: Hafner Pub. Co., 1959.

Youngken, Heber W.   *Textbook of Pharmacognosy.* New York: McGraw-Hill, 1948.

Bibliography of Regional Plant Life Books

Anderson, J.R.   *Trees and Shrubs, Food Medicinal and Poisonous Plants of British Columbia.* Victoria, B.C.: Dept. of Education, 1925.

Bagdonas, C.R.   *Observations on Edible Native Plants of Colorado.* Unpublished, 1964.

Balls, E.R.   *Early Use of California Plants.* Berkley: Univ. of Cal. Press, 1965.

Bartlett, K.   *Edible Wild Plants of Northern Arizona.* Flagstaff: Northern Arizona Society of Science and Art Museum of Northern Arizona, 1943.

Berrigan, D.   *The Native Fruits of North Dakota and Their Use.* N. Dakota Agric. College Bul #281, April 1935.

Blankenship, J.W.   *Native Economic Plants of Montana.* Bozeman, Montana: Mont. Agric. College Exper. Station, Bul. #56, April 1905.

Bourke, J.G.   "The Folk-Foods of the Rio Grande Valley and of Northern Mexico." *Journal of American Folk-lore* (1895).

Budrow, J.T.   *Some Useful Native Plants of Colorado.* The Courier Printing & Pub. Co., 1895.

Christensen, B.V.   *Some Drug Plants in Florida.* Dept. of Agriculture, Florida, Bulletin #14, Aug. 1935.

Colyer, M.   *Observations on the Edible Native Plants of Southwestern Colorado.* Unpublished 1962, 1963.

Craighead, Frank C. and John J.   *A Field Guide to Rocky Mountain Wild Flowers.* Boston: Houghton-Mifflin Co.

Curtain, L.S.M.   *Healing Herbs of the Upper Rio Grande.* Santa Fe: Santa Fe Lab. of Anthropology, 1947.

Dalgren, B.E. and Standley, P.C.   *Edible and Poisonous Plants of the Caribbean Region.* Washington, D.C.: Bureau of Med. and Surgery, Navy Dept., Govern. Printing Office, 1944.

Douglass, J. and M.   *Observations on Edible Native Plants of Colorado.* Unpublished 1961, 1962.

Gaertner, E.E.   "Freezing, Preservation and Preparation of Some Edible

Wild Plants of Ontario." *Economic Botany* (Oct.-Dec. 1962).

Gilkey, Helen. *Handbook of Northwest Flowering Plants.* Portland, Ore.: Binford and Mort Publishers, 1951.

Gillespie, W.H. *A Compilation of the Edible Wild Plants of West Virginia.* New York: Press of Scholar's Library, 1959.

Gunther, Erna. *Ethnobotany of Western Washington.* Seattle: Univ. of Wash. Press, 1945, 1949.

Hardin, James W. *North Carolina Drug Plants of Commercial Value.* N.C. State Coll. Agric. Bul. #418, 1961.

Harrington, H.D. *Edible Native Plants of the Rocky Mountains.* Albuquerque: Univ. of New Mex. Press, 1967.

Haskin, Leslie. *Wildflowers of the Pacific Northwest.* Portland, Oreg.: Binsfords and Mort.

Heller, C.A. *Edible and Poisonous Plants of Alaska.* College, Alaska: Univ. of Alaska Press, 1966.

Jacobs, Marion Lee and Burlage, Henry M. *Index of Plants of North Carolina with Reputed Medicinal Uses.* Austin, Texas: Henry M. Burlage, 1958.

Josselyn, J. *New England Rarities Discovered.* London, 1672.

Kirk, Donald R. *Edible Wild Plants of the Western United States.* California: Naturegraph, 1970.

Krochmal, Arnold, Walters, Russell S., and Doughty, Richard M. *A Guide to Medicinal Plants of Appalachia.* U.S.D.A. Handbook #400, 1968.

Leighton, Ann. *Early American Gardens for "Meat and Medicine".* Boston: Houghton-Mifflin, 1970.

Mardy, G.A. *Fifty Edible Plants of British Columbia.* Brit. Col. Provincial Handbook #1, 1942.

Martinez, Maximo. *Plantas Medicinales de Mexico.* Ediciones Botas, 1944.

Mexican Plants—Badianus Manuscript, 1552. E. W. Emmert, trans. Baltimore: Johns Hopkins Press, 1940.

Michalowski. *Florida Edible Wild Plants.* St. Petersburg, Fla.: Great Outdoors Publ. Co., 1963.

Morrell, J.M.H. *Some Maine Plants and Their Uses "Wise and Otherwise."* Rhodora, May, 1901.

Morton, J.F. *Wild Plants for Survival in South Florida.* Miami, Florida: Hurricane House, 1963.

Oswald, F.W.   *The Beginners Guide to Useful Plants of Eastern Wilds.* Hawthorne, N.J.: Anderson Press, 1956.

Pesman, M.W.   *Meet the Natives of Colorado.* 5th ed. Denver: 1966.

Porsild, A.E.   "Edible Plants of the Arctic". *Journal of the Arctic Institution of North America,* Vol. 6, No. 1 (1953).

Rose, J.N.   *Notes on Useful Plants of Mexico.* U.S. National Museum, 1899.

Santander, Carlos U.   *Diccionario de Medicacion Herbaria.* 5th ed. Santiago, Chile: Ed. Nascimento, 1953.

Standley, Paul.   *Some Useful Plants of New Mexico.* Washington, D.C.: Annual Rep. of the Smithsonian Institution, pp. 447–462, 1912.

Stratton, R.   *Wild Greens and Salads of Oklahoma.* Stillwater, Okla.: Okla. A.M. College, 1943.

Sweet, Muriel.   *Common Edible and Useful Plants of the West.* California: Naturegraph, 1962.

Szczawinsky, A.F. and Hardy, C.A.   *Guide to the Common Edible Plants of British Columbia.* Victoria, B.C.: Brit. Col. Provincal Handbook No. 20, April 1962.

Tanaka, Yoshio.   *Useful Plants of Japan.* Japan, 1888.

Tehon, Leo R.   *The Drug Plants of Illinois.* Ill. Nat. Hist. Surv., Cir. 44, 1957.

Yaeger, A.F., and Latzke, E.   *The Native Fruits of North Dakota and Their Use.* N. Dakota Agric. College Bul. #281, April 1935.

United States of America Department of Agriculture.   *Common Weeds of the U.S.* New York: Dover Press, 1970.

The Dictionary
of Useful Plants

Plants as Families

The pages which now follow in this book offer to the reader a very miniscule knowledge of plant life, touching only upon the known or reliably reputed values in various areas of usefulness. No complete descriptions of the plants themselves have been given, either from the common appearance or the scientific botanical viewpoint, and no illustrations included, beyond sketches that give a rough appearance of some of the plants or their parts.

As will be quickly noted, all discussions are in the headings of "Families" because so often a knowledge of the values of one commonly known member of a family will quickly lead one to equal or interesting values of close relatives. Some readers may feel that the studying of plants under the family heading may require more than common botanical knowledge, but if references to the material presented here do lead one gently into some knowledge of botany, surely no harm will have been done.

On this subject of families, almost everyone knows that the household kitten belongs to the same family as a lion, or that dogs and wolves may have many familial characteristics in appearance and habits. With every other field from birds and bees down, even into minerals, the observant scientist knows family connections; and certainly this is true in the human world where there are large "families" such as the European and the Chinese—right down to you and your children who have appearance and characteristics which identify the "family."

Thus, one should, in using this book, do a little delving into the world of botany, and have at hand one of the new (and sometimes regional) botanical dictionaries or encyclopedias which are easily available. The regional series now offered by the New York Botanical Garden are good examples of this.

THE MAPLE FAMILY

ACERACEAE

In the history of "plant uses" of American plants, it is probable that the story of the production of maple sugar, which was first written up in the late eighteenth century in a supplement to Culpepper's herbal, was given wide prominence. The famed Dr. Benjamin Rush of Philadelphia (a signer of the Declaration of Independence), allowed that it might well equal in importance the sugar from the cane then being grown in the East Indies, and that it certainly was as good as, or better than, such sugar. Sugar from the maple tree is, however, only one of the many uses of the product of various species of the maple family.

Acer grandidentatum—Big-tooth maple.
  This is a maple of the higher mountain areas of the southwest and, like others of the family, maple sugar can be made from it. A shrubby tree, it is not tall growing.

Acer negundo—The box elder, ash-leaved or cut-leaved maple, stinking ash.
  This tree, which is not usually identified as a maple because of its cut-leaved appearance, is a short-lived, coarse tree, which does, however, have sap that may be boiled into sugar. There are a number of references to the use of this tree for sap from sections in Canada where the sugar maple does not grow so well.

Acer pennsylvanicum—Striped maple, goosefoot or northern maple, moosewood.
  A smallish tree notable in appearance for its striped bark. It grows in the mountains from Canada to the South, and the only values which have been ascribed to it are that an extract from its juices has been used for skin eruptions.

Acer platanoides—The Norway maple.
  Although negative comments are not usual as an inclusion in this book, a comment can be quoted from another writer who rightly says: "Its faults are great, chiefly in that it is surface-rooting, which is bad for lawns and sidewalks."

Acer rubrum—Swamp maple, red, scarlet, or water maple.
  Usually found in the East growing in low or swampy ground, the tree is beautiful, the first one to color in late summer. Sugar may be made from the sap and there is a record of the use of a strong decoction of this maple combined with sugar to be used for an

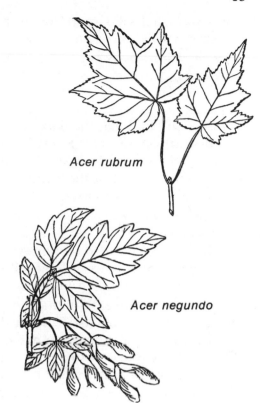

Acer rubrum

Acer pennsylvanicum

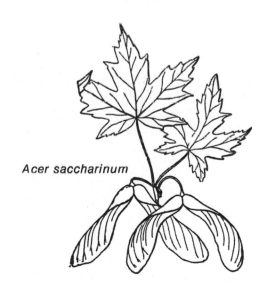

Acer negundo

Acer saccharum

Acer saccharinum

eye wash. Selected wood from trees has been used for the famed "curly maple" in cabinet work.

Acer saccharinum—Silver, soft, or white maple.

A rapid growing tree, widely spread in this country, it is not to be recommended as a lawn or street tree, nor is the small amount of sweet sap worth gathering. Persons interested in dye plants will find that the bark, used with one or another type of mordant, will produce a variety of good brown colors. A blue-black ink can also be made of the bark. The scientific name is so similar to that of the sugar maple that the two are nomenclaturally easily confused.

Acer saccharum—Sugar or rock maple.

Growing in the East and as far south as Texas, no American tree is finer nor possessed of more value than the sugar maple. Nor indeed are any trees of finer fall color, making its home areas places of autumn pilgrimage.

As indicated in these notes, maples have many values of beauty as a shade tree, as the source of fine hard lumber, some possible medicinal uses, and minor value as a dye material. However, with a knowledge of the maple as a source of sugar, which came to us from the Indians, we have a true culinary value, quite unequaled.

Today after tapping the trees in early spring and leading off the sweetish sap through a spile, made (possibly) from hollowed stems of elderberry bushes, one can boil down the sap either out-of-doors over a woodfire, or at home with plenty of gas, as the reduction into syrup is slow. Further boiling reduces the syrup to the harder sugar.

There are many recipes for using syrup or sugar in cooking, substituting the maple sugar or syrup in place of white or brown sugar.

Maple Money Candy

Boil equal amounts of maple syrup and dark corn syrup until the mixture forms balls when dropped in cold water. Drop them onto a buttered pan to form thin discs about the size of a quarter.

Maple Butternut Cream Fudge

Mix two cups of maple sugar with half a cup of cream and boil until it strings from a spoon. Mix in one cup chopped butternuts (or other native wild nuts) and cool in buttered pan.

THE WATER PLANTAIN FAMILY
ALISMATACEAE

Widely distributed in this family are mainly two genera, both of them aquatic plants and of value for food or medicine.

Alisma plantago-aquatica—Water plantain, mad-dog weed, devil-spoons, great thrumwort.

Here the words "mad" or "devil" indicate a poisonous nature, which some books say it has when uncooked. It was used by early herbalists as a diuretic and by the Cherokee Indians for application to sores and for wounds and bruises.

'The plant when growing can well be studied, as it was by the great John Ruskin, who noted in the relationships of the ascending stem a great principle of architectural proportions that had been used by the Greeks in building the Parthenon.

Sagittaria latifolia   Alisma plantago-aquatica   Triglochin maritima

Sagittaria latifolia—Arrowhead, swamp potato, wappato.

These names, as do those of the Alisma, show its whole story, for in whichever local species, it grows along the borders of streams and ponds and has, under water, potato-like tubers growing at the end of long runners. A major source of vegetable food for many tribes of Indians, as the plant is spread from East to West. In cooking like a potato, the rather unpleasant taste of the raw tubers is dissipated.

In addition to this species there are several local forms native to the East Coast, the Midwest, and one, the *S. montevidensis*, the giant arrowhead, found in the southern states. The species *S. sagittifolia*, noted in many old herbals, is the European form.

***Triglochin maritima*—Arrow grass, sourgrass, goosegrass.**
A plant of salt marshes and sometimes found inland, it is prevalent on both coasts. The seeds were parched and ground into flour by some western Indian tribes. However, in droughts, the plants are poisonous to cattle, although this poison disappears in parching.

THE CARPET-WEED FAMILY
AIZOACEAE

This family can only be defined as a "weed," and, as such, a plant which is quite widely distributed. Some grow on land and some in the water as with the sea-purslane, while an Asian plant *Tetragonia* is a summer substitute for spinach and is especially good in providing this pot green from early summer until frost.

***Mollugo verticillata*—Indian chickweed, carpet-weed.**
Reputed to have been used by the Indians as a poultice, demulcent, and ointment and possibly also as a potherb, today it has relatively minor value.

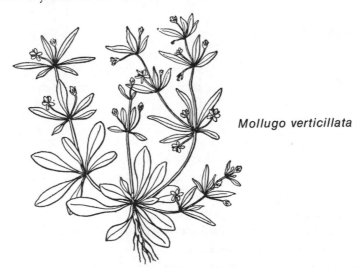

Mollugo verticillata

***Tetragonia expansa*—New Zealand spinach.**
This garden vegetable from Asia has become established along

the West Coast near salt marshes and is becoming popular in home gardens. It has the same uses as regular spinach.

Mesembryanthemum crystallinum **and** *M. edule*—Ice plant, sea fig. Two African species planted as erosion controls along the coasts of California, the juicy stems and leaves are fleshy and may be used in salad. The little fruit is edible, if not delicious. The first species has reddish or white flowers while the other has showy magenta blooms.

THE AMARANTHUS FAMILY
AMARANTHACEAE

Many of the plants of this book, while certainly "wild," are by no means to be considered as weeds, in the usual meaning of this word, although such appellations of many members of this family, such as pigweed, tumbleweed, careless, etc., are happiest at home in a rich farm yard. And yet, in a small way, there are values of one kind or another, or at least "reputed" ones.

Amaranthus graecizans—Tumbleweed, amaranth, white amaranthus. It bears the name of tumbleweed because as the plant dies in the fall it "tumbles" over the fields. It is found throughout North America, and has a minor reputation as an herb to be used against fevers.

Amaranthus hybridus—Smooth pigweed, amaranthus, green amaranth, love-lies-bleeding, pigweed, prince's feather, red cockscomb, wild beet, spleen amaranth.
Just as with so many common names, quite similar species can be noted as *A. melancholicus*, *A. caudatus*, *A. tricolor*, *A. paniculatus*, and *A. hypochondriacus*.
   While few would include this in the area of a food weed, it is used as a pot-herb in Jamaica, while in India, it is extensively cultivated for its seeds, which are ground into flour. Hence this plant should be noted for a possible use for those in need of a new "nature food." Medicinally amaranthus has been used in treating dysentery, ulcers, and hemorrhage of the bowels, all because of its astringent quality.

Amaranthus lividus—Purplish amaranth.
An introduced plant found in waste places in the northern states, it is distinguished by the erect flower head. It doubtless

Amaranthus graecizans   *Amaranthus hybridus*

has much the same values as other members of the family. Here
should be noted the aspect of the various colors found in this
family, color that may or may not have given rise to assigned but
doubtful medicinal value. In the old days of the Doctrine of
Signatures, such a plant would have been assigned values
related to the blood, because of the red or reddish colors.

In this connection one wonders whether or not one should
disregard the values of color as a curative agent. Who, for instance, would want to eat a green beefsteak or who would think
that perfume would be of any value unless it had a "cider" color?
Surely one cannot disregard the psychological value of colors in
any part of our life.

Amaranthus retroflexus—Green amaranth, pigweed, red-root.
A weed widely spread, coming likely from Mexico where one
finds it listed as a medicinal plant in explorations made of plant
use among the Zapotec Indians. Here also, as with other species,
one finds reputed values as a hemostatic. But again one knows
that the seeds are of food value, being formerly cultivated for
this by the Indians of Arizona. In the Northwest, it has been used
as a cooked pot-herb or used as a salad green when young. One
authority suggests that the young shoots which arise in early
spring make a good "asparagus" substitute, but there are cautions against ever using the roots or the red leaves in the fall,
as they may well be poisonous.

In the Amaranth two other members of the family have listed values.

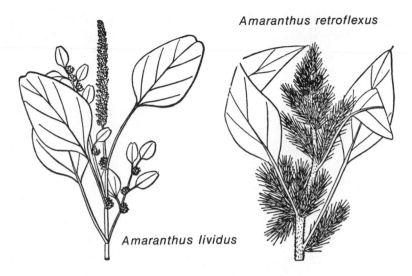

Amaranthus retroflexus

Amaranthus lividus

Achyranthes repens—Forty knot.

It is a tropical garden plant, and with an alternate scientific name of *Alternanthera*, found growing in dry places in East Coast areas. It has values reputedly diurctic and one recipe for this use notes that "a decoction made by treating a handful of herb in a pint of water in doses of a wineglassful three times a day is useful."

Telanthera polygonoides—Piss-a-bed.

Given this common name it should hardly be necessary to indicate its use.

THE AMARYLLIS FAMILY

AMARYLLIDACEAE

The Amaryllis family, the flowers of which seem to belong to the lily family, gives for those who like house plants the big, bright, Amaryllis flowers. For those who are interested in economic plants, this family gives us the great group of plants called agave or maguey, plants that in Mexico are said to have some 400 possible uses, all the way from house shingles to potent alcoholic drinks. Some of such uses are within the purview of this book.

Agave Americana—Maguey, century plant, American aloe, agave.

Found across the dry parts of the American Southwest, this is but one of many, many species of agave, which has served the

Indian so well. Leaf fibers give us thread (sisal is from a different species), the leaf has soap-like properties, the heart of the growing plant is used as a roasted salad plant, while the juices become pulque and stronger drinks. The fresh juice has been used as a laxative and diuretic. A century ago the tubbed specimens of variegated forms of agave were considered fine forms of decoration on lawns.

Agave parryi—Mescal.

Found in New Mexico and Arizona, the common name should not confuse one with the hallucinogenic "Mescal button." Rather this species has constituted a staple food of the Apaches.

Agave utahensis—Utah aloe.

Found in the arid parts of the southern Rocky Mountains this plant can be used as a food plant, using the succulent parts.

Hypoxis hirsuta—Coville, yellow stargrass.

Sometimes called the Star-of-Bethlehem, this grows in the Appalachian chain from Maine to Georgia. Its use, other than that of being a lovely flower, seems to stem from its possible medicinal value in the treatment of ulcers of long standing, with a preparation of the root (bulb).

Manfreda virginica—False aloe, rattlesnake's master, Virginian agave.

A tincture of the root has been used in the treatment for snake bite (hence one name). The plant grows from Maryland to Texas, while other species are from Texas southward. Some species of *Manfreda* has roots which are much used in Mexico as soap, where the plant is commonly called Amole (soap).

THE SUMACS

ANACARDIACEA

Most of the plant families of this book are classifiable under one or another use, but here we come to a plant which while it is most always beautiful, may vary in value from the most dangerously poisonous to delightfully useful.

Nomenclaturally it presents problems, too, for even its common name is or has been spelled "sumac," or "shumach," while the scientific name may be found under *Rhus* or *Toxicodendron,* and among the species the scientific name may vary according to author or locale. Here, as with many plants of this book, the reader should consult his local botanies.

A sample of this confusion will be found in the first species listed below, which seems to be known variously as *Rhus trilobata, R. canadensis,* or *R. seronina.*

Rhus aromatica—Fragrant or sweet-scented sumac, stink bush, skunk bush.

Under *R. trilobata* this would be known in the Rocky Mountains as squaw bush, where it has been used as a beverage, while, listed as *R. canadensis* from North Carolina to Louisiana, it is listed for its oils and resins and its use as a red coloring matter.

Rhus copallina—Shining sumac, varnish sumac, common sumac.

An Eastern plant, it too contains tannin. Roots were used by the Indians as an ointment for hemorrhoids, while the hairs on the berries possess a strong acid which, as an infusion, is used as a gargle for sore throat.

***Rhus glabra* (also *R. trilobata R. integrifolia*)**—Scarlet sumac, upland sumac, Shernoke, vinegar tree, squaw bush, lemonade berry.

The first is an Eastern species, the second is from the Midwest to California, and the third is solely from California. However, they all have similar red fruit clusters which were long used by

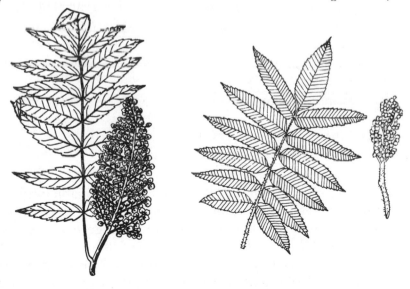

Rhus glabra   Rhus typhina

the Indians as the source of a cooling summer drink, which you yourself can prepare. Take a couple of cups of the berries, bruise and wash them until the juice turns a good pink color. Strain carefully to remove the little hairs found on the seeds, sweeten with sugar and chill before serving. In the Appalachian region the leaves are smoked to treat asthma, while the stem produces a yellow dye and the berries a good tan or beige dye.

In many books on medicinal plants, various suggestions are made for the use of all parts of the plant, most of them depending on the generally astringent qualities found. The bark boiled in milk is indicated for healing wounds, for which the Iroquois used it.

Rhus typhina—Staghorn sumac, hairy sumac, velvet sumach, vinegar tree.

A large growing shrub or small tree, this is an ornamental of the eastern United States. The bark and branches, because they contain so much tannin and malic acid, have been used in tanning.

The Poison Ivy Group of Rhus

Rhus diversiloba—Western poison oak, yeara.

These three species can well be treated as one in a book of this nature, as in one kind or another it is found pretty much over the entire country. The commonest form is *R. radicans* with its three shiny leaves, but there is a variance as to habit of growth as a shrub or a vine, while the oak-leaf form truly does have leaves with an oak-leaf shape and color. The West Coast form is also similar in leaf shape.

Rhus radicans—Common poison ivy, three-leaved ivy, poison creeper, climbing sumac, poison oak, mercury.

This is the eastern low-growing poison ivy which may be found listed in some botanies as *R. toxicodendron*. Even the smoke from dried burning foliage may cause serious poisoning and the main thing is to treat this and other poison forms with great respect.

Rhus vernix—Poison sumac, poison elder, thunderwood, poison dogwood.

A very beautiful shrub found widely throughout the East with many leaflets on a stem, with greenish flowers and then with very delightful-looking white berries in the fall.

In some ways it seems to be even more poisonous than the

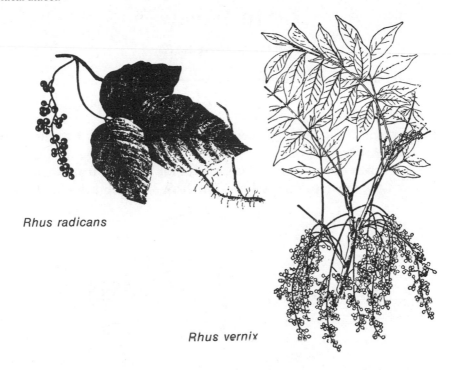

Rhus radicans

Rhus vernix

poison ivy, and handling it should be avoided, especially as the foliage is somewhat similar to *Rhus glabra* as above. It usually likes a wet place as against the dryer homes of other species.

One of the most important things for a nature-lover or plant-using enthusiast is to learn to identify your local kind of poison ivy and to understand methods of protecting or treating yourself if infected. Camp counsellors have used a boiled-down lotion of jewelweed (*Impatiens pallida*) or rubbed on leaves of the sweet-fern (*Comptonia peregrina*) or perhaps washed well with Fels-naptha soap or with unleaded gasoline. Anything will do, which will dissolve the poisonous volatile oil.

Readers who may wish to know more about poison ivy can secure Farmer Bulletin No. 1972 for 10¢ from the Supt. of Documents, Washington, D.C., 20402.

THE PAPAW
ANNONACEAE

This member of what is known as the custard-apple family somewhat resembles a large banana or in early times was thought to be similar to the papaya.

Asimina triloba—Common pawpaw, American custard apple, fetic shrub.

A tall shrub or good sized tree, this plant is found from western New York down to Mississippi. The fruit about four inches long

Asiminia triloba

has a rich luscious taste with a pulp like egg custard. As with such a plant as the yew tree, the pulp is edible but the seeds are poisonous. Reports are that for some people the bark foliage or the fruit may cause dermatitis, hence experimentation is not suggested.

THE DOGBANE FAMILY
APOCYNACEAE

A widely spread plant in the United States, the family is largely a medicinal one for, as the name with "bane" in it should indicate, it is baneful in its effects, while names like "rheumatism weed" would indicate a value. Other names for some species such as "American ipecac," "catchfly," and "honey trap," indicate similar uses. The long central stems are full of fibers (cf. the name "silkweed") and in California, Indians used the dried fibers to make twine, nets, and even clothing.

Of more than these minor values, however, is the fact that one species (not native here), *Vinca rosea,* has been proposed as being of great value in treating bronchial cancer in children, and other uses are being explored.

Apocynum androsaemifolium—Spreading dogbane, American ipecac, bitter dogbane, bitter-root, black Indian hemp, catch fly, colicroot, common dog's-bane, dogbane, fly trap, honey bloom, Indian hemp, milk ipecac, milkweed, rheumatism wood, wandering milkweed, western wallflower, wild ipecac.

This dogbane is found throughout the United States and the great number of common names suggesting medicinal uses should suggest that it has a wide usage, but here, as with so many plants used medicinally, it should be remembered that overuse makes it dangerous. The values are found in the roots and dried

Apocynum androsaemifolium

rhizomes, and a "dose" would be not more than one grain or a simple infusion of one teaspoon of roots to a pint of boiling water, taking two teaspoons, six times daily.

The reported medicinal values are listed as emetic, cathartic, diuretic, and cardiac stimulant, while one authority suggested it as a medicine to use in cases of the bites of mad dogs.

In sum, this and other dogbanes are plants to respect and use with discretion.

Apocynum cannabinum—Indian hemp, bowman's root, Indian physic,
        wild cotton, coctaw-root, glabrous hemp (and others).
Much the same may be said of this plant as the one above in that
its effects are emetic, cathartic, and diuretic. Poisonous to stock
as well as man and yet medicinal when used by the knowing, it
should be used only with great care.

The Cree Indians and others, in parts of the West, used it for
making ropes and twine.

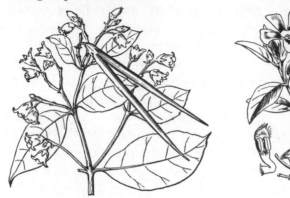

Apocynum cannabium   Vinca minor

Vinca minor—Periwinkle or myrtle.
All gardeners know the blue myrtle as a fine groundcover plant,
always green, and, while not a true native plant, it has widely
escaped, and may be recaptured and taken into the home garden. It has little known medicinal value.

THE HOLLY FAMILY

AQUIFOLIACEAE

Of the three genera in this family, the hollies are the only important
one in this country—important for beauty, use, history, and medicine. In the last fifty years, beautiful additions and hybridizations
have been accomplished, bringing into the horticultural field many
fine hollies which have incorporated the hardiness of the American
holly, the beauty of leaf and berry of the hollies from England and
the Orient, as well as a variety of plant habits highly useful in landscaping our homes. But of the true American hollies here are the
important, useful ones.

Ilex cassine—Dahoon, yaupon, cassine, black vomit.

This is a shrub or small tree found from Virginia to Florida and a holly from which the "black drink" of the Indians of that region was made. Extractions of this and *I. vomitoria* produced violent vomiting as well as an extended period of freedom from hunger and thirst. Among early herbalists it was used for treatment of gout, catarrh, pleurisy and smallpox.

Ilex glabra—Inkberry, gall-berry, evergreen winterberry.

Beyond the fact that a drink made from the plant would well be an emetic, this East Coast dwarf and evergreen shrub is a truly excellent landscape plant. Although the berries are black instead of holly-red, the neat rounded character of the plant makes it an all-year-round fine shrub.

Ilex opaca—American holly.

This coastal tree growing down to Florida and in Texas is highly variable in beauty but the holly enthusiasts have segregated many fine natural variations and it (or the inter-specific breeds) is one of our finest ornamental trees. Medicinally it has been used much as other hollies, the berries being emetic, or in excess, poisonous.

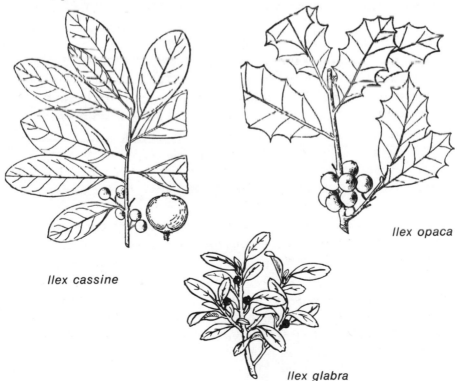

Ilex cassine

Ilex opaca

Ilex glabra

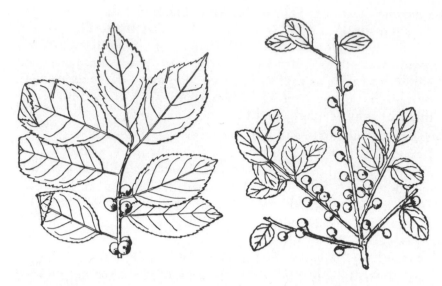

Ilex verticillata   *Ilex vomitoria*

Ilex verticillata—Winterberry, black alder, red-berried alder, feverbush.

A good landscape shrub for which a better common name would
be the "deciduous holly," for the berries are a bright red, pro-
lific, and fine for winter display, although poisonous to eat. Its
medicinal usefulness is reputed to be much as the other species.
One authority cites its use by the Indians as "astringent, antiseptic, and tonic." For those interested in dyeing, the unripe berries
will dye wool green while the bark gives a good yellow.

Ilex vomitoria—Yaupon, cassine, Caroline tea, black drink, Indian tea,
emetic holly, cassiaberry bush.

Early explorers of America beginning with deVaca in 1542, reported the ceremonial use by the Indians of an emetic and
a cardiac stimulant "tea," a ceremony which was pictured in
deBrys book in 1591. Sometimes thought to have been the extract of the Dahoon holly, recent investigations have pointed to
the descriptively named *Ilex vomitoria*. It is a smallish evergreen
tree, occurring from Virginia to Florida. The leaves of the plant
are emetic, cathartic, and seemingly both stimulant and depressant. Mainly, from the modern viewpoint, one looks on this
plant and its uses as an Indian religious ceremonial plant of the
East Coast.

THE ARUM FAMILY
ARACEAE

All of the members of this family are natives of wet spots, along the edges of streams and, in one species or another, are widely distributed. Indeed, the great number of common names of each plant shows this, as does the fact that so many folks know about some ordinary uses.

Unfortunately, there is not room here to give detailed instructions for cooking and other uses.

Acorus calamus—Sweet flag, calamus, myrtle flag, pine root, pepper-root, beewort, sweet rush, sweet sedge, sweet cinnamon.

Of all the plants of this book, the use of sweet flag for a pleasant chew and as medicine has been widespread among people from ancient Greece, through the American Indians, and among people today. Very widespread in its habitat, the part most used is the rhizome (thickened root), as well as the sweet and fragrant stem of young leaves.

In gathering, note the flowering part (the spathe) protruding from the leaf, as this is the cue that the plant is safe to use, rather than being a similar appearing and quite poisonous species of iris which grows often in the same kind of wet spot that the arums all love.

Principally as a stomachic and for other problems of the digestive tract, it was considered so valuable that Indians used it as a medium of exchange.

As a food plant, the rhizomes have been cut into, sliced, and candied.

Beyond long known and much used medicinal values, the forager in the wild will want to gather the roots and use them perhaps, for candy. Here one cuts the rootstocks and boils them until tender, then reboils them in a thick syrup and possibly adds some candied ginger for additional flavor. Or perhaps one can just dig and clean the rootstocks and use them for a pleasant chew. Or when camping, they can be dug and used as part of a tasty salad, possibly adding wild onions or wild chives for additional flavor.

Arisaema dracontium—Green dragon, dragon root.

Similar to Jack-in-the-pulpit, but without the pulpit, it has had

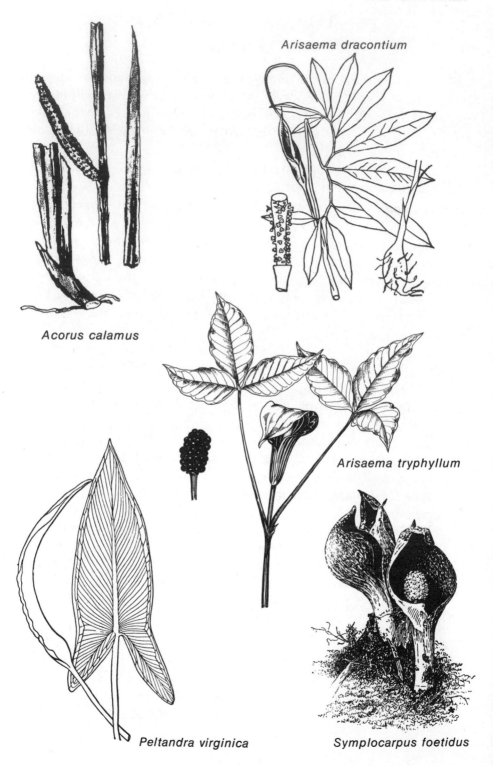

Acorus calamus

Arisaema dracontium

Arisaema tryphyllum

Peltandra virginica

Symplocarpus foetidus

some medicinal uses, though it is notable principally because it is poisonous to insects and vermin.

Arisaema triphyllum—Jack-in-the-pulpit, Indian turnip, bog-onions, priest's pintle, wake robin, cuckoo plant, and others.

The raw corm (bulb) is poisonous and produces skin irritations and yet the Indians in many parts used the corms boiled as a main item of their diet. They also used dried corm-dust as a headache cure, as it probably was a counter irritant. Corms were dug in the fall. But beyond these uses, the unusual physical feature of the "pulpit" makes it a fine plant to use to introduce children to the wonders of plant growth.

Peltandra virginica—Arrow arum, Virginia tuckahoe, Indian bread, poison arum.

Growing widely in all of the eastern part of the country, it is a plant with similar qualities to *A. triphyllum*. The arrow-shaped large leaves have a tropical look, making the plant useful for pool-edge planting. Much used by many Indians as a food plant after extracting the acrid principle with heat, it is not, however, recommended as a "quickie-wayside-food."

Symplocarpus foetidus—Skunk cabbage, rockweed, swamp cabbage, etc.

Just about the first flower of spring and a fine example of "beauty in the beast," a bouquet of this species usually adorns my dining table in spring. Indians and others have gathered and cooked the first leaf growth, and the roots have been used to prepare "flour." The dried, powdered root was also prepared as a wound dressing, while the root-hairs were used as a styptic and for alleviation of tooth-ache pains. In the Northwest a related plant, the yellow arum (*Lysichiton*) is similarly named and used.

THE GINSENG FAMILY
ARALIACEAE

Here is a family of plants widely spread, with family members at variance with each other in appearance and most of them of no value other than medicinal, unless one should rate the English ivy as a landscape plant, or the imposing Hercules club as a valuable shrub.

Aralia nudicaulis—Wild or Virginian sarsaparilla, American spikenard, shotbush, spignet, sweet root.

This is an aromatic plant found in the woodlands from the East
to Missouri, the extraction of the root being a gentle stimulant,
diaphoretic, and cough remedy. It has been used as a substitute
for true sarsaparilla.

Aralia racemosa—Indian-root, American spikenard, life-of-man, old
man's root, spignet, pigeon weed.

Roots and rhizomes have been used to treat rheumatism, coughs
and, in the Appalachian area, they have been used for backache.
The purplish berries are not considered edible, but a principal
use has been as a major ingredient of root beer.

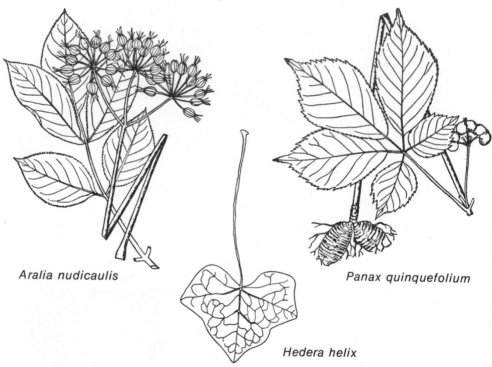

Aralia nudicaulis

Panax quinquefolium

Hedera helix

Hedera helix—English ivy.

Though not a native American plant, it is so much used and
naturalized that it is a part of our national flora. Basically it
should be regarded as a poisonous plant, but extractions of the
plant have been used as a cure for the itch, ulcers, and other skin
troubles.

Oplopanax horridum—Devil's club.

A shrubby plant covered by yellow prickles, which grows north to Alaska from the mountains of Oregon. The young stems may be eaten cooked as greens while the roots may be peeled and chewed.

Panax quinquefolia—Ginseng, tartar root, five-finger, red berry, etc. Here is a plant native to Canada, the Appalachian and Ozark regions, and the Pacific Northwest. It has been hunted and dug as a medicinal plant for many years and the U.S.D.A. Bulletin 2201 (10¢) offers help in growing it commercially. While there seems to be no scientific evidence of its actual medicinal value, the Koreans and the Chinese have considered it a drug of immense value as a stimulant and an aphrodisiac.

THE BIRTHWORT FAMILY
ARISTOLOCHIACEAE

Only two plants in this family are of special interest in the "useful" category, both bearing at times similar common names. Widely spread in the woods in the area from Canada to Texas, the family is notable mostly for the modest flowers or the distinctive ones of the so-called Dutchman's pipe *(A. durior)*, a fine screening vine.

Aristolochia serpentaria—Virginia snakeroot, pelican-flower, snakeroot, thick birthwort, serpentary.
In spite of the "snake" names, it does not seem to have been used for snake bites. Mild infusions are reported to be useful for general tonic purposes, for mild fevers, and in any place where

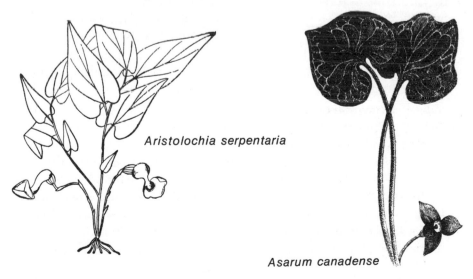

Aristolochia serpentaria

Asarum canadense

an aromatic bitter was suggested. Once listed in the U.S. Pharmacopoeia, it is no longer considered important.

Asarum canadense—Wild ginger, Canada snakeroot, Indian ginger, false colt's foot, heart leaf.

There are a number of suggestions as to the use of the thickish root stock for medicinal purposes, but they are likely all based on its qualities as an aromatic stimulant. But the dried root has often been used as a substitute for "tropical" ginger, a use in Colonial times that likely came from the Indians.

George Washington Carver, the great man who did so much for the peanut industry, was much interested in the use of wild foods. In one essay on wild ginger, he says that one can pick or dry the leaves, powder very fine (and the same with the root) and "shake over the food as eaten or drop a few leaves into the food while cooking. I know one person who will not drink a cup of tea without a sprinkle of wild ginger powder in it." Continuing on what he calls the "heart leaf," he says it is "the acme of delicious, appetizing, and nourishing salads."

THE MILKWEEDS
ASCLEPIDACEAE

It is interesting that the generic name of the plants considered here should be that of the reputed "Father of Medicine," Aesculapius, a Greek doctor who lived about 100 years before the time of Christ. Why the name was given to this family by Linnaeus is not known, especially since all the plants considered here are American in habitat, although one West Indian species is highly valued as an emetic. In references to the useful plants of the Rockies and the Northwest, note is made of the edible shoots of one species, and all through the East, these and others discussed are commonly known and used.

Asclepias currassavica—Blood-flower, cancerillo.

Here is a species native of tropical America, somewhat naturalized in parts of the United States, which contains a substance some researchers think may be useful in some forms of cancer (*Science*, 12/25/64), it having been called "cancerillo" and used for this in Costa Rica. It has also been used for warts, a use other species of Asclepias are known for. A further case where scientists are taking another look at anciently known herbal values.

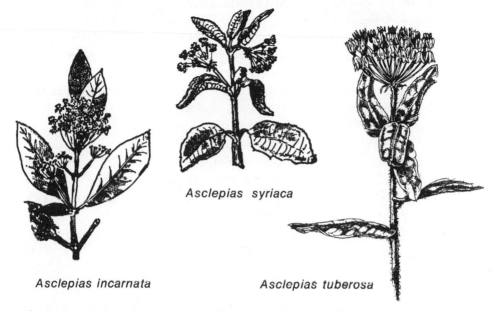

Asclepias syriaca

Asclepias incarnata   Asclepias tuberosa

Asclepias incarnata—Swamp milkweed, white Indian hemp, water
    nerve root, rose-colored silkweed.

A strong growing species found widely, it grows in wet areas
with flowers in July. Medicinally (as indicated by the names), it
is listed as a stomachic and quick diuretic, the thickened roots
being used medicinally.

Of more general value is the spring-time use of the growing
tips as a substitute for asparagus, it being recommended that
water be changed when cooking, to remove any mild bitter taste.

Asclepias speciosa—Showy milkweed.

This species is found from the West to British Columbia, but in
general is much like eastern species except that the flowers are
purplish-green. The young shoot, leaves, and even flowers are
served as cooked greens or boiled in soup with meat. Milkweeds
are said to contain esclepain, a good meat tenderizer.

The Hopi Indians believe that one species increases the flow
of milk in women.

Asclepias syriaca—Milkweed, silkweed, swallow-wort, wild cotton.
    This plant has many uses and, from the name and the botanical
    studies, it seems to be an introduced plant, perhaps from Syria.
    Among its uses are as young cooked shoots, possible medicinal
    values, the developing seed-pods as cooked vegetables (as ap-

parently used by the Dakota Indians), the opening seed pods for home decoration and flower arrangements (as has long been done), or perhaps using the fibers for making twine. One additional reference calls for using the juice to cure warts, and, considering its many other uses, perhaps this is so, also.

Possibly the only negative thing about the milkweeds is that they have a bitter quality, which should be removed when preparing them for the table.

You choose milkweed stalks no more than six or eight inches high, then remove all leaves except the tiny tender ones at the tip. Cook them just as you do asparagus, but in several waters, to get rid of the milky juice which may have that bitter taste. Serve them with melted butter.

Asclepias tuberosa—Butterfly weed, chigger flower, fluxroot, pleurisy root, Canada root, Indian-nosy, and many other local names.

Found in dry, barren grounds throughout the Northeast, this surely is one of the most beautiful of all wild flowers, with its brilliant orange heads. The plant grows where little else will. There are some reports of poisonous qualities, and this might be suggested by the fact that Appalachian Indians used it to induce vomiting. Other references show that it was cultivated by the Indians for the roots to be cooked; the Sioux prepared from the flowers a crude form of sugar.

Sarcostemma (**various species**)—The climbing milkweed.

This member of the milkweed family has fruits that may be eaten raw or cooked. The plants are found only in the Southwest.

TOUCH-ME-NOT-FAMILY

BALSAMINACEAE

Commonly called jewelweed, these species are found wild in the East, and as far west as Nebraska, north to Oregon, in cool, damp places, often alongside a stream. There are European species and cultivated ones such as the garden balsams, which, with modern improvements, are becoming one of the fine plants for shady spots.

Impatiens biflora—Jewelweed, touch-me-not, snapweed, lady's earrings, quick-in-the-hand, balsam weed, celandine.

This plant will also be found in botanies under *I. pallida* or

I.capensis, thus representing one of the many cases of disagree-
ment among botanists.

A few mentions are found of some minor medicinal qualities,
but rarely much mention of a use that makes it one of the most
important plants of this book, in that the juice of the stems
seems to be one of the best cures known for ivy-poisoning.
Newspaper reports and personal conversations all indicate that
the juices of the crushed stems applied to the skin where there

Impatiens biflora

has been contact with poison ivy, will often prevent, and partly
cure, the ivy-itch and later complications.

One camp counselor, a friend of the writer, explains how he
boils down messes of this plant at the beginning of summer
camping and uses it on those who have been in contact with ivy.

On this subject it should be noted that the ivy-poisoning result from a plant oil, and by using jewelweed, Fels-naptha soap,
pure unleaded gasoline, or the crushed leaves of sweet fern, the
oil is dissolved, and bad attacks of poison may be prevented.

THE BARBERRY FAMILY
BERBERIDACEAE

The barberry family is widespread—a few species native in the United States, some fine ones from South America, and perhaps the best of the cultivated forms from China and Japan. Common in the East, where it has been naturalized from Europe, is *Berberis vulgaris*, the common barberry, while common in the far West is the broad-leaved barberry, *Mahonia*. One very tiny plant, fine for gardens, is the ground cover plant, the *Epimedium*, which hardly looks like a barberry. But of the others there are many uses.

Berberis vulgaris—Common barberry, wood-sour, jaundice-berry.
As a jaundice-berry, it is said to cure jaundice, but one wonders if this is not because of the very yellow under-the-bark wood. One reference book says that jelly made from the berries is poisonous. But if so, this dictionary would not have been written, as barberries make a beautiful and tasty jelly. They can be picked from plants in the wild or in the yard, where the barberry makes a fine landscape shrub.

The juice has been used to dye Moroccan leather. Barberry has long been known and treasured in Europe, from whence it escaped to our shores. In Italy, barberry was known as holy thorn, as it was said that the branches formed part of the crown on Christ's head.

Berberis vulgaris

Caulophyllum thalictroides

One lady interested in craft uses of plants wrote the author that she picks the berries before they are quite ripe and before they have become fully colored and soft, then strings them up in necklaces. When dried they crinkle beautifully and look like odd little bits of coral, with varying shades. Delightful, she said, to wear with summer dresses.

Because this common barberry is the host plant for a rust of wheat, the growing of it is prohibited in many states, but where found it should be deemed very useful.

Caulophyllum thalictroides—Papoose root, blue berry cohosh, squaw-root, blue or yellow ginseng, blue cohosh, leontice.
Once an "approved" drug, but no longer "official," evidence indicates that it was used by the Indians for stimulating uterine contractions and thus to hasten childbirth, and hence the name papoose root. For this purpose the root was dug and an infusion made. It is native through the eastern mountain range.

Mahonia aquifolium—Oregon grape, mountain grape, mahonia.
A native of the Northwest, this is a fine ornamental plant for use in the East, with wide holly-like leaves and dark blue berries with a wax-like covering. The berries may be eaten raw or used for jelly. Actually there are several species, one being a creeping form. The yellow roots were used by western Indians to make a yellow dye for their basketry, while in the dyeing of cloth it produces a nice brown.

Mahonia aquifolium

Podophyllum peltatum

Podophyllum peltatum—May-apple, mandrake, hog-apple, ground
     lemon, Indian apple, vegetable mercury, vegetable calomel,
     duck's foot.
This plant is very widespread throughout the states and is a
delightful plant to discover in the wild, being distinctive in having only two leaves, one of which is a flowering stem. The roots
are the part used medicinally for its effect on the liver. Once a
commonly dispensed drug, it disappeared from our pharmacopoeia in 1930. At times called wild jalap because it causes
cathartic action, it should be used only under proper medical
supervision and yet, as a "proper" drug, it is one of the good
ones of this book.

THE BIRCH FAMILY
BETULACEAE

Almost everyone, except those who live in dry, hot flatlands know the
lovely birches with their papery bark, often snow-white in color. The
tree and its bark have many values besides making the birch-bark
canoes of the Indians.

Alnus rugosa—Smooth, red, or hazel alder, green, speckled, or black
     alder.
This tree is easily distinguished as a birch by the long "fruit."
Its values as a medicine are minor, but it was used by the Cree
Indians for dropsy. Its chief economic value, however, is in the
fact that it is a good dye plant, the roots giving a brown dye, the
leaves a yellow-green, and the bark a yellow-brown, with the
dyes being used for both wool and leather.

Betula alba—Canoe birch, white birch, paper birch.
As with the alders, above, the white birch gives dye material
from the dry leaves and bark. There are a number of references
both here and abroad to the birch sap being used as a sweetener,
or to ferment as a mild wine, while the leaves have been used
by Indians and others to make a mild tea. Beyond that there are
references to the bark being beaten, ground and used as a food
additive, while one report notes that in Scandinavia the sawdust
is boiled, baked, and added to white flour. Some folks, such as
the author, like best to see the white logs adorn the unused
fireplace.

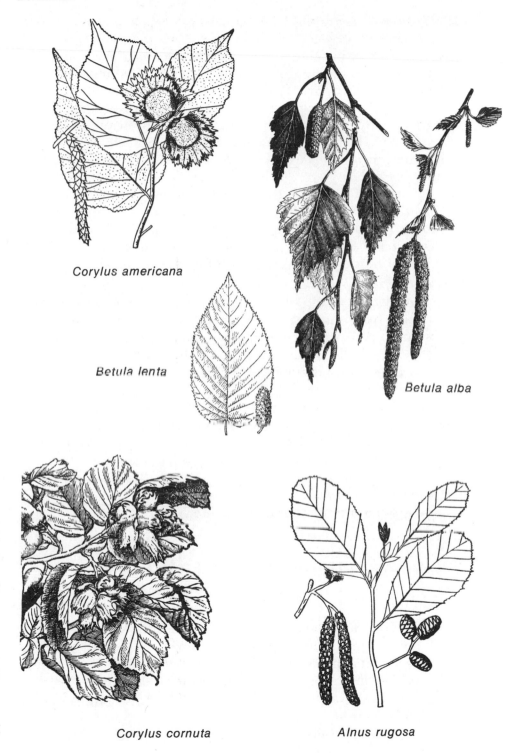

Corylus americana

Betula lenta

Betula alba

Corylus cornuta

Alnus rugosa

Betula lenta—Sweet or black birch, mountain mahogany, river birch,
cherry birch.

Again a tree of the colder and less fertile areas of the country,
this species has reddish bark, rather than white. In times before
the use of so many synthetic drugs an "oil of sweet birch" was
distilled, and produced both an aromatic flavoring agent and an
alleviant to rheumatism, because of the active principle of methyl-salicylate. The flavoring quality comes out much like the oil
of wintergreen and is used to make birch beer, a popular mild
drink.

Again, in the case of dyes, the decoction of the bark, with
copperas, is used for dying wool a lovely wine-colored drab.
Also, this birch and others have been used in earlier times for
making birch brushes by splitting down the wood into strips,
while among cabinet makers, birch furniture is much desired.

Corylus americana—Hazel nut, filbert.

Growing largely in thickets, the hazel nuts are found over much
of eastern North America, and when the nuts are ripe in August,
it is fun to gather and enjoy them. A good way to use them is
to toast the hulled dried nuts, crush them a bit, and add to
pancake batter, using honey or maple syrup on the cakes for a
truly tasty bit of natural food.

There are many other species, not American in origin, which
have better and larger nuts, but it is well to know this large shrub
and hope that one can find the nuts without worms inside.

Corylus cornuta—Beaked hazelnut, western hazel.

This, from northern California and the Cascades to Canada, is
the western form of *C. americana* with fruits that are especially
good ground into meal and made into bread.

THE BIGNONIA FAMILY
BIGNONIACEAE

This is not too important a family. It includes the *Bignonia radicans*
or trumpet creeper, found in woods over much of the eastern states
area. It is a rambling vine with scarlet trumpet flowers, a bright spot
wherever the vine rambles over stumps and dead trees.

Catalpa bignoniodes—Indian bean, catalpa, cigar tree, Indian cigar,
candle-tree.

One medical reference says that the pods are "tonic and vermi-

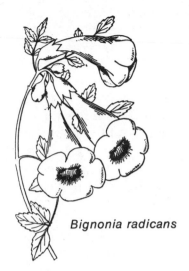

Bignonia radicans

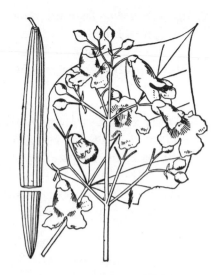

Catalpa bignonioides

fuge" and that they may afford, when smoked, some relief from asthma. The odor of the flower is "said to be poisonous," but to those brought up as the author was, in the shade of this huge and beautifully flowered tree, this is doubtful. In my youth, smoking of the cigarette-like seed pods was the "in" thing.

The huge flower-heads are really lovely on a big spreading tree, but the tree should not be planted unless there is a vast expanse of lawn where it can be displayed.

Stenolobium stans (syn. *Tecoma stans*)—Trumpet bush.
Found in dry slopes from New Mexico south into tropical America, this shrub bears funnel-shaped, bright yellow flowers. In Mexico, the roots are crushed into water and allowed to ferment to make a sort of beer. The roots are also used as a home medicine.

THE BORAGE FAMILY
BORAGINACEAE

In every part of the country there appear plants called "wild," which are escapes from gardens, or brought into the country perhaps as ships' ballast or with imported hay or grains, or even brought by birds and animals. It is said that some 30 percent of our native flora is not really native.

Borago officinalis—Borage, star-flower, false bugloss.

This plant, known and used since Roman times, is suggested to have an exhilarating effect, when used medicinally. Called Euphrosynon by the Greeks, it was said that, put in a cup of wine, it helped to make one merry, and it is still considered a good addition to a cooling drink.

There is quite a story to all the supposed effects of this plant, and it is a must for herb gardeners, as the leaves add a delightful touch to salads. Quite beyond this is the fact that it is a "bee-plant"—the lovely star-like "true-blue" flowers being always covered with honey-suckers. Often found in the wild, it should certainly be a part of every home herb-garden.

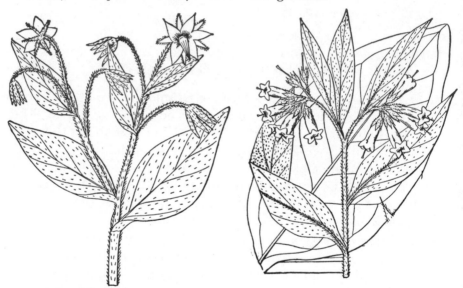

Borago officinalis   Symphytum officinale

Lithospermum incisum—Gromwell, puccoon.

A hairy-leaved mountain plant, it is found in foothills and mountains from Montana to Arizona. The roots have been found edible when cooked.

Symphytum officinale—Healing herb, knitback, comfrey, ass-ear, consolida, knitbone, bruisewort, gum plant.

Long known as having many medicinal values, modern herbals list comfrey chiefly as a demulcent, esteemed as a remedy in pulmonary complaints and as a soothing ingredient in herbal preparations of various kinds.

Like borage and other familiar plants of the same family such as anchusas, heliotropes, and mertensia, the hairy nature of the foliage is noticeable and the blue flowers are too.

The name of Symphytum was given by Dioscorides nearly 2000 years ago, a name which meant "to unite," indicating its use as a possible cure for broken bones.

THE PINEAPPLE FAMILY

BROMELIACEAE

In the field of house plants, the bromeliads are fast becoming the "in" thing, and rightly so, as they thrive in heated atmospheres and require only water and fertilizer in their centers. Being, however, mostly tropical plants, our main contact with the family is the pineapple, and the very familiar Spanish moss which grows on trees from Virginia southwards.

Tillandsia usneoides—Spanish or Florida moss, tree-beard.

This "moss" has been gathered for cushions. It could be used

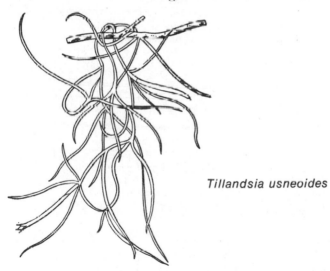

Tillandsia usneoides

as a garden mulch. Medicinally it has been used, mixed with lard, as an alleviant for hemorrhoids and some records list its internal use as a stomachic.

THE BOXWOOD FAMILY
BUXACEAE

Not a large family, but one which includes not only the commonly known boxwood, a plant of origins in the Near and Far East, but also one Japanese plant much used as a garden ground cover, the pachysandra or spurge.

***Buxus sempervirens*—Boxwood.**

Boxwood has been grown commonly in our eastern states since Colonial times and is widely spread in this species (or as *B. suffruticosa*). It is well to mention it is a lovely evergreen edging, hedge, or specimen plant. There are a number of references to

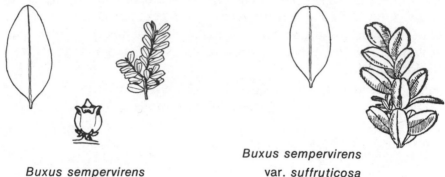

Buxus sempervirens

Buxus sempervirens
var. *suffruticosa*

its use medicinally (of doubtful value) and more especially that the foliage of boxwood is rated as poisonous, and most especially so to animals.

THE CACTUS FAMILY
CACTACEAE

Although commonly thought of as being resident only of the dry deserts of our Southwest, certain of the more than 1,000 species known are widespread; one kind being found growing in the upper Hudson Valley in New York. Many species are valuable mostly for the beauty of their flowers or as indoor plants, but many kinds in their natural desert habitats are otherwise useful.

***Cereus caespitosus*—Tufted hedgehog cereus.**

The little fruits, purple in color, which follow the lovely flower, are esteemed by inhabitants of New Mexico. The fleshy part, after spine removal, is eaten as a vegetable.

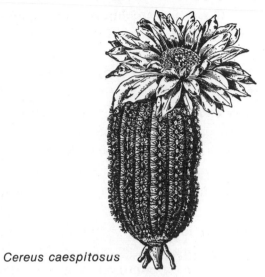

Cereus caespitosus

Cereus giganteus—Suwarrow, harsee.

In the Southwest, Indians collect the sweet juice from this species to make a conserve. One writer, from Arizona, calls the fruit "delicious," with a combined flavor of peach, strawberry, and fig

In using the name "cereus," it should be noted that there is a great divergence in the scientific names of the cactus family; some are called *Cereus* in some books, while others designate the same plants *Echinocereus* or other names.

Cereus variabilis—Pitahaya.

Here again, in the markets of Mexico, a variable number of fine cactus fruits are called "pitahaya" and the author can testify that they are fine to eat as well as huge and beautiful to look at. Traveling in the Southwest, one should ask the local residents of an area which is the best to eat. Mostly the plants are huge and high, and the often squash-sized fruits vary in color, according to variety and habitat.

Echinocactus wislizeni or **Ferocactus wislizeni**—Visnada, biznacha.

With the some 1,000 possible scientific names for this group and almost no common ones, one can but admire many of the tall tree-or-barrel-like cacti for the great amount of water of which they are made, and which offer water to quench a desert thirst.

A native of Texas and Arizona, it is used by the Apache Indians.

Lophophora williamsii—Peyote, mescal button.

This small-growing member of the family is a hallucinatory plant, which has long been used in religious ceremonies, with such use now permitted in several states by authenticated Indian groups. But it is a highly dangerous alkaloid, and its non-liturgic use should be avoided.

Lemaireocereus thurberi—Organpipe cactus.

This great cactus is found across from Arizona to lower California and aside from its being part of a great landscape, the spiny fruits may be used as food.

Opuntia vulgaris—Prickly pear, Indian fig, devil's tongue, tuna, nopal.

On the Atlantic coast and in many other places, one will find the common "broad-leaved" cacti listed under many names in various scientific catalogs.

They are a very common "super-market" fruit in Mexico, where they are known mostly as tuna or nopals. They should, of course, be washed and after cutting off bottom and top; the slit

Opunta vulgaris

skin can be peeled. They can now be used as green salad or with omelettes.

When chopped up, they are known as nopalitos and one recipe from an old southwestern cookbook gives this recipe.

> Mix nopalitos with chopped pimentos and tomatoes. Add a bit of fresh cilantro (also known as Mexican or Chinese parsley), if desired, and top with a spicy vinegar dressing to which a touch of chili powder has been added.

Peniocereus greggi—Night-blooming cereus, deerhorn cactus, reina de la noche.

This plant is found among the Creosote bushes from western Texas west and south to Mexico. The large root is baked or boiled. There seems to be a number of species of cacti with similar flowers and fruits, some of which are eaten. But the real joy in this plant is the enjoyment of the beauty and fragrance of the blooms when they are open after sunset.

THE CALYCANTHUS FAMILY

CALYCANTHACEAE

Calycanthus floridus—Sweet shrub, strawberry-bush, spice bush, Carolina allspice.

Native from Virginia southwards, this wonderfully sweet-smelling eight foot shrub is one of the finest wild plants to be brought into cultivation. Its purple-brown flowers are not beautiful, but are most delightfully fragrant. The aromatic bark has been

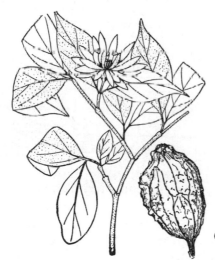

Calycanthus floridus

noted as a substitute for cinnamon and one medical book rates a decoction of the root-bark or seed as an antispasmodic and as a "cure for chronic agues."

Mainly it can be recommended as a shrub no garden should be without.

THE BELLFLOWER FAMILY
CAMPANULACEAE

If this book were about useful plants for the flower garden there would be many fine species and varieties to discuss here, but in the bellflower family, there are only two.

Campanula rapunculoides—Harebell, creeping bellflower.
In a reference book on the edible plants of the Rocky Mountains, the roots of this lovely blue-flowered plant are noted as being edible, with a good nut-like taste, if boiled for 20 minutes.

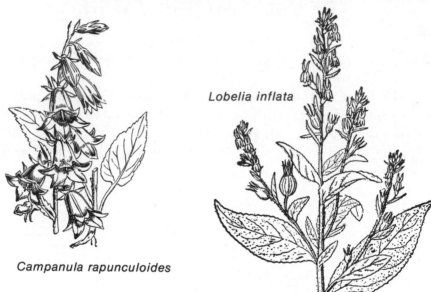

Lobelia inflata

Campanula rapunculoides

Lobelia inflata—Indian or wild tobacco, eyebright, asthma weed, vomitwort, bladderpod, gagroot, emetic weed.
About 150 years ago, this plant was considered as "one of the most valuable remedies ever discovered" and, because it then was found in all of the United States (east of the Mississippi), much use was made of it. Actually the plant contains dangerous alkaloids and while under administration by Indian experts was, perhaps, safe enough, it is known now only as an early quack medicine. There is some evidence that one of the alkaloids is a specific stimulant to the respiratory center and that its use for asthma, croup, and whooping cough had a basis, but there are many other modern drugs which take this once famous plant from the list.

THE HONEYSUCKLE FAMILY

CAPRIFOLIACEAE

Lonicera **(various species)**—Honeysuckle, American or fragrant
woodbine, Japanese honeysuckle, scarlet or trumpet honeysuckle.

In the honeysuckle group of plants there are many fine shrubs
and plants useful in various ways, though most are plants from
other countries.

Here we are concerned with the vining types, which are more
or less fragrant, especially the Japanese species, *L. Japonica,*
which easily escapes from cultivation and may form veritable
weedy jungles. This plant is useful for holding a bank, and is
simply a must for having at least one plant in every garden for
the joy of evening fragrance. Medicinally, a number of references are made to the juice of the stems being an antidote for
bee stings. The fragrant flowers have also been used for perfume making.

In the Appalachian area, a number of medicinal uses have
been made of plant extracts of *Lonicera*, qualities including that
of an emetic and cathartic, and for alleviation of asthma and
other lung troubles.

Sambucus canadensis—Common elder, elderberry.

There are a number of species of the elder growing in differ
ent climatic sections, but the common one is widely distributed and as such possibly known to all readers of this
book. When you go out hunting elderberries, seek the blue
variety *(Sambucus canadensis)* and not the red *(Sambucus pub-
ens)*. The latter are distasteful and in some areas even poisonous. Don't worry about confusing the two, though, for
they look quite different. The toxic plant produces bright-red
fruit in dome-shaped bunches, while its edible cousin bears a
flat cluster of rich-blue to purple-black berries with a whitish
"dusted" surface appearance.

The European species is quite similar and has much the same
value as ours, and mention of its name and its use go back into
dim history. One finds, for instance, Shakespeare, making reference in *Henry V,* to:

> That's a perilous shot out of an elder
> gunne, that a poor and private displeasure
> can doe against a monarch.

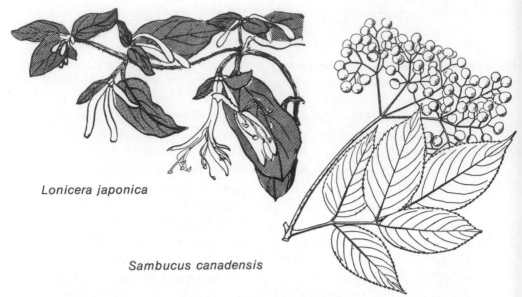

Lonicera japonica

Sambucus canadensis

This, of course, refers to the making of a blow gun with the hollowed-out stems of elder, something known to every country lad.

Basically, of course, one brought up in the country remembers, as does the writer, that elderberries make the best of all pies. One recipe for an elderberry pie would be this:

> 3 1/2 cups elderberries
> 1 cup of sugar
> 1/4 teaspoon salt
> 2 tablespoons cornstarch (or tapioca)
> 1 tablespoon lemon juice
> 1 tablespoon butter

> Use two crusts and cut venting holes in pie top, bake at
> 400°F and serve with vanilla ice cream.

The partially ripe fruits make a fine jelly, while the unopened flowers can be dipped in batter and fried. When pickled, these make a good substitute for capers.

Possibly the most widely known use of elderberries is in the making of wine, something not too easy to do, but excellent when successful. Recipes for elderberry wine appear in many nature books. Also, from the white flower heads, one can brew what is known as elder-blow wine, something extremely tasty and beautiful to behold.

As a craft plant, the elder is important because the soft pitch in the stems is easily hollowed out to make a flute or (as noted) a blow gun or, indeed, anything needing a pipe.

As a dye plant it also has much written about it, the leaves giving a green dye, and the berries a lavender or purple dye.

Less well-known, however, are the various medicinal properties of elder, which, because the literature on the subject is so exhaustive, can only be hinted at here.

BARK—The dried inner bark of the stem has been used for centuries as an active purgative of a dependable nature, but should be used with caution, as in large doses it is emetic. The bark of the *root* is violently purgative and dangerous.

LEAVES—There are alkaloids and poisons in the leaves, which make them safe only for external use, but here we find that an ointment made from the leaves is recommended for bruises and sprains. The juice of the leaves was recommended as an eye-wash, also a possible alleviant of ivy poisoning. A countrywoman wrote me that her grandmother "for headache warmed the leaves of elderberry and applied them to the forehead."

BERRIES—The heat-thickened juice of elderberries forms "an invaluable cordial for coughs and colds," while a draught of hot elder wine before going to bed would be not only soporific, but would promote perspiration and help to ward off the ill effects of a chill.

FLOWERS—It is, however, the *flowers* of elder which receive the most favorable notice in the extensive literature on elder, and it is the plant part which has achieved recognition in the National Formulary. The fresh flowers, carefully dried and cleaned of stems are, says Youngken (and many others), "employed as a diaphoretic and stimulant and in the preparation of elder-flower ointment and water."

A tea made from the dried flowers and peppermint leaves (1 teaspoon each to 1 1/2 cups of water) is an excellent and soothing drink for those with colds, such a drink being also used, says a correspondent, by the Pequot Indians, for baby colic. In fact, studying all the references to the medicinal plants of the American Indians, shows that they fully appreciated the values of elder.

The elder-flower water, for which there are a number of recipes, was a favorite cosmetic for the suppression of freckles, alleviating sunburn, and to relieve the itching and other effects of salt-water bathing.

One quite unusual recipe suggests making an ointment from the elder flowers to heal sores on animals. The flower-heads are rubbed into pure lard, the mixture heated in a moderate oven, then strained in jars, this ointment used for sores and to keep away flies.

Triosteum perfoliatum—Fever-root, horse ginseng, feverwort, wild coffee, wild ipecachuanha, and many other local names. A decoction of this plant was used by the Cherokee Indians in fevers, colds, and female obstructions. In fact, a great number of common names, which it has, shows that an interest and knowledge of it was wide-spread in the past.

The low, shrubby, weed-like plant is common from north to south in the East and is altogether like the larger-berried shrubs of most of the family.

The Viburnums

The balance of the plants of this family are in the genus *Viburnum,* a group of shrubs or small trees which are wide-spread. Of course,

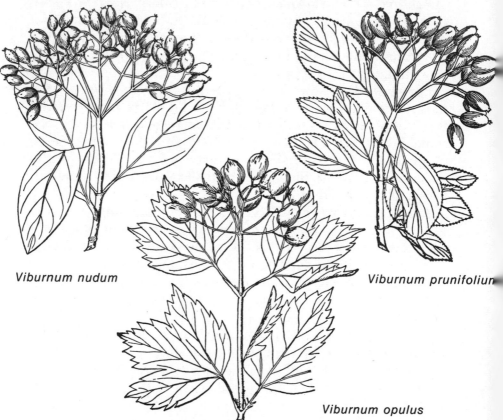

Viburnum nudum

Viburnum prunifolium

Viburnum opulus

many viburnums are of foreign or hybrid origin. As a group they give us some of our finest landscape plants.

Viburnum edule—Squashberry, mooseberry, arrowhead, viburnum. This is one member of the family that grows in the North and the West, and is among those listed as a good edible-fruited plant of the Rocky Mountains. The red or orange fruits are useful for jam.

Viburnum nudum—Possomhaw, withe-rod, shawnee haw, swamp haw. One of the larger growing "haws" (to 20 feet) liking wet places, it produces bitter black berries. The bark of the root or stem is a uterine sedative, diuretic, and tonic.

Viburnum opulus—High-bush cranberry, wild guelder-rose, cramp-bark, pimbina, snowball-tree, whitten-tree. Although the fruit and uses are similar, the true *V. opulus* is European in origin and the native form is *V. trilobum.* Both have maple-like leaves and similar fruits. The fruit, which looks like the real cranberry, is edible but of small value.

THE PINK FAMILY

CARYOPHYLACEA

Almost everyone knows the pinks and the carnations, which give the common name to this family. Quite possibly even the most non-botanical person knows the wildflower called bouncing bet, but hardly would that person guess there was much useful about any of the family other than beauty and fragrance. Yet here are four plants of minor value.

Agrostemma githago—Corn cockle, corn rose, corn campion, mullein pink, crown-of-the-field, bastard nigelle. Like so many other "weeds," this is a plant introduced from Europe and basically is a poisonous plant with certain properties which have been used in medicine. There is some report of its having been processed for the manufacture of starch, but basically it is a plant to be avoided.

Paronychia species—Whitlow-wort, nail-wort. A tiny tufted, white-flowered perennial of wide distribution, there are three or four species found, mostly in the western states, growing in poor, dry, and hot soils. Mostly valueless, it has been applied as a poultice reputed to offer relief from the intense pains of hangnails or any other acute inflammation of the finger or toenails, the latter being known medicinally as "whitlows."

Saponaria officinalis—Soapwort, bouncing bet, bruisewort, London pride, chimney-pink, latherwort, dog cloves, world's wonder.

Another introduced plant that even as a weed is lovely and long-blooming, with pink and sometimes partly double flowers. The common names of the plant should give some indication of its value, for the word "wort" indicates a medicinal value and the "soap" indicates that it may be used for washing. The roots or leaves may be conjured into a soapy foam, a knowledge valuable for campers. Although early listed, as were many other plants, as a cure for venereal disease, its present value might be only as an alleviant for skin irritations. Learn to know it as a nice garden weed and its value as an aid to cleanliness.

Possibly the greatest value of this plant would be the soapy suds that may be extracted by soaking the roots in water when the plant is in flower. The mucilaginous saponin so extracted can be used for washing not only wool but especially for washing silk. With silk it not only cleanses but leaves a luster on the dried cloth. It is so used in museums especially, for restoring rare old fabrics.

Silene cucubalus* and *S. acaulis—Bladder campion, catchfly, campion. These plants are found throughout the West, the first a plant of waste places, and the second in high altitudes. The mossy campion *(S. acaulis)* may be gathered as a plant, boiled until tender, and eaten. It is a tufted and purple-flowered plant.

Spergula arvensis—Spurry, poverty weed, corn spurry, pine cheat, sand-weed.

A weed from East to West, it is another adventive plant. The only values listed for it in various works are that it is a "nutrient for cattle" and that the seed has sometimes been used as an emergency bread-flour.

Stellaria media—Chickweed, adder's mouth, satin flower, starwort, stitchwort, bird's eye.

An introduced plant and a genus with several minor differentiated species, it is of national distribution. It has food values either cooked or raw. It grows best in cooler climates (even in winter under snow) and while, to the author, it is a prime pest,

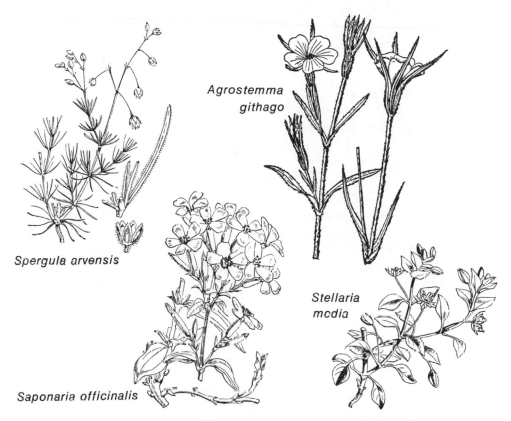

Agrostemma githago

Spergula arvensis

Saponaria officinalis

Stellaria media

a number of references from the East, the Rocky Mountains and the Northwest all recommend it as a salad green or, gently cooked or fried, as a green vegetable.

Some medicinal values have been noted but they are not important.

THE STAFF TREE FAMILY

CELASTRACEAE

Taken as a family group, there is little of generally useful value among its members, except that, for landscape purposes, many of the introduced *Euonymus* varieties are exceedingly useful.A number of the American species have been rated as quite poisonous to man and beast, and the only one much noted in medicinal books would be the following.

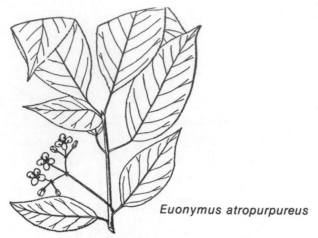

Euonymus atropurpureus

***Euonymus atropurpureus*—**Wahoo, burning bush, skewer wood, American spindle tree, bitter ash.

Found throughout the entire East, this is a large growing bush with capsule-like seeds. The bark of the bush and the root have been used medicinally as a tonic, diuretic, and laxative, but in this last case, it can be drastic in action.

THE GOOSEFOOT FAMILY
CHENAPODIACEAE

Some years ago in a peat-bog in Denmark, the completely preserved body of a man was found who was thought to have been thrown there more than 1500 years ago. Investigation showed his stomach to contain, among other seeds used for food, a great many of the seeds of what is called "fat-hen" or "lamb's quarters," *Chenopodium album,* one of the plants of this family. There is other evidence in the names of this and other members of the family that the seeds and leaves of the goosefoots have long been regarded as good food, widely so in our country, as well as abroad. Here are some of them.

***Atriplex* (various species)—**Orach, mountain spinach, jagged sea orach.

Names of various forms of *Atriplex* are *A. patula, A. hastata glabriuscula,* and *A. hortensis,* and variously they are found across the continent. Fernald and Kinsey in their book say, "The succulent leaves or young tips, especially when the plant grows along the seashore, are juicier and somewhat impregnated with salt." The

Rocky Mountain flora indicates that there, too, the plant is so salty that it is used to flavor food.

Chenopodium album—Lamb's quarters, pigweed, fat-hen, white goosefoot.

Eaten by early man in Denmark, and by the lake dwellers in Switzerland, it was much used by the Navajo and other Indians, boiled or raw. A researcher in the Northwest suggests it as an excellent vegetable to freeze. The seeds may be ground as flour. The crushed fresh roots may be used as a mild soap substitute. Regarded by most users as better than another member of the same family, common spinach, it is one of the most basically useful of all "weeds."

Chenopodium ambrosioides var. amthelminticum—Wormseed, Jerusalem tea, Jesuit tea, ambrosia, stick weed, stinking weed, goosefoot, epazote (Mexican).

Somewhat similar in appearance to *C. album*, this is a plant which grows somewhat taller and has come from Mexico. Medicinally it is used in the making of chenopodium oil, which is used to treat intestinal worms, in both man and beast. In Mexico it is cooked and eaten as a vermifuge while in our Southwest a tea is made of the leaves to encourage milk flow and to relieve post-delivery pains. Although from the South, it has spread widely in the states.

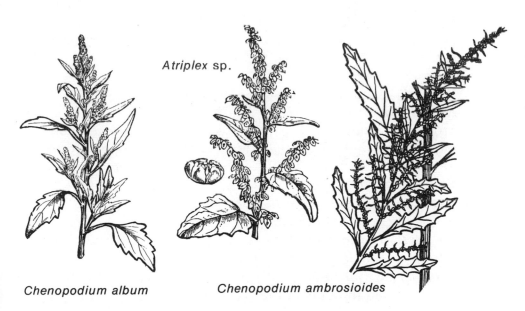

Atriplex sp.

Chenopodium album   Chenopodium ambrosioides

Chenopodium berlandieri—Pigweed.

Chenopodium botrys—Ambrose, feather geranium.

Chenopodium capitatum—Strawberry blite, blite goosefoot.

     The three above are all plants with somewhat similar appearance and all generally listed as possible food sources, similar but not as basically good as the ones above.

Cycloloma atriplicifolium—Winged pigweed.

     A weed which grows up to one and one-half feet, it is found in dry ground in the Southwest. The ground-up seeds may be boiled as mush or made into cakes.

Kochia scoparia—Summer cypress.

     This escape from gardens may be found growing in waste areas throughout the West and, indeed, in some places becomes a pest. It is a plant from Asia, grown sometimes as an annual hedge. The tips of young shoots may be eaten and the seeds ground and cooked.

Monolepsis nuttalliana—Poverty weed, patata.

     A family member found in the Rocky Mountains, it is rated as a "very good pot-herb, to be cooked and boiled 20 to 30 minutes with one change of water."

Salicornia europaea—Samphire, prickly-weed, glasswort, chicken-claws, saltwort.

     Widely spread on both coasts, this species has succulent stems. Because of the salty nature of this little plant of the saltwater marshes, it is rated as a good salad herb and is particularly recommended for pickling. Because of the salt content it is relished by cattle.

Salsola kali—Saltwort, tumble-weed, Russian thistle.

     A common weed of dry plains, fields, and roadsides, it is found across the country and does, when older, break loose and tumble with the wind. The young, rapidly growing shoots, three or four inches tall, make a good cooked vegetable when boiled for about 15 minutes.

Sarcobatus vermiculatus—Greasewood.

     A spiny branched shrub which grows in arid, alkaline areas of the West. The growing twigs can be boiled until tender and eaten with salt and butter.

Suaeda (**various species**)—Seep weed, desert blight.

     A plant found throughout the West, it is a succulent annual or a perennial herb and grows in alkaline soil. The seeds may be

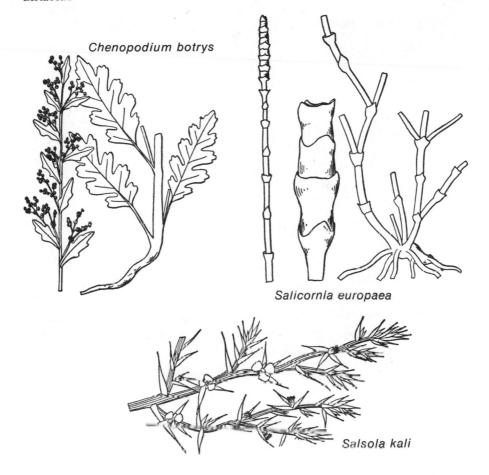

Chenopodium botrys

Salicornia europaea

Salsola kali

eaten raw or parched, with young plants being used as greens.
A black dye can be made by soaking the plant in water for a long
period.

THE ROCKROSE FAMILY

CISTACEAE

Helianthemum canadense—Frostweed, frostwort, ice plant, rockrose,
        scrofula plant, holly rose.

The frost in the common name refers to the fact that in late fall
crystals of ice may shoot from the base of the stem. It grows
widely in dry areas in the eastern United States. It was used by
some Indian tribes as a diuretic and astringent, and a North

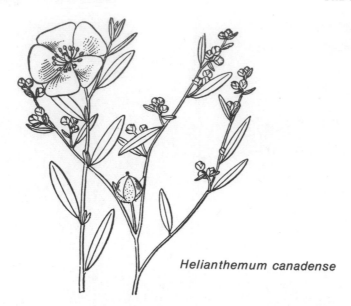

Helianthemum canadense

Carolina authority credits it as a "valuable remedy in scrofula, syphilis, cancerous affections, and as a gargle." Other reports that counter this indicate it should always be used with care, and it is not, therefore, an important medicinal plant.

THE WHITE-ALDER FAMILY

CLETHRACEAE

Clethra alnifolia—White alder, clethra, sweet-pepper-bush, Indian soap.

A shrub growing about six feet high in moist areas, mostly along the East Coast to Texas. This plant is notable mostly for its fragrance in late summer, yet one outdoor enthusiast has told of how the stalk of blossoms has all the properties of a mildly scented soap.

Clethra is also included here because of its value as a bee-plant. It provides a subject for a discussion in this book of the secondary usefulness of clethra and of many other plants which provide, somewhere in their flowers, the pollen and nectar which becomes through the action of the honeybee *(Apis mellifera)* that product called honey, which is at once a delightful, healthful, sweetening agent and a medicine, with possibly far more values than perhaps are known.

With so many health food groups recommending the use of honey in place of other sugars, all this is known, but for a further comment some years ago, one can go back to the book by Dr. D.C. Jarvis, *Folk Medicine,* in which he enumerates the more or less common medicinal values which every nature lover should know about.

Honey, according to Dr. Jarvis is valuable for: producing sleep, relief from burns, an alleviant in coughs, nutrition for athletes, control of bed-wetting, easing kidney complaints, valuable in infant feeding, and controlling muscle cramps.

The constituents of honey which make such things possible, are the easily digested sugars, dextrose, and levulose; volatile oil; mucilage; wax; and formic acid.

The good cook hardly needs instructions in the many valuable ways in which honey may be used, and today with so many adjurations against the use of ordinary granulated sugar because of its ill effects on the body, honey should certainly be used whenever possible.

In the case of using the bounties of the wayside, a good way to combine the values of wild fruits with that of honey would be to make honey-jellies which are made from clear fruit juice and honey. Make a small amount of jelly at one time, using not more than two quarts of juice at a time. Wild fruits which could be so used would include: wild apples, currants, grapes, cranberries, huckleberries, blueberries, wild sweet cherries, chokecherries, beach plums, blackberries, and any others having good juices.

Since some fruits do not jell easily, it is necessary to combine

Clethra alnifolia

them with one or more pectin-producers, such as apples, or to
add commercial pectin.

There is much more in the literature on the subject of honey
worth exploring by those interested in using the bounties of
nature, and certainly the clethra here mentioned and pictured,
is one of the fine sources of good honey.

THE DAISY FAMILY
COMPOSITAE

This is one of the largest of plant families (with the possible exception of orchids) and, to people in the States, certainly the most
commonly known. There are some 800 genera, countless species,
and endless varieties, all of them in a greater or less configuration in
the form of the common daisy.

Achillea lanulosa—Yarrow.

This is a slight variation of *A. millefolium,* found in the forest
edges throughout the West with the same statements applied to
it as with the eastern form, below. The association of the name
of Achillea is with the famous Greek Achilles, who may have
used a plant of this genus to treat the wounds of his warriors,
but one gathers it was not useful for heel trouble.

Achillea millefolium—Yarrow, milfoil, woundwort, sanguinary, thou-
sand-seal, dog daisy, nose bleed, thousand-leaf clover, sol-
dier's woundwort.

A widely distributed plant throughout the world, this common
and beautiful weed has feathery, fern-like leaves and quite
beautiful heads of white to pink blooms.Actually its name comes
from the legend which said that Achilles applied the leaves to
the wounds of his soldiers after the battle of Troy, while the
specific name comes from the "mille-" or thousand leaflets of
the foliage. Whether or not infusions of the leaves will heal cuts
or relieve baldness, or even be better in beer than hops, or
whether it will cure colds or purify the blood, it is listed in the
Youngkens *Textbook of Pharmacognosy* as an "aromatic bitter, diaphoretic, and emmenagogue." Generally we know that the Indians of our country used it widely for a variety of purposes varying often from tribe to tribe. One researcher, Eva Moody, has
noted the variable uses among a dozen tribes of the state of

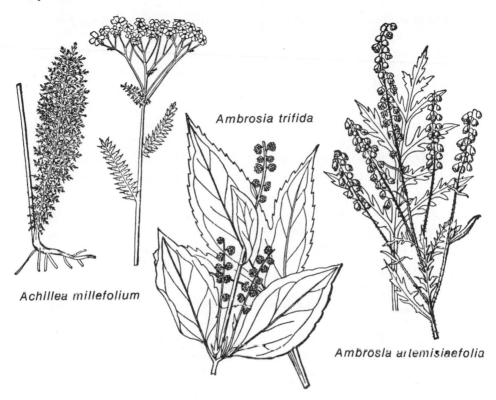

Ambrosia trifida

Achillea millefolium

Ambrosia artemisiaefolia

Washington, and similar reports are found from other parts of the country. An infusion made of one ounce of the dried whole plants to one pint of water can be taken in a wineglassful dose and combined, says one writer, with elder flowers and mint in the case of colds. A further and final use may be indicated by one common name of "devil's plaything," indicating that it once was used for divination. Thus one sees in this one plant how many values there may be in a common wild plant, suggesting further the interest in the study of botany and nomenclature and, indeed, of all the interplay between the history of our American Indians and of ourselves.

Ambrosia artemisifolia—Ragweed, Roman wormseed, hogweed, stammerwort.

It can hardly be said that this produces any "ambrosial" drink, for it is the ragweed which distributes the pollen which is quite possibly the worst cause of hayfever.

Ambrosia trifida—Great ragweed, horse-cane, wild hemp, Buffalo-weed.

Anaphalis margaritacea—Pearly everlasting, cotton-weed, live-long, poverty weed.

Many of the composites perhaps do not look like a "daisy" until one explores them closely, with their petals outside and seeds in the center, and this is a good sample of such a seeming variance from the norm.

A common weed almost everywhere, these flowers can be picked and dried (and dyed) to be used for winter bouquets, and additionally some use has been made, medicinally, of the juices of the plant as a relief for mouth ulcers and similar conditions.

Antennaria (**various species**)—Pussytoes.

In the West this low-growing, wooly perennial is found in mostly arid situations. Gum from the stalks of the plant has been used to make a (possibly) nourishing chewing gum.

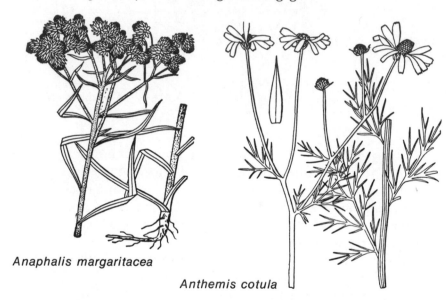

Anaphalis margaritacea

Anthemis cotula

Anthemis cotula—Mayweed, dog-fennel, poison daisy, chiggy-weed, fetid chamomile.

A plant used medicinally for its "irritating properties", but, as overuse may cause blisters on the skin and an infusion may cause vomiting, it is not as valuable as other members of the genus.

Anthemis nobilis—Camomile or chamomile, ground-apple, corn feverfew, barnyard daisy, turkey-weed, may-weed.

This European plant has long been grown for use as a medicinal plant, the common name seeming to have come from two Greek words meaning "fruit on the ground," and there is evidence that it was used also by the Egyptians. Who, indeed, has not heard of chamomile tea? Pharmacologically an "aromatic bitter," it is soothing, sedative, and completely harmless. As an example of its great repute, a bath of chamomile is said in Rumania to be an "old age cure." It should be considered as a principal plant for home herb gardens.

This anthemis is considered to be the English or Roman chamomile, while the Germanic people use, under a similar name, the plant of the same family—*Matricaria chamomila.*

Anthemis tinctoria—Golden Marguerite, dyer's chamomile, ox-eye chamomile.

The very word "tinctoria" would indicate that this is a dye-plant, which with gold flowers, produces dyes of yellow, gold, and khaki. Some medicinal uses are noted, such as the oil of the seed being good for earache and deafness.

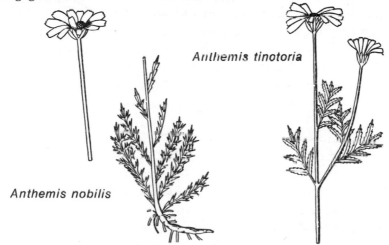

Anthemis tinotoria

Anthemis nobilis

Arctium lappa—Great burdock, beggar's button, burdock, clot-bur, lappa, and others.

Possibly the first plant with which children become acquainted as "beggar's lice," but for this book the use would be as a food plant which is much used by the Japanese, under the name of Gobo. Here the long roots (often up to two feet) are used as a cooked vegetable. Once considered a good medicinal plant, it is no longer "official."

Arctium minus—Common burdock, clot-bur, cuckoo button.

The burdocks are widely distributed plants, although it is a plant introduced into the country from Europe where, as well as in Japan, it is valued as a food plant. The young stems can be gathered and cooked as asparagus while the roots, gathered in the fall in the first year of growth, may be cooked, or dried and saved, as did the Iroquois Indians in the years after the plant came from abroad. And may it not be that the more it is used in such manners, the sooner, as a weed, it will be exterminated from our gardens.

Artemisia absinthum—Wormwood, absinthe, madderwort, old woman, mugwort.

An adventive plant from Europe, the wormwood is found in most of the eastern states. It grows to about three feet with odorous gray-green leaves. The leaves are gathered in fall in Europe for the flavoring of the drink absinthe, and it has been used somewhat for flavoring beer. No longer listed as a medicinal herb, it was once recommended for improving appetite and other stomachic problems. In olden days this was one of the "strewing herbs" used to take ancient odors from even more ancient places of public assembly, notably churches.

Artemisia tridentata—Big sagebrush.

This silver-gray-colored shrub of which there are a number of botanical variations is found throughout the Great Basin Desert in our West. The seeds or fruits may be dried, pounded into meal to make pinole, or eaten raw. The oil in the foliage of a number of the sages is used in the manufacture of absinthe, while tea made from the leaves has been used in treatment of colds and even in what is said to be a good hair tonic.

Balsamorhiza (**various species**)—Balsamroot.

A mostly basal-leaved plant with large roots with heads of sunflower-like blooms. It is widely found in the dry areas of the West. All parts of the plant are edible, especially the root, eaten raw or cooked. The roasted seed when ground and used with white flour makes an excellent tasty bread.

Bidens bipinnata—Spanish needles, beggarticks.

A weed of the Southwest, growing to about two feet with yellow flowers, it offers only leaves which might be used as a potherb.

Calendula officinalis—Pot-marigold, marigold, goldbloom, may-bud.

This is the annual plant, long known in gardens abroad, which always has yellow or orange flowers of good size and which, because of this similarity to the plants of "Tagetes" brought into

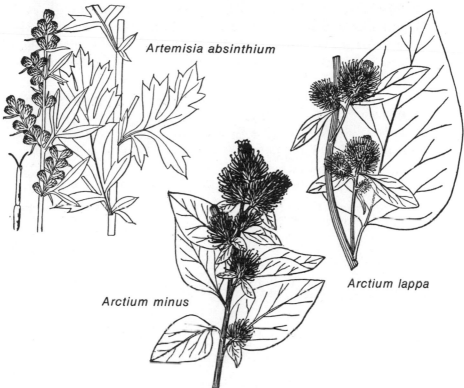

Artemisia absinthium

Arctium lappa

Arctium minus

Europe in the sixteenth century, that bright flower of Mexico was thought to be the well-known marigold. Hence when one sees the word "marigold" in the literature of England, it is this calendula rather than the Tagetes plant which we know by the marigold name.

Throughout Europe, the petals of calendula have been used for coloring broths and soups, and because of this use and a long history, it is usually a denizen of herb gardens.

Carduus (**various species**)—Plumeless, Italian and bristle thistle. Similar to the thistles call *Circium* and widely found in the West, the pith of the stems may be boiled and eaten, while the dried flowers may be used as rennet to curdle milk.

Carthamus tinctorius—Safflower, false saffron, bastard saffron. Unrelated to the true saffron, which belongs to the iris family, the flowers of this (probably) Asian plant, have been used for a yellow color in dyeing silk, and, when mixed with talc, became "rouge." Some medicinal values are known, but are unimportant.

Cichorium intybus—Chicory, blue sailors, succory, wild endive.
Whether or not this is a weed depends on how much one loves
a fine blue flower. Some people plant it in their gardens and
others protect the fields in which it grows. Again an introduced
plant, it is now common everywhere in open fields. For our
country, its use is largely for adding the dried, ground roots to
"bitter-ize" coffee, especially in the South. Among people of
European ancestry it is a spring tonic green, cut when just
emerging; while in Belgium, it is a main item of export in the
growing and sending to us and elsewhere, the forced roots
which we know as "Belgian endive" or "witloof chicory." Noted
as valuable by writers from the East to the Far West, it is one of
the most notable of our wayside bounties.

Cirsium (**various species**)—Thistles, Canada thistles, creeping thistle, roadside thistle.
Noted in books concerned with edible plants, from East to West,
and from Canada, several species of thistles, all with the lovely
light purple flowers, are noted as having food value. For this the
roasted roots are sweetish in taste while, rated as the best food
is the peeled young flower stem, which may be eaten raw in salad
or cooked. The thistle "down" (for those camping) makes an
excellent tinder for starting fires. Ornamentally the fresh flower
heads make a beautiful bouquet and thus it may be said that
however prickly or badly reputed the thistle may be as a weed,
it has a surprisingly useful value.

Cnicus benedictus—Blessed thistle, Our Lady's thistle, blessed carduus, etc.
A name such as this (and much written about it in books from
ancient times) would indicate this European annual weed, now
widely spread in this country, had valuable properties. Actually
it seems to have few great medicinal values except that
Youngken rates it as a "bitter tonic in the form of a decoction,"
and it may be safely used as such, preparing the dried foliage.
   Interestingly enough the many "holy" names seem to have
come from the story that white veins of the foliage were marked
by the Virgin's milk as she suckled the Christ child, as well as
from any actual medicinal values the plant, in olden days, was
supposed to have. The herbalist Culpepper says that this thistle
was ruled by the planet Mars.

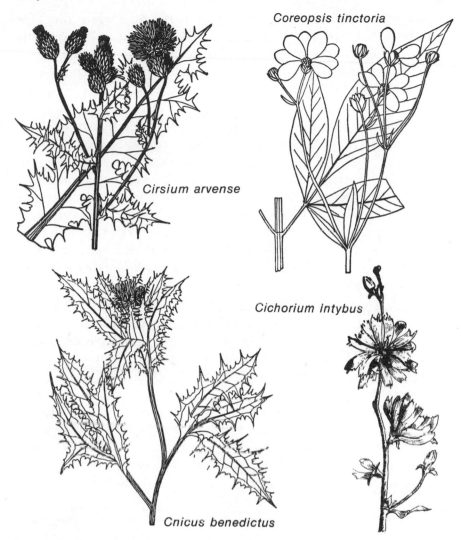

Coreopsis tinctoria

Cirsium arvense

Cichorium intybus

Cnicus benedictus

Coreopsis tinctoria—Coreopsis, tickseed.
A plant of the Midwest which has spread as a weed very widely, is this rather lovely yellow flower, which produces as a dye plant, the colors of bright yellow and burnt orange. Variations of coreopsis have come into our gardens as a good perennial plant, and it is often seen making a lovely bright spot along roadsides.

Echinacea purpurea—Cone flower, black sampson, hedgehog, red sunflower.
This is a tallish growing perennial widely found in the Midwest. The large flowers usually are cone-shaped and with mostly pur-

ple petals. The roots are the part used, and while the U.S. dispensatory says that medicine made from it "increases the body's resistance to infection," a pharmacological book says that it "is employed in the treatment of ulcers and boils."

Erigeron canadensis—Canadian fleabane, horse-weed, hog-weed, colt's tail, etc.

An American plant, truly, which was first noted by explorers as early as 1640, and soon appeared in herbals abroad, although it never seems to have been fully accepted by medicine. Although the name "fleabane" would indicate it as good as an insecticide, actually this name came because the little seeds looked like fleas. Its uses as a home remedy over the centuries has been as a tonic, astringent, diuretic, and even for the reduction of pimples. It is taken as an infusion made from the whole dried plant. There are a number of species all more or less with the same values.

Eupatorium perfoliatum—Boneset, thoroughwort, Indian sage, ague weed, vegetable antimony, sweating plant.

A widely spread weed which, with such names, would be assumed to be valuable medicinally, but apparently the only value it would have would be to produce sweating and help break a fever. Fevers were called in the old days breakbone fevers, and it would appear from all reports that the Indians used it thus to break a fever. Long a favorite home remedy, it is mostly interesting to the botanist for the way in which the opposite leaves sort of perforate the stem, and with this it is easily recognized.

Eupatorium purpureum—Gravel root, joepye weed, trumpet weed, queen of the meadow, kidney root, purple boneset, Indian gravel root, motherwort, niggerweed, quillwort, hempweed, trumpet weed, etc.

A plant with as many common names as this is surely one known to people all over the East and South where it grows in generally moist situations. Purplish to white heads of flowers in August make it one of the finest of tall wild flowers. Its Latin name comes from an early user of the plant, Mithridate Eupator, while the name joepye is said to be that of an Indian who cured typhoid fever with extractions of the rhizome or root. Among herbalists it is claimed to be of value as a diuretic and tonic.

Galinsoga parviflora—Galinsoga, quick weed.

Widely spread, this rather unimportant plant is included in the

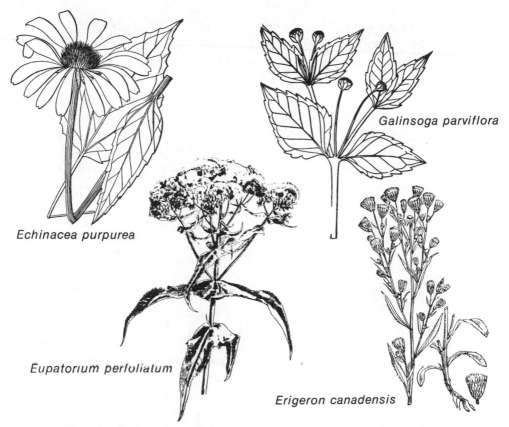

Echinacea purpurea

Galinsoga parviflora

Eupatorium perfoliatum

Erigeron canadensis

list of Rocky Mountain edible plants as a good pot-herb, cooking just the tops after removing the roots.

Gnaphalium obtusifolium—Cud weed, life everlasting, silver leaf, cotton weed, rabbit tobacco, none-so-pretty, fragrant everlasting, etc.

This plant is found pretty much everywhere throughout the United States and into Canada. It has been used by the Indians and by the people of the country of India and of China. In Mexico and in France, various values are ascribed. The most reliable authority lists it as used for "pulmonary and intestinal catarrh, for diarrhoea, and as a fomentation for bruises."

Grindelia (**various species**)—Gum plant, gumweed, rosin weed.

A common roadside plant of the dry open places of the West, with large yellow flower heads. Indians and pioneers both made use of the dried leaves for tea, with a broth made of the leaves used for indigestion, and externally for skin irritations.

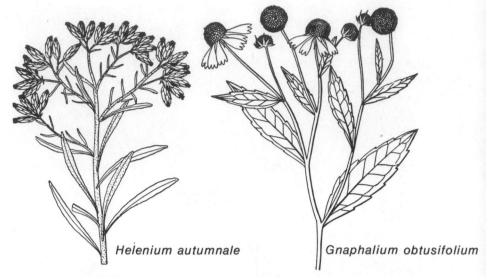

Helenium autumnale   *Gnaphalium obtusifolium*

Grindelia camporum—Gum plant, scaly grindelia, rosin weed, tar
    weed.
  The dried leaves and flowering tops of this plant of the Far
  West, are used to make infusions which are expectorant and
  sedative, with an action resembling atropine. One good authority says that it's often smoked with stramonium and other drugs
  in cases of asthma. Many references are made to the use of the
  juices of the grindelia as a cure for ivy poisoning.

Helenium autumnale—Sneezeweed, false sunflower, staggerwort, yel-
    low-star.
  A plant of wet places in many sections of the East, the name
  staggerwort may indicate the fact that it is poisonous to cattle,
  but there is record that the Indians in some areas used the dry
  flower heads in powdered form to sniff for colds, and an infusion
  of the leaves as a laxative.

Helianthus annuus—Common annual or giant sunflower.
  If there is any one plant which should be regarded as America's
  contribution to the "flower world" it would be the sunflower,
  which originated not in Mexico or South America, but in mid-
  United States, from whence it has spread around the world, with
  the present greatest use made of it as a crop in Russia. The
  interest of many wild birds in the seeds should alert one to its
  food values. It forms a highly nutritive food for man (as the
  "natural foods" people consider invaluable) and, as well, it pro-

vides a good oil for cattle food. Some medicinal uses have been known, but essentially one should think of it as one of the best of food plants, something well known to the Indians of the Missouri region, as reported on by the Lewis and Clark expedition in 1805.

Helianthus tuberosus—Jerusalem artichoke, artichoke, earth apple, Canada potato.

Here we have a perennial sunflower, which produces tubers which may be dug in the fall and baked with oil or butter, or may be used in pickling. A true native American, the name Jerusalem comes from the French name, girasol, for a sunflower. As a potato-substitute it may be used by diabetics, without ill effect. There is good evidence that these were cultivated in a mild sort of way by the Indians, as a basic article of diet.

Hieracium (**various species**)—Hawkweed.

A world-wide weed, getting its name from an ancient belief that hawks ate the sap to sharpen their eyesight. Usefully the green plants were used as sort of a chewing gum by Indians of the Northwest.

Inula Helenium—Elecampane, scabwort, elf dock, horseheal, wild sunflower, velvet dock, inula.

An introduced, tall-growing, daisy-like flower which has spread very widely to mid-country, the names given above should reveal much of its value, going back to its uses to Greeks and Romans by whom the "Helenium" names were given perhaps

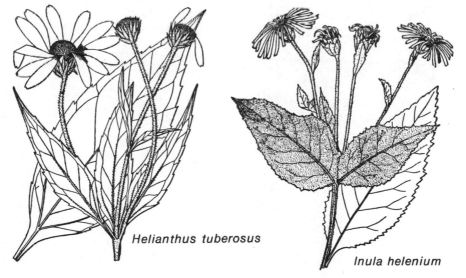

Helianthus tuberosus

Inula helenium

in honor of Helen of Troy. Scabwort indicates its use as an antiseptic, while horseheal means a long-time use for pulmonary diseases in horses. "Wild sunflower" puts it in the daisy family, while "velvet dock" tells of the softness of the under-side of the leaves. Inula is an old common name. And then one comes to "elf-dock," which goes back to Anglo-Saxon times when under a complex prescription involving magical rituals and an over-night rest on a local altar, it was prescribed for elf-sickness, which might today be described as mild mental aberration. Thus, as with many, many plants of this book, common names tell much more than one would think. On the actual pharmacological values of Inula, the most reliable authority says that "its active constituent, helein, has been employed as an antiseptic and bactericide in pulmonary diseases," with these values being obtained by crushing the dried, thick-

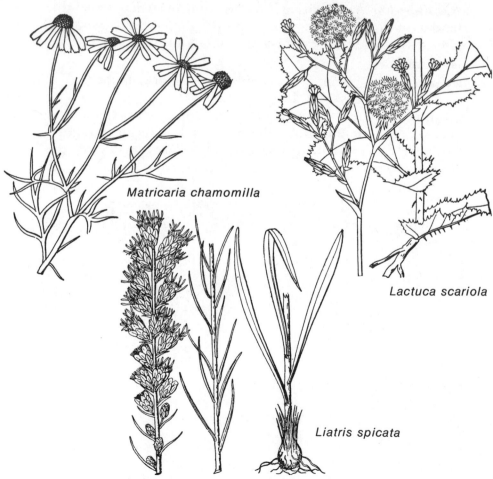

Matricaria chamomilla

Lactuca scariola

Liatris spicata

ened two-year old root, and steeping, with a cupful of the infusion taken once a day.

Lactuca scariola—Prickly or wild lettuce, wild opium, milk or horse thistle.

Widely spread and found even in the Rocky Mountain area, this close cousin of our garden lettuce can provide a salad basis when the plant is young and tender. One common name of wild opium indicates that it is mildly soporific and sedative, but, because of certain constituents, care should be taken not to get the milky juice in the eyes. It is interesting to note that even the common garden lettuce is rated in one book on the subject "as a narcotic where opium is objectionable."

Liatris spicata—Button-snakeroot, gay-feather, backache root, devil's bit, blazing star.

A lovely wild plant of wet places, this plant may be best known for its beauty in the landscape. Tall and brilliant when in bloom, it is allied to some of our good garden sorts. It is listed as being medicinally valuable as a diuretic, stimulant, diaphoretic, and emmenagogue.

Matricaria chamomilla—Scentless false chamomile, Mayweed.

Here is another escaped weed, and one which is quite similar, except that it is an annual, to *Anthemis nobilis* (q.v.). They are both known as chamomile. A plant long appreciated in various cultures, it has a fragrance like pineapple, and is used to flavor Manzanilla wine. The French use the leaves for making one of their healthful tisanes or teas, while in Germany it is a medicinal plant. A different use is noted by a well-known botanist, Albert F. Hill, in that the dark amber liquid of an infusion has been used to restore live color to hair, especially to darken blonde or red hair. Medicinally it is said that an infusion will cut short an attack of delirium tremens or is a cure for nightmares. Another writer, Francatelli, suggests a tea so made is an excellent drink for the aged, or that a hot fomentation will relieve pains of inflammation and neuralgia.

This is one of the mainstay plants of the herbal garden and should be better known and more used.

Petasites speciosa—Coltsfoot, butter burr.

The foliage of this shade-loving plant can be cooked and eaten and some salt can be made by burning the leaves and using the ashes as salt.

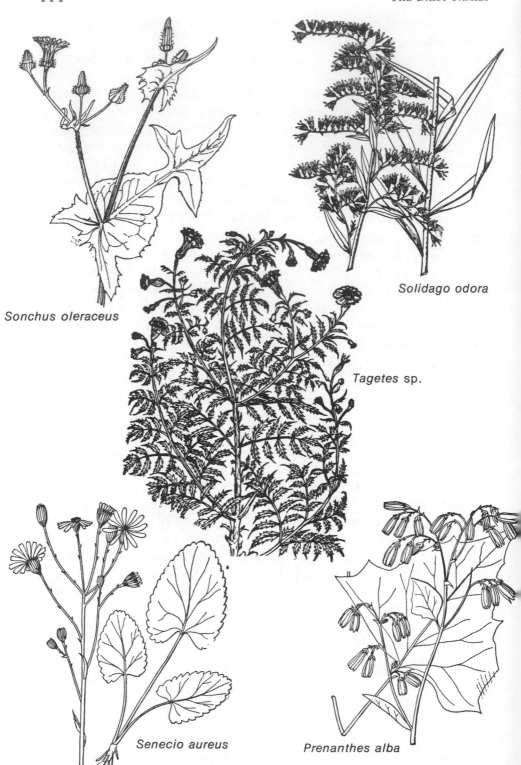

Sonchus oleraceus

Solidago odora

Tagetes sp.

Senecio aureus

Prenanthes alba

Prenanthes alba—Rattlesnake-root, gall-of-the-earth, white lettuce, cankerweed.

The statement in one good reference work says that "a decoction of this plant has proved beneficial in cases of rattlesnake bite in North Carolina," thus showing the reason for the first name. It makes a bitter tonic and has been used for dysentery. It is found in the woods from East to the Midwest.

Senecio aureus—Wild valerian, coughweed, cocashweed, female regulator, golden senecio, ragwort, squaw weed, uncum, waxweed, golden groundsel, life-root plant, butterweed, etc.

Very wide-spread in the United States, the names above should show that it was one of the Indian medicinal plants, one certainly known to the "squaws," who basically were the doctors of the tribe, rather than the "medicine men" of whom one reads. At one time, an American "official" drug useful in female disorders, its many names suggest its wide usefulness. The part used is the root, or the entire plant before flowering.

Solidago odora—Sweet-scented golden rod, Blue Mountain tea, anise-scented golden rod.

One of the most appreciated of wild flowers, elevated to a place in European gardens, has been the golden-rod, but it is so common throughout much of the United States, that we do not half appreciate its beauty. This particular species rates as a "tea" made from the dried leaves, and as such rated to be an aromatic stimulant and a diuretic. A western sort (*S. Californica*) has been used to make lotion for "sores and cuts for man and beast, finishing off with a sprinkling of powdered dried leaves." Among the practical uses of golden-rod are that it is one of the better-known dye plants, the flowers producing a yellow-green. Appreciation of uses such as this should make us take a second look at golden-rods, and transplant some of the improved forms into our flower borders.

Sonchus oleraceus—Sow thistle, milk thistle, snow thistle.

A widely spread plant with rather bitter juice which has been rated as a salad plant when used with milder tasting "greens." On the medicinal side, it is rated as a cathartic and used with belladonna and aromatics in the treatment of dropsy. The Chinese in California have used it as an anti-opiate.

Tagetes (**various species**)—True marigold.

A plant which is basically Mexican, and is one which is well known in its improved forms for all gardeners. All species of it are a source of yellow and orange dyes. Most recently, however, a great deal of interest has been focused on certain tall and not so beautiful species, which provide anti-insectidal values in the garden, supposedly because of the acrid oils which give most marigolds such a pungent smell.

Tanacetum vulgare—Tansy, bitter-buttons, ginger plants, hind heal, English cost.

Although there are native species of this genera, this particular species is another introduced plant and one long used by herbalists. Although used at times as medicine, it is perhaps too hazardous for the uninitated to consider. It was, however, used in olden times as a substitute for pepper, using the crushed dried leaves. Also it was much used then for discouraging ants and for a deterrent for flies on meat, in the days before refrigeration. Perhaps, at the moment, its principal value would be as a decorative plant, as the flower heads are easily dried and used for winter decorations.

Taraxacum officinale—Dandelion, blowball, doon-head, clock, piss-a-bed, and possibly fifty other names.

If everything could be said about the dandelion, it would take more than five pages in this book, for it is a plant appreciated and used since the cultures of Egypt, reliably described by Theophrastus in 300 B.C., and used medicinally by Arabian physicians who named it Taraxacon. Listed in every herbal medicinal text,it is rated with values as a diuretic; a laxative; tonic; hepatic; aperient and stomachic; the actual medicinal properties being found in the white juices of the living plant.As a fine and healthful salad green made from the new foliage in spring, it is much used by those of European ancestry. Later it may be cooked and the bitter principle eliminated by changing cooking water after a first boil. As with its cousin, chicory, the roots can be dried, roasted, and made into a coffee substitute or the younger roots can be boiled and used as carrots. Again as a final and wonderful use, the yellow flowers can be picked in quantity and used for making a most delightful wine. To have this vegetable in winter, one could dig the roots carefully and force them in moist sand in a cellar, producing thus an equivalent of Witloff chicory or Belgian endive. Appreciation of this most widely spread ancient weed should bring children and nature-novices into a basic appreciation of the bounties of nature.

Tragopogon porrifolius—Salsify, vegetable oyster, purple goat's
  beard.

Another weed introduced from Europe, this is found from coast
to coast. It is a plant long cultivated as a food, because of its
unusual flavor, which resembles oysters. If found in the wild, the
roots from young plants are best, and used before the flowers
develop. Scrape, slice, and cook like carrots.

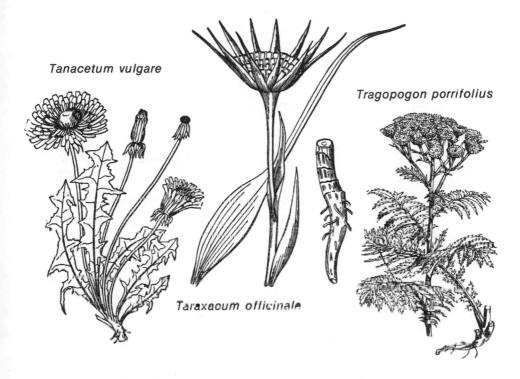

Tanacetum vulgare

Tragopogon porrifolius

Taraxaoum officinale

Tussilago farfara—Coltsfoot, coughwort, tussilago, foal's foot,
  horsehoof, butter-bur.

As with so many plants of this book, the common names, as well
as the scientific, give a cue as to the value of the plant, and here
"tussilago"—translated—means "cures a cough." This knowledge is repeated in the common names, while the shape of the
leaf is that of a horse's hoof. The yellow color of the flowers is
indicated by "butter-bur," while another common name "clay-
weed" would indicate its habitat. For centuries it has been definitely known as a good ingredient in cough remedies, to the
value of which the writer can testify. An ounce of leaves boiled
down in a quart of water to which honey is added makes a good

Tussilago farfara

remedy. A very interesting plant, it flowers in early spring before the leaves appear at all, which may be several months later; and it is, like so many other plants, an introduction from abroad.

THE MORNING GLORY FAMILY
CONVOLVULACEAE

***Ipomoea leptophylla*—**The bush morning glory.
Found out on the plains from the Dakotas down to Texas and over into the Rockies, this perennial is a bushy vine, but otherwise with flowers like the more familiar morning-glory. Growing

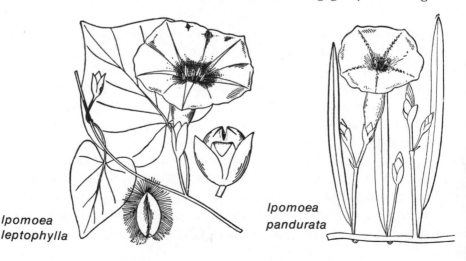

Ipomoea leptophylla

Ipomoea pandurata

up from year to year with an enormous root, a writer on the useful flora of the Rockies says that it is "one of the very best of plants to be eaten." This root may be eaten raw, boiled, or roasted and then becomes, says Harrington, "one of the most palatable of all the wild foods we have ever tried."

Ipomoea pandurata—Wild potato vine; man-root; wild jalap; scammony; mecha-meck.

A similar plant to that above with more vine-like growth and growing in the eastern United States. Possible to use as food, but as one name would indicate, it has a reputation as a strong purgative, and is not recommended.

THE DOGWOOD FAMILY

CORNACEAE

Cornus canadensis—Bunchberry, crackerberry.

A low-growing, bright-berried little plant, with fruit which, while edible, is rather tasteless. It is related to a species, quite similar, which is found largely in woodsy, peaty places in Canada, and so over into Scandinavia—a form named after Sweden—*Cornus suecia*, with slightly tart, palatable berries used there by the Laplanders, to make a pudding by mixing the crushed berries with whey. The suggestion is made that our tasteless bunchberry could be so used by the addition of a little lemon juice to add some "zip."

Cornus florida—Flowering dogwood, Indian arrow-wood, cornel, bitter redberry, false box, and Indian names—mon-ha-can-ni-min-schi and hat-ta-wa-no-min-schi.

Beyond any usable values, this is surely one of the fine ornamental small trees for planting in a shady, acid-soil position. In looking at the names, we note the word "arrow-wood" and because the wood is very hard, it has a number of possible uses. The Indians used the split stems as toothbrushes, the astringent properties of the bark being valuable for hardening the gums.

As to the pure medicinal properties of dogwood bark, it was once used as a bitter tonic and febrifuge and even as a substitute for quinine. But it is no longer an "official" drug, and its best use might well be as a treatment for a sore mouth or as a poultice

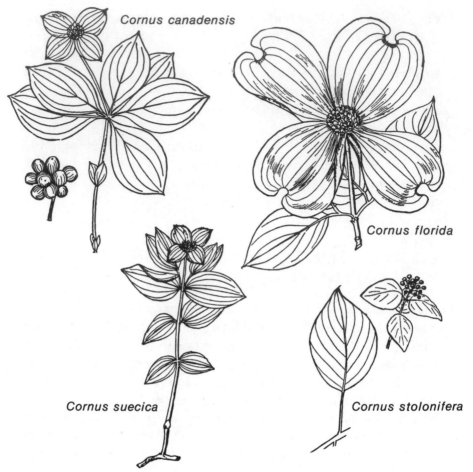

Cornus canadensis

Cornus florida

Cornus suecica

Cornus stolonifera

for external inflammations. A final value, known to the Indians, was as a calendarial guide to the right date for planting corn, for this major crop was planted when the dogwood bloomed— probably a much better guide to planting time than some of the moon signs still used today.

Cornus stolonifera—Red osier, red dogwood, red willow.
Here is another member of the dogwood family which is good as a landscape plant, for its bright red stems make a colorful spot in winter against the snow. It is wide-spread, in one variation or another. It is reliably reported that the Indians of the West and the early pioneers used to gather the inner bark of the stems, dry and smoke it, and that such smoking gives a narcotic effect, which if overdone, may cause stupefaction.

Cornus nuttallii—Western dogwood.

A dogwood tree to about 50 feet which is found south from British Columbia. The red berries have been eaten raw or cooked, while the inner bark of twigs has been added to tabacco for smoking.

THE ORPINE FAMILY

CRASSULACEAE

Sedum roseum—Stonecrop, roseroot, Queen or King's crown.

An "alpine" plant found in many mountainous places both east and west in which the rose-scented roots as well as the young leaves are rated as being good for salad use.

Sempervivum tectorum—Houseleek, hen and chickens, Jupiter's beard, healing blade.

Here again the last three names tell something of its values which might be called real or imaginary. The steeped leaves are deemed to be a cooling application for bruises and burns with likely the same effect as the *Aloe*(q.v.). Deemed by some to be a wart remover or corn remedy. One writer reports that in Italy he saw such juice administered to a newborn infant, presumably to "guard against convulsions and ensure a long and healthy life."

The Jupiter name comes from the fact that for millenia it was thought that plants of sempervivums planted on a roof would protect against lightning—from the bolts of Jove.

The "hen and chickens" comes from the way in which the

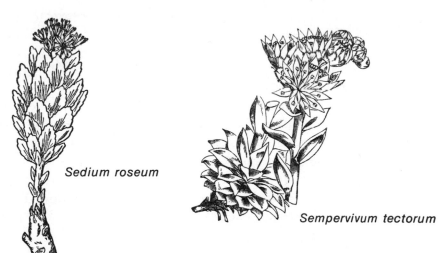

Sedium roseum

Sempervivum tectorum

plant sends out little plants from a central mother, the mother dying after blooming. A case where "live forever" means the clump and not the main plant. An interesting genus of plants of which this species is the most common, but not the most beautiful.

THE MUSTARD FAMILY
CRUCIFERAE

In no sense is the list of useful wild members of this family presented here as being all-embracing. A great percentage of the 1800 widely-distributed family members have peppery and piquant qualities; many of them are essential cultivated vegetables such as cabbage, mustard, turnips, cauliflower, and radishes, while there are an equal number of favorite garden flowers such as the sweet alyssum, wallflowers, stock, and candytuft. But for the person likely to sample some of the naturally growing American plants in this family, here are a few.

Barbarea verna **and** *B. vulgaris*—Winter cress, yellow rocket, scurvy grass.

A bitter and winter-hardy weed which can be used in raw salad to make a biting taste, but when cooked needs two changes of water to remove this bitter principle. The first species is grown and sold in the South. Other genera such as the *Cardamines* and *Caulanthus*, which grows in the West, may be used as above.

Brassica nigra—Mustard—black, brown or red, kerlock.

Mustard is not known as a desirable adventive into the vegetable garden or farm, but it appears widely everywhere and could be well listed as a pot-herb. The greens can be gathered in early spring and should be cooked about a half-hour. The biting taste suggests they be cooked with and used to brighten the flavor of other greens. The mustard is actually rich in vitamins as well as having trace minerals. The seeds, of course, when ground, become the mustard of commerce.

Capsella bursa-pastoris—Shepherd's purse, St. James wort, pick purse, etc.

A common weed, brought in by earliest settlers, it is found from East to West. There is some reference to its use as a salad herb

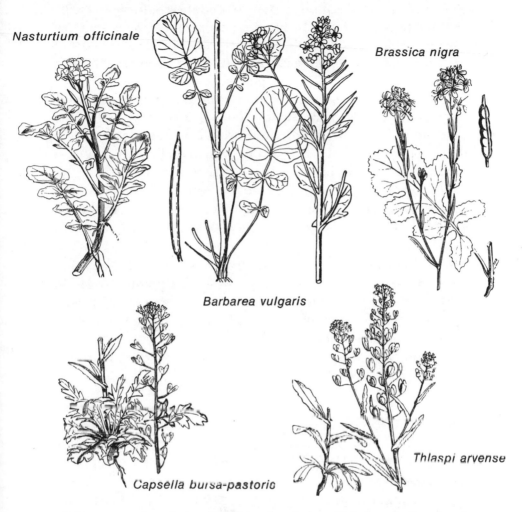

Nasturtium officinale

Brassica nigra

Barbarea vulgaris

Capsella bursa-pastoris

Thlaspi arvense

when young, but it is of little value here. Mainly use has been made of its astringent properties and it was used by the Germans in World War I as a styptic when other materials could not be imported.

Lepidium fremontii—Pepper grass.

This and other species are widely spread in the West as either annual or perennial herbs. The seeds mixed with vinegar make a flavoring for meat dishes, while the young shoots of the plants are said to be good as salad material.

Nasturtium officinale—Watercress, sisymbrium.

Here is one of the common and wide-spread plants of our country in which scientific nomenclature is confused, for in botanies one will find it variously as above or as *Radicula, Sisymbrium,* or *Rorippa,* while of course one can associate the name *Nasturtium* with the quite different garden flower, but one which has a "nose-turning" pungency not unlike this valuable water plant.

It is hardly necessary to talk much about using watercress in the form of a salad herb, or for cooking for flavor, with other vegetables. The only caution here would be about gathering it from any stream where it's growing, which might be polluted—such as a stream which runs through a cow pasture.

Watercress is truly a highly valuable source of vitamins A, B, C, and B_2, as well as iron, copper, magnesium, and calcium.

Thlaspi arvensee—Pennycress, hedge mustard, and other local names.

The young tender shoots of this field pennycress are rated as good for salad among the Rocky Mountain plants, while for cooking it is suggested that the water be changed once or twice to take out the bitter principle. The fact is that there are a number of plants of the general mustard family which are rated to be "possibly useful," but most contain the strong mustardy taste which suggests their use solely for their "peppery" quality.

THE SEDGE FAMILY

CYPERACEAE

Cyperus esculentus—Chufa, nut-grass, earth-almond, edible galingale, rush-nut.

A widely spread weed which, for its tiny tubers, has been known for many centuries as a good edible plant, has come to us from southern Europe and India. The little tubers which grow just below the ground may be boiled, peeled, and seasoned, or even, as done at times, toasted and used as a substitute for coffee. In Europe they were often ground and made into flour, and going back even further, there is evidence that they were so valued in ancient Egypt that supplies were put into the tombs for celestial eating.

If found to be growing in the reader's garden, they should be dug and used, for, as a weed, it is otherwise perhaps the most difficult-to-eradicate garden pest known.

Scirpus **(various species)**—Tule, tall bulrush, black rush, boulder bast.

A number of species of this genus such as *maritimus, robustus, validus, acutus,* and others all have rootstocks which seem to have been used by Indians, both in this country and the East. Similar in use to Cyperus above, the roots have been ground into flour.

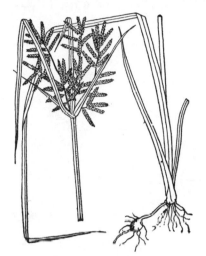
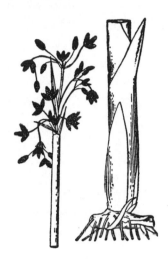

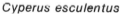
Cyperus esculentus   Scirpus validus

Fernald and Kinsey report that "the bruised young roots, boiled in water, furnish a sweet syrup," but "that the labor of digging it, precludes its becoming a popular food for those whose squaws are not inclined to gather it." There are further reports of the seed being used as food as well as the pollen used to make cakes.

THE CYPRESS FAMILY

CUPRESSACEAE

Juniperus communis—Common or dwarf juniper, horse savin, hackmatack, ground juniper.

It may seem odd to the reader to find the junipers and cedars listed under cypresses, but this is one of the decisions of the botanists followed in this work. Twisting this around it is also noted that some authorities put cypresses among the pines, with many other plants appearing in odd classifications.

In this particular species we have a plant that bears the fruits which are used principally in flavoring gin and the fact is that the word "gin" itself is a contraction of the word in several languages for the juniper itself (French-genievre).

Medicinally, if you are not interested in the flavor of gin, the berries have been used as a diuretic and also to treat arteriosclerosis, while in more ancient times the berries were swallowed to produce abortion, from whence came a name of "bastard-killer."

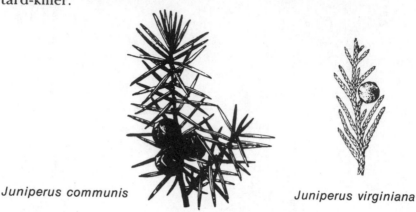

Juniperus communis   Juniperus virginiana

Juniperus virginiana—Eastern redcedar, juniper, red savin, Virginia cedar.

Also note that a western cedar, *J. scopularum,* which bears the name red cedar, is, similarly to the above, used as a flavor for gin and the berries are noted as an "emergency food," while for many birds, and especially the cedar waxwings, the berries are a basic food.

Especially notable is the use of the bark, berries, and twigs of this and other cedars (Junipers) as a material for dyeing wool a good khaki color.

Considering the pungency which is found in all the species of juniper, it is not hard to think of them as having some medicinal values, and this is especially true of the red cedar. In Appalachia, a mixture of nuts, leaves, and twigs is boiled, and inhaled as a treatment for bronchitis. In New Mexico, people of Mexican background use a boiled mixture of bark and water to treat skin rash.

It so happens that the writer of this lives in a section where most trees are of this species, and it is very interesting to see how variable seedling trees are in shape, color, and growth characteristics, circumstances which have given rise to a number of named horticultural varieties. This further suggests that the best plants for your garden should be grown from cuttings rather than from the highly variable seeds.

THE GOURD FAMILY

CUCURBITACEAE

Curcubita Pepo—Summer and autumn pumpkins.

One associates the pumpkin and squash as being part of our heritage from the Indian culture, but the botanists are not at all certain about the origin of the many sorts of these vegetables. Possibly some came up North from Mexico and Texas. In any case it should be noted that the seeds of any of these forms are nutritious and that oil can be extracted from them. Some note

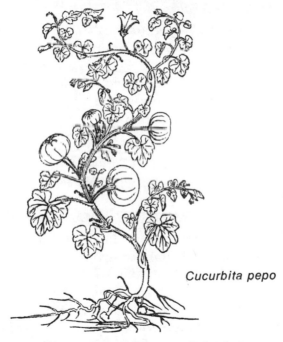

Cucurbita pepo

has been taken of the value of the seeds in the treatment of tape worms and "affections of the urinary passage." And who does not know of pumpkin and squash pie as good food?

One lady who claims an Indian ancestry has sent me her recipe for squash pie, which, feeling it is truly "American" you might like to try.

Squash Pie

2 1/2 cups cooked squash (any kind)
2/3 cups brown sugar (loosely packed)
1 1/3 cup white sugar
4–6 eggs
1 teaspoon salt
4 cups milk (I use 1/2 milk and 1/2 cream)
2 teaspoons vanilla
1/2 teaspoon nutmeg
1 teaspoon cinnamon
1 heaping tablespoon cornstarch (or flour)
Bake in a 450° oven for ten minutes. Reduce heat to 375° and bake 30 minutes more, if needed, same as you would pumpkin or persimmon pie. I use this recipe for squash, pumpkin, sweet potato, and persimmon pie. Wild plums are good with this recipe. On your next pumpkin pie, add a few black walnuts for a taste that's different.

***Cucurbita foetidissima*—Buffalo gourd, calabazilla.**

One of the many members of the gourd family, this is a rough and coarse perennial which bears egg-shaped gourds, which can be eaten, cooked, or dried. Here the raw gourd and the root of the plant make a usable lather when crushed in water and rubbed between the hands. It grows in dry ground in much of the Southwest.

THE YAM FAMILY

DIOSCOREACEAE

***Dioscorea villosa*—Wild yam root, colic root, China root, devil's bones, dioscorea, rheumatism-root.**

The names given above indicate the uses of this plant in herbal medicine, but one should not be fooled into thinking that "yam" implies that it is the common yam found in the markets. It is rather a twining perennial vine found in moist places in what one would call the climatic zone 7, down the East Coast across into Texas. The part used is the smallish root, dried, powdered, and made into a decoction. This is variably recommended to be used for the nausea of pregnant women, for flatulence, for various intestinal disorders and even for hiccough.

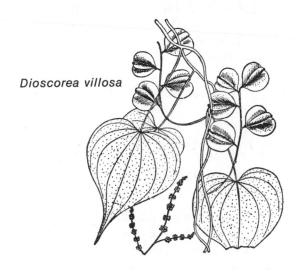

Dioscorea villosa

THE PERSIMMON FAMILY

EBENACEAE

Diospyros virginiana—Persimmon; sugar, winter, or date plum; possom wood.

This tree grows from the mid-Atlantic south and to the Middle West, producing fruits which, when allowed to thoroughly ripen on the tree (and not necessarily freeze) are a real delight.

Perhaps they are not as nice as the huge Japanese persimmons now available in autumn in our markets, but it is interesting to note that the name Diospyros in translation means "fruit of Jove" or "heavenly fruit."

Some note has been taken of the medicinal values of the great astringency in the unripe fruit, and of the bark. This astringency

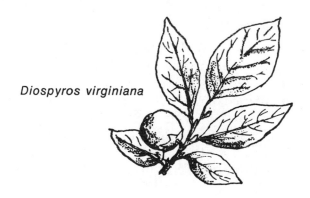

Diospyros virginiana

suggests its use for diarrhoea, as a tonic, and, combined with alum, it might be helpful in an ulcerated sore throat.

A correspondent tells of how her Indian grandmother used to make pies, after removing the seeds, cooking as for pumpkin, adding eggs and honey and spice and cream, making sort of a custard dessert. Again persimmon butter would be made much as apple butter, fine in mid-winter with hot biscuits and honey.

THE OLEASTER FAMILY
ELAEAGNACEAE

Eleagnus commutata—Silverberry.
A large shrub also growing along streams in parts of the Rockies, the silver-green berries may be eaten raw or cooked, good for making soup or an excellent jelly.

Shepherdia argentea

Shepherdia argentea—Buffalo-berry, wild oleaster, silver-leaf.
This is a tall shrub native to the western plains and out to the Northwest, growing in moist valleys and low meadows. The great abundance of nice olive-shaped scarlet fruit has provided Indians and campers with a fruit which, when ripe, is tasty and nutritious, especially if beaten up with a little sugar. Like others in this family, it is often grown for ornament in its natural area and, as well, the fruit has been used as a source of red dye.

THE CROWBERRY FAMILY

EMPETRACEAE

Corema Conradii—Crowberry; empetreum; poverty-grass; curlew-
  berry.

Common in the Northeast and the Northwest states, in swamps
or sandy or rocky slopes, one writer on the plants of British
Columbia says that the fruits "being abundant and available all
year round, they are considered as the most important fruit of
the Arctic region." It is a low matted evergreen with blackish

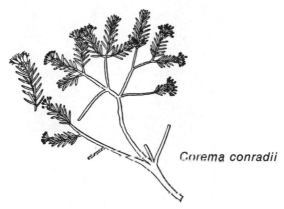

Corema conradii

fruits with a hard seed. The fruits have a mild medicinal flavor
and are best eaten after freezing.

A very similar plant is *Empetrum nigrum*, called by the same
common name and, as differing from *Corema*, is found in dense
mats on the northern West Coast. The berries, while not too
tasty can be cooked, while at times they have been used to make
a fermented beer with brown sugar or molasses.

THE HORSETAIL FAMILY

EQUISETACEAE

Equisetum arvense—Scouring rush, joint weed, bull pipes, shave
  brush, pewterwort, common horsetail, etc.
Equisetum fluviatile—Swamp horsetail, scrub grass, joint grass.
Equisetum hyemale—Common scouring rush, Dutch-rush, gun-bright,
  mare's-tail.

When one realizes that the giant forms of this plant, now totally extinct, were the trees from which much of our coal was formed and that certain botanists list this genus as "Plant No. 1" in their classification, it will readily be understood that what we have here is a real leftover from ancient times.

The first listed species is a small one growing about one foot or less while the others are possibly up to two feet. Usually found in waste places and on the edges of swamps, one can, by picturing them as great trees, envision the appearance of the Carboniferous era millions of years ago.

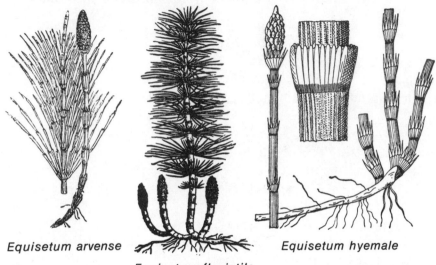

Equisetum arvense   *Equisetum hyemale*

Equisetum fluviatile

On the practical side the common names should give an idea of the uses of the horse-tails, for actually, the stems contain silica which once made them useful for scouring pewter, for brightening gun-stocks, and for kitchen scouring. Indeed, it was so used by the Indians and the colonists, and may today be useful to campers. Again the larger species can be used as sandpaper. Another practical use is for those interested in dyeing, the stalks giving an interesting yellow-gray color.

On the food side, one authority suggests that the young heads can be used as asparagus or boiled and fried. Medicinally, however, more values are imputed to the horsetails, and in Grieve's *Modern Herbal* we find this:

> The barren stems only are used medicinally . . . either fresh
> or dried . . . diuretic and astringent. Horse-tail has been
> found beneficial in dropsy, gravel and kidney infections.

The decoction applied externally will stop bleeding of wounds.

Thus, historically and practically, this is one of the very interesting wild plants with a variety of uses.

THE HEATH FAMILY
ERICACEAE

A FAMILY NOTE—The Heaths are a widely spread family, almost always to be found in conditions of an acid soil, often of light shade, and in many cases in mountainous areas on both the East and West Coasts. The family name of "heath" indicates that the heathers are a basic family member to which we add the lovely azaleas and rhododendrons; the mountain laurel; the arbutus and others which will be discussed here, with many uses for food and other things.

Arbutus menziesii—Madrona.

Although bearing the scientific name of the fragrant and lovely trailing arbutus of early spring in the East, this is a tree of the West Coast with a beautiful red bark which provides the material for an excellent brown dye.

Arctostaphylos uva-ursi—Bearberry, kinnikinnick, mealy-plum vine, crowberry, hog cranberry, brawlins, bear's bilberry, etc.

A widely spread plant both in our country and abroad. It is first of all interesting in its name, the generic name meaning "bearberry," from Greek, and the specific Latin name also meaning bearberry.

Its usefulness begins with its landscape value, with a fine two inches high growth, as a ground cover in sunny spots, with suitable soil.

As a food plant, the lovely red berries are listed in some books as being edible when cooked, but the tasteless quality would not recommend it for this. On the West Coast the Chinook and other Indians mixed the dried leaves to add to smoking tobacco. As a dye plant it is a source of a yellow-gray dye.

Medicinally, the bearberry is rated in many books as a good diuretic and tonic. One noted nature-lover and botanist, Thomas Mechan, in whose nursery I worked some years ago, wrote that a simple way to take bearberry medicinally would be to soak the dried-powdered leaves in brandy and take it at night

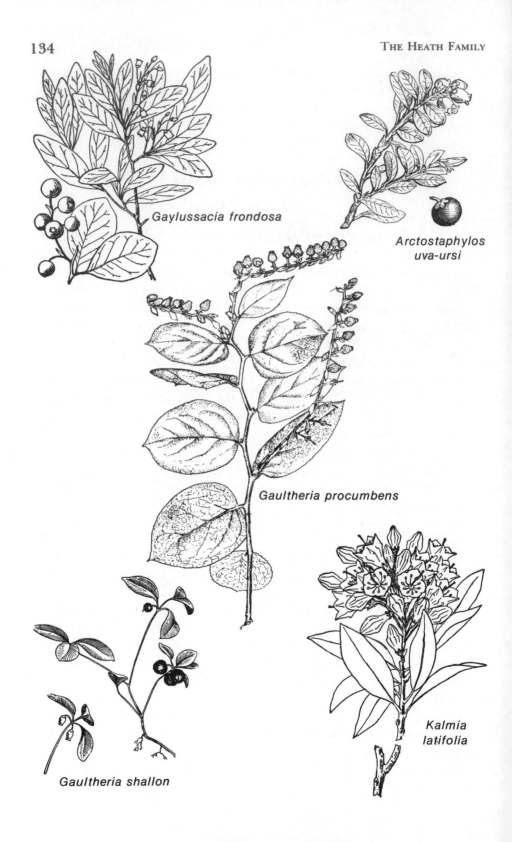

Gaylussacia frondosa

Arctostaphylos
uva-ursi

Gaultheria procumbens

Gaultheria shallon

Kalmia
latifolia

in a cup of hot water, with the quantity or frequency not given.

In sum, the bearberry is a very humble plant but one of much interest.

Gaultheria humisfusa—Western wintergreen.

A tiny little northern West Coast ground cover with fruits and leaves which taste like the related wintergreen. Here the small red fruits may be eaten cooked or raw as with the eastern species.

Gaultheria procumbens—Teaberry, boxberry, partridgeberry, wintergreen, checkerberry, pigeon berry, clink, tea of Canada, and a host of other names.

As with so many plants, the common names are a key to the uses and here the first given name "tea" tells us that the dried leaves of this plant were used as a substitute for real tea, especially after the famed Boston Tea Party. It is a tiny little plant about five inches high growing widely in the open woods, with nice red berries in the winter.

It is the source of the true "oil of wintergreen" used as a flavoring agent, and in earlier days as a source for methyl-salicylate, which as a medicine, is a valuable tonic, stimulant, astringent, and aromatic.

Mostly it is fun for the ordinary woods-lover to pick and chew the tasty leaves when walking in early spring.

Gaultheria shallon—Salal.

A plant found along the West Coast from Alaska to California, this is a two foot shrub bearing purple-black berries and with lovely leathery leaves. A West Coast writer says that, "Jams, jellies, and pies made from salal berries are excellent, and there is usually no difficulty in picking large quantities of them in late summer. . . . The Northwest Indians mashed the berries and dried them in cakes to be used during the winter."

Gaylussacia baccata—Black huckleberry.

Gayluccacia frondosa—Dangleberry.

Gaylussacia dumosa—Dwarf huckleberry.

Kalmia latifolia—Mountain laurel, calico-bush.

Aside from its quite wide use in the East as an evergreen shrub for landscape planting, especially in the selections which have been made with flowers of a delicate pink, the Kalmia species here is useful mostly for the yellow-tan dye which comes from the leaves.

Vaccinium oxycoccus **and** *V. macrocarpum*—Small or European cranberry.

Vaccinium vitis-idea—Rock cranberry, cowberry, lingenberry, mountain cranberry.

Vaccinium vitis-idea **var.** *minus*—Small mountain cranberry.

As will be seen below, there are other species of *Vaccinium* which are important fruits, but here are put together those which represent what are known as cranberries—"the what-goes-with-turkey" kind and found in one sort or another on Cape Cod, in the upper midborder states, and in the Northwest.

Although the cranberry is now mostly cultivated with improved selected varieties, they still may be gathered in the wild in the naturally swampy areas where they grow. As their use is known to everyone, no cooking instructions are needed here. Experimental medicinal use in the Albany College of Pharmacy with some 60 patients with acute urinary tract infections produced beneficial results by giving the patients 16 ounces of cranberry juice per day. Reports in *Prevention* magazine indicate that one mother cured her child of bed-wetting by a dose of four ounces of cranberry juice at 5 PM daily.

Medicinal values thus show themselves in even the most humble wild fruit.

Vaccinium ovatum—The western box-blueberry.

Vaccinium arboreum—A southern form commonly called farkleberry.

Vaccinium angustifolium—Blueberry and low-bush blueberry.

Vaccinium caespitosum—Dwarf bilberry.

Vaccinium corymbosum—Highbush or swamp blueberry, whortleberry.

Vaccinium hirsutum—Hairy huckleberry.

Vaccinium myrtillus—Whortleberry.

Vaccinium uliginosum—Bog bilberry.

A listing of the various genera and species as above should make the ordinary blueberry picker not feel upset when confronted first by a bush of blackish blueberries, then by low spreading ones on the ground, or finally by giant bushes of choice berries all more or less in the same area.

Some of these sorts of berries are found in the North, some in the South or in the West, and for all of them there are other common names than those given, as well as a number of species

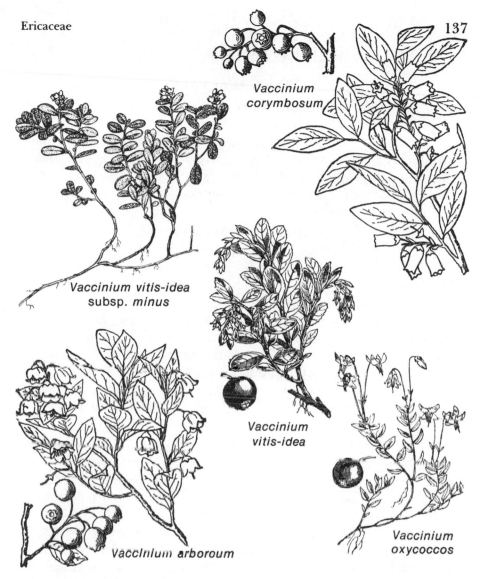

Vaccinium corymbosum

Vaccinium vitis-idea subsp. *minus*

Vaccinium vitis-idea

Vaccinium arboroum

Vaccinium oxycoccos

which the botanists are not too ready to name. A 75-page scientific monograph published in 1945, (W.H. Camp, *Blueberries*, Brittonia) fails to untangle all of it. One can only say that the blueberries are all good or better, and may be eaten fresh, dried like the Indians used to do, or more modernly, frozen.

Meanwhile, it is just plain fun to "go a-blue-berrying."

On the "useful" side of the blueberries, several dye authorities say that the juice of the fruits provides a good blue-gray dye, or when used with the addition of nut-galls, it gives a nice dark brown.

THE SPURGE FAMILY

Euphorbiaceae

Croton corynbulosus—Chaparral tea.

A plant of the dry rocky areas from Texas to the West, this belongs to the Spurge family, which includes many poisonous plants. It has been used for making tea of the flowering tips, but as any strong use of the plant oil is a purgative and may, with cattle, be deadly, it is not a recommended plant to use. It is a shrubby perennial herb.

Euphorbia serpyllifolia—Spurge, prostrate spurge.

This species of a large genus happens to be one which grows widely in dry open ground in the West, the roots of which were used, after chewing, to mix with cornmeal to make a "tasty" bread.

But more importantly it should be noted that this spurge genus with possibly 150 species widely spread around the world, contains many kinds (often succulent with milky exudates) which are possibly poisonous, or medicinal if properly used. A few of these mostly from the Southwest would be:

E. ALBOMARGINATA—said to be good for rattlesnake bites.

E. HIRTULA—for treating asthma and bronchitis.

E. MARGINATA—an eastern garden plant *(Snow-on-the-mountain)*

E. PULCHERRIMA—the favorite Christmas poinsettia.

Ricinus communis—Castor-oil plant, castor bean, palma Christi.

This familiar plant, of garden decorative use for its palm-like foliage, comes to us from Africa, but is, in a way, perhaps first among the plant-products with which children become acquainted when they are given castor oil. It *is* a decorative tropical-looking plant in any garden, but the ultra-poisonous character of its unaltered seeds place it high on the list of poisonous plants. Admire, use, and beware are three good terms for it.

Simmondsia chinensis—Jajoba, deer nut, goat nut.

This tall evergreen shrub is a native of an area from Arizona to lower California, and at one time, the bitter nuts were prepared as a coffee substitute, while the oil in the nuts has been used in the manufacture of hair oil, or as a substitute for beeswax in various products.

A recipe for using the seeds called for roasting the seed and grinding the kernels together with the yolk of a hard-boiled egg and then boiling the mixture a while, and using with milk and sugar.

Stillingia sylvatica—Queen's delight, cock-up-hat, nettle potato, silver leaf, yaw root.

From Virginia to Kansas and south, this is a perennial which grows to about three feet. Like other Euphorbias, it is a milky-juiced plant, with variably-shaped leaves and yellow flowers. The part used medicinally is the root-stock, of which, after extracting the properties in alcohol, it might be used as an emetic, cathartic, or diuretic.

Ricinus communis

Stillingia sylvatica

Actually, this is not an important drug plant, but its inclusion here brings up two points. First, that a standard reference refers to it as an "empiric" drug, which means more or less that it is a hand-me-down drug of somewhat doubtful value. Secondly, that reference to this one member of the Euphorbia family shows that the family all has a milky exudate, and that a number of members of this family are poisonous, and thus it is a good rule to be shy of the entire family. True, some of the Spurges are useful as garden plants or as house plants, such as the crotons and acalphas.

THE BEECH FAMILY

FAGACEAEA

Castanea (**various species**)—The American chestnut.

It may seem foolish to discuss a genus of plants which, because of disease, is almost a thing of the past; but, for the author, who used to go "chestnutting" when a boy, it can be said that this was one of the most edible of nuts, while the wood of the trees was valuable in many special ways. Presently one can plant some Chinese species which, through the many centuries, have grown up with disease resistance, and also which makes us hope that a few healthy young seedlings of our own American form will come along to service future generations.

Castanopsis (**various species**)—Chinquapin.

In the Northwest, the nuts of these species are sweet and pleasant to the taste when they ripen in September. There are usually from one to three nuts in a cluster.

Fagus grandiflora—The American beech.

A widely spread tree in the United States, it is not as notable for its beauty as the European beech, but with its beautiful bark, erect growth, and solid character, it is one of our best trees.

On the useful side surely the trade name of "beechnut" is well known, coming from the days when the beech oil was used commercially. Actually the beechnuts are delicious eating. Fernald and Kinsey say that it is one of the "sweetest, most delicious products of our northern forests," once widely sold in markets. Dried and roasted it was once used as a coffee substitute, while in parts of the South the emerging leaves were used as a potherb. In Maine, reports have it, the Indians ate also the emerging buds.

Quercus alba—White oak, stone oak, tanner's oak, stave oak.

Names such as the above common ones should give indication as to the uses of oak. There are, indeed, many varieties of oak and many have the same or similar uses. First to be noted is the use of the very hard wood of this and other oaks, a "stone"-like value; then the use of the astringency of the bark for tanning; plus the various colors of dyes, from chartreuse to light brown.

For medicinal purposes, the inner bark of the oak is cut, dried, powdered, and used an an infusion. As might be supposed, the inherent astringency suggests its value in dysentery and diarrhoea. One authority lists a dose as a decoction made from one ounce of bark to a quart of water, boiled down to a pint, and taken in wineglass doses. As a gargle for cases of sore throat, as a possible mild haemostatic, and as a vaginal douche, the same astringency would be operative.

The bark from a number of species of Quercus, such as the red oak, the black oak, and other native and hybrid forms may also be useful, but herbalist James Meyer suggests that while such barks may be used as an external astringent, they are "rarely employed internally, as it is liable to derange the bowels."

One notes in studying a book of drug formulas that tannic acid is a usual ingredient of healing ointment, and from personal experience the author can vouch for the efficacy of a healing herbal salve containing the extract of oak bark.

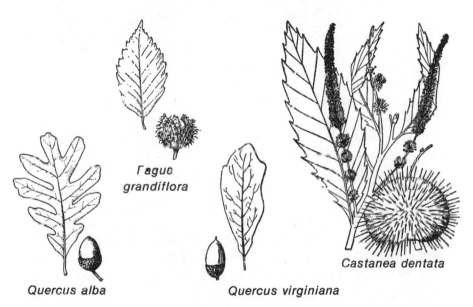

Fagus grandiflora

Castanea dentata

Quercus alba

Quercus virginiana

The same valuable property of astringency is found in oak galls and in the acorns. Acorns in powdered form are an old remedy for diarrhoea. Some Indian tribes crushed the acorns in water for food, others dried and boiled them, while some boiled them for oil. In the western United States, varieties of white and other oaks are similarly used for food, often being a staple of the Indian diet. One species, *Q. gambelii,* is especially recommended for food quality.

Surely from every standpoint, the oaks, the white oak especially, is one of our great native plants.

Quercus velutina—Black oak, red oak, quercitron, dyer's quercus, yellow bark.

This species of oak has bark with about the same properties as *Q. alba*, speaking medicinally, but it is especially notable for the material "quercitron," used in dyeing wool and silk. This oak like many others is widely spread in growth in the United States.

Quercus virginiana—Live oak.

This is an oak growing mostly in the South and having a sweet palatable acorn and a wood much used in the old days for shipbuilding. Get acquainted with all the oaks in your part of the country.

THE FUMITORY FAMILY

FUMARIACEAE

Fumaria officinalis—Fumitory; earth smoke; beggary; sax-dolls; fumaria.

This is the family to which belongs such plants as Dutchman's breeches *(Dicentra)* and Mexican poppy *(Argemone)* and here we find that in a number of family members there are certain principles which are mildly poisonous to man or beast. The particular plant above, by name "officinalis," shows that it has been on the medical plant list from earliest times as a mild tonic, and for eruptive skin diseases, but presently is not much used. Grieve's *Herbal* notes that it has been used in the past by French and German physicians as a purifier of the blood and thus one wonders, because so many of the chemical medicines have reactions, if doctors today will not come back to some of the old and useful herbs.

Fumaria officinalis

THE GENTIAN FAMILY

GENTIANACEAE

Centaurium umbellatum—Centaury; feverwort; bitter herb; red centaury.

Here is another one of the many plants which have become widely naturalized in our country right out as far as the plain states, and also a plant which must be distinguished from others of the name "centaury" which are found in the daisy family. And likewise it is known botanically by some authorities as *Erythroea*.

The flowers are of a pink-purple color, bringing in the famed "gentian-blue," and for those who work with dyes, it produced a blue dye. There is much of history about the plant, the name coming from that of a Centaur by the name of Chiron.

Medicinally the centaury has been used for centuries without seemingly having much value except that it has bitter qualities which make it hopefully useful in aiding digestion, general stimulation, and perhaps through suggestion providing a tonic effect on the system.

Those readers religiously inclined will be interested that among early Christians it was a holy plant, and on the Isle of Man is known as "Steps of Christ" since it was said to have grown along the path used by Christ on his way to Calvary.

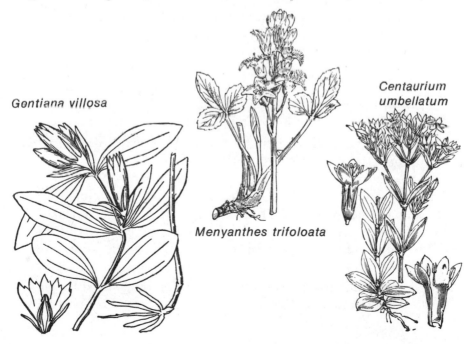

Gontiana villosa

Centaurium umbellatum

Menyanthes trifoloata

Altogether a good example of the interest one can find in some very simple, much-traveled herb.

Frasera speciosa—Elkweed; deer tongue; green gentian.
In the higher elevations of the West, this perennial is noted by its greenish-purple spotted flowers. Reports are that the fleshy root may be eaten raw, roasted or boiled and is good when mixed with other cooked or raw greens.

Gentiana villosa—Sampson's snakeroot; marsh gentian; striped gentian.
A perennial plant widely found throughout the East, growing in meadows, brooksides, and among calcareous rocks, and flowering in the fall with purplish-green gentian shaped blooms. In the Appalachians the root tea is drunk as a tonic with values much as the plant above. It is said that wearing a piece of the root will "increase one's physical powers."

Menyanthes trifoliata—Buckbean, marsh trefoil, bog myrtle, bitterworm, marsh clover, water shamrock, butter root, bog hop.
A plant widely spread in the northern hemisphere which, with its tri-foliate leaves, easily acquired the name of trefoil. Medicinally the part used is the foliage, which is dried and then used for hot infusions, as a simple tonic. For many years it was a recognized drug in this country and one writer claims that "it is the most serviceable of all known herbal tonics." At times in the past the bitter roots have been used for flavoring beer, and there is a report that the Laplanders used to feed the roots to cattle.

THE GERANIUM FAMILY

GERANIACEAE

Erodium cicutarium—Stork's bill, alfilaria, pin cloves, pin-weed, pingrass, pin needle.
An interesting wild plant which grows variously from the Pacific to Utah and again in the East in the mountains of North Carolina. When young, the fern-like leaves may be used in salad, while medicinally, it has been used as an astringent and diuretic. The sharp pointed outgrowths of the seeds may possibly cause injury for tender skins.

Geranium maculatum—Cranesbill, wild geranium, storkbill, dove's foot, chocolate flower, shameface, tormentil, crowfoot, etc.

A widely spread plant of North America, it is a hairy perennial growing to about 18 inches. The rosy-purple flowers in late spring are lovely and it is one of the nicer wild flowers.

Medicinally it has long been known as a strong astringent and the part thus used is the knobby rhizome, dried and made into

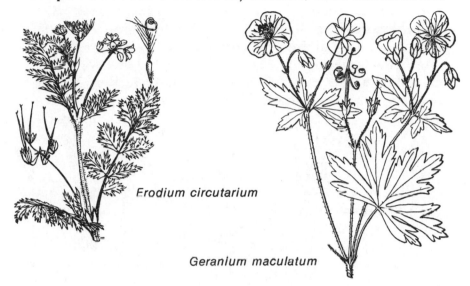

Erodium circutarium

Geranium maculatum

a chocolate-colored powder and used as a mild infusion, which because of the high tannin content is useful for a sore throat and ulcerated mouth.

The tannin content makes it of possible use in home tanning, and for such use the leaves and roots are collected just before flowering when its value is greatest.

A caution is necessary here that when used as medicine, it may cause severe constipation, which in its turn may have to be treated.

THE GRASS FAMILY

GRAMINEAE

Agropyron repens—Witch-grass, couch-grass, quack-grass, quitch-grass, dog-grass, blue-joint, Colorado blue-grass, and other common names.

One of the worst (if not quite *the* worst) of weed grasses is this grass which spreads by underground roots and is well known to most gardeners. And yet it should be noted that in British Columbia and other temperate climate areas, the roots have been dried, ground, and used as flour. Reports are also given that a drink made from this plant has values for irritations of the bladder. Thus it is a good example of how something good may come from the worst.

A further example of a use to be made of this grass is that the roots are a source of dye which produces a pleasing gray color.

Again the name dog-grass comes from the fact that dogs when sick will often seek out and chew the stems, which by causing vomiting, will have a curative effect.

Holcus lanatus   Andropogon virginicus   Agropyrum repens

Andropogon virginicus—Broom-sedge, Virginia beard-grass.
Almost everyone knows how grass will stain, and hence it is not strange that some of the grasses can be used for purposes of dyeing wool. With this species, colors can be obtained going from yellow, to gold, to greenish-yellow, and to brass. It grows throughout the East and in tropical America.

Avena fatua and *A. barbara*—Wild oats.
The wild oats are a rather tall plant related to the cultivated oat plant, a native of Europe, but found widely growing in the West. The seed is edible after the grain hairs are singed off.

Digitaria sanguinalis—Crabgrass.
Perhaps one of the few grasses which most gardeners can iden-

tify and a real troublesome weed. Yet in parts of Europe the seeds are used as cereal or ground as flour. Perhaps if readers of this could harvest all the crabgrass seed, their troubles would be over.

Eleusine indica—Goose grass.

Another introduced grass of which the seeds may be parched and eaten, as is true with many grasses. Grows widely in waste spaces.

Glyceria (**various species**)—Manna grass, sugar grass.

This plant grows in the West in marshy habitats and here the seeds produce an excellent flour when parched or ground, or boiled as in the manner of rice.

Holcus lanatus—Velvet grass.

This is an introduced grass and one widely known, but the fact that grasses are usually considered non-poisonous is not true with this grass, which contains a very virulent poison, hydrocyanic acid. Thus while the soft velvety appearance of the plants make this an attractive grass, it should be remembered as a real poisonous plant.

Oryzopsis hymenoides—Indian ricegrass, ricegrass, mountain rice.

One of the grasses that grows in the arid parts of the West, the seeds of this and other grasses are best when dried and ground into flour for making breads and cooked mush.

Phalaris canariensis—Canary grass.

This grass which came from southern Europe is the one producing canary food and it does grow as an escaped annual in parts of the West. The seeds are good for your birds, while the green plants can be used as a part of a dish of greens.

Phragmites communis—Reed grass, reed, carrizo.

Throughout the country and especially among the Indians this grass has given food through its seeds, but especially the roots, which may be eaten raw, roasted or boiled or, as in the case of some Eastern tribes, made into a sort of sweetish confection.

Other uses of the strong six to 12 foot stalks of reed grass by the Indians were for arrow shafts, mats, screens, pipestems, cordage, huts, and thatching. A sort of string can be made by simply twisting together the fibers obtained from the reeds.

Always and everywhere the reed grass is found growing in swampy ground.

Setaria (**various species**)—Foxtail grass, bristle grass, millet, bristly
     foxtail.
   Foxtail grass is widely spread in this country, though an import
   from abroad. The seeds are quite sizable and are used, even
   today in Europe, in breads and soups.

Sorghum halapense—Sorghum, Johnson grass, Columbus grass, Su-
     dan grass.
   There are several species of sorghums, some with sweet qualities, and in some areas the grass is a pest. But it has a wide
   distribution and some species have been grown in countries like
   Egypt for centuries. The seeds may be used to make meal or
   mush, and are parched, ground, etc.

Zea mays—Corn, maize, Indian corn.
   It should not be possible to talk about grass in our country
   without a gesture to the one grass which has made America
   prosperous, and provided one of the major food crops of the
   world—the wonderful, early-Indian-bred corn, in all of its many
   selections and varieties. No need to discuss its many uses as
   food, but it is well to study the ancient Mexican religions and
   note how it, and the rain which made it possible, were treated
   as gods. In one of the notable Protestant missions to the Navajos, the worshippers today add a pinch of pollen to sanctify the
   altar, and use communion wafers made of cornbread. Corn is
   indeed worthy of veneration.

Zizania aquatica—Wild rice.
   A native of our Great Lakes area over to Idaho, wild rice is
   generally recognized as a valuable food grain, having a flavor
   superior to cultivated rices. But being gathered only from the
   wild from shallow waters, it becomes expensive.

ST. JOHN'S WORT FAMILY

GUTTIFERAE

Hypericum perforatum—St. John's wort, God's wonder plant, devil's
     scourge, Llamath weed, goat weed, Grace of God, rosin
     rose, amber touch and heal, terrestial sun, hundred holes,
     etc.
   Here is another of the many plants now growing widely as a
   weed, which has come to this country from Europe, where as an
   herb it has been widely esteemed. The many names above

Hypericum perforatum

would give much information as to its uses. Because of the bright sunny yellow blooms it was long associated with the summer solstice, which again was related to St. John. Strangely, when the flowers are used in various medicines the juices are red, which is called St. John's blood or sometimes Mary's sweat. A reliable correspondent of the author tells of a great value as "touch and heal" when blended with olive oil. Many records go back to veneration of the plant in Ireland, while in England it was hung over doorways to bring prosperity.

Every reputable herbal book tells of many values of this Hypericum, most of them reducing to uses for healing through astringency. As a dye plant the plant tops produce a good dark yellow color.

THE WITCH-HAZEL FAMILY
HAMAMELIDACEAE

Hamamelis virginiana—Witch hazel, snapping hazel, spotted alder, winter bloom, wood tobacco.

There are few people interested in nature who do not know this rather tall-growing shrub which blooms, quite unusually, with yellow, thread-like flowers in late autumn. With their knowledge of a cousin of this species in Europe, early settlers soon found that the liquid infused from the leaves and bark of this wide spread plant of the East would, because of its tannin content, have a healing and astringent effect on cuts and sprains, although by modern doctors it is not so much recommended.

Presently commercial extraction of the properties of the plant is done in Connecticut and it will likely be long in demand because of its nice tingling medicinal effect rather than because of any real inherent value.

In another area, the supple hazel branches have been used in divining for water, a practice still extant, though often questioned by the scientists.

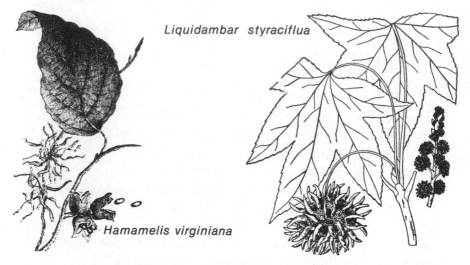

Liquidambar styraciflua

Hamamelis virginiana

Liquidambar styraciflua—Sweet gum, American styrax, red gum. Generally a tall tree of the Southeast, the gum from wounds in the bark is the source of an approved drug, storax, which is an expectorant and a weak antiseptic, long used by settlers in that area. In Appalachia, it is said that brandy-soaked twigs of this tree are chewed to clean the teeth.

THE HORSECHESTNUT FAMILY
HIPPOCASTANACEAE

Aesculus californica—Buckeye, California buckeye. This plant of the West Coast and especially California produces a "chestnut" much like the Eastern species and yet neither of the nuts of these two species is good to eat. Indians in the West used the nut of this species as one of the fish-stupefying poisons. There are reports that there are ways to remove the poison for human consumption, but it is well to leave that to others.

Aesculus hippocastanum—Common horsechestnut; buckeye tree.

If perhaps 30 percent of the wild flowers of North America have been introduced from Europe and elsewhere, so too have many of the good ornamental trees, as here in the case of the common horsechestnut which originated in the Balkans. It can hardly be said to be an important useful tree, but what child in the country has not had the fun of playing with the falling "nuts" from this tree?

Aesculus hippocastanum

But just as the nuts are not edible and may be mildly poisonous, so the properties in them have been used to treat hemorrhoids, while down in Appalachia, country folk used to carry a nut in a pocket to ward off rheumatism.

And here, as an ornamental tree, something may be said about its usefulness on the street. It is of medium height, spreading, and beautiful, especially in some of the double or pink variations, but let it be noted that it is the dirtiest tree you can have, shedding dead flowers, then brown leaves, later the hard nuts, and after that the nut shells. Thus, from experience, it is not a tree to be recommended.

THE WATERLEAF FAMILY
HYDROPHYLLACEAE

Eriodictyon californicum—Yerba Santa, mountain balm, consumptive's weed, bear's weed, holy herb.

Here is a plant which is to be found growing on the dry hillsides of California, and which received its name of holy herb from the padres who early learned the medicines of the country from the Indian natives.

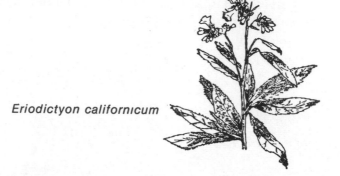

Eriodictyon californicum

A number of references to this plant indicate its value as an expectorant and again for making an aromatic syrup used as a vehicle for quinine. For those with asthma, recommendations are to dry the foliage, make "cigarettes" and be helped by smoking them. Youngken, a reliable writer, says that "its aqueous fluid-extract is diluted with water and used locally for poison-ivy dermatitis."

THE IRIS FAMILY
IRIDACEAE

Iris versicolor—Blue flag; poison or water flag; snake, liver, or flag lily. There are many, many kinds of iris growing throughout this country and more especially along the lower Mississippi River, while one authority lists some 200 species which are cultivated. But for the subject of this book, only one of these many is of interest and this because, in spite of its regal beauty growing on shores of ponds, the roots contain a poison called iridin. Yet, used properly, the "poison" had values for the Indians. It is said that they used the root alone for colds and lung troubles; poultices of the roots applied to soothe burns, while a half inch of

Iris versicolor

the root was steeped and applied to boils to reduce them.

Apparently with many tribes the root of this iris was thought to protect the wearer against snakes, while in Arizona it was used as a fumigant to protect the body against snake bite in their dance.

Thus, as with so many other things in the world of nature, the bad can be balanced against the good.

THE WALNUT FAMILY

JUGLANDACEAE

Carya laciniosa—Big shellbark hickory (New York to Oklahoma).

Carya ovata—Hickory, shagbark hickory (Quebec to Texas).

Carya tomentosa **(formerly *C. alba*)**—Hickory (Massachusetts to Texas).

These three members of the Carya genus are lumped together as, with their natural hybrids and basic similarity, their uses are quite alike, differences being much in the appearance of bark and other "tree" characteristics.

We know that the word "Old Hickory" was associated with a strong president, Andrew Jackson, and from early writers on native plants we know the value placed on the nuts by the Indians. Bartram and others tell of how the Indians made a sort of cream or butter out of the oil coming from the nuts, after cooking.

The wood of the tree has always been treasured and here again we know that another president, Abraham Lincoln, was known as the "railsplitter," splitting hickory for rail fences, for which the straight grain of the wood is valuable. Again, in early days, the wood was highly valued as a long-burning fireplace wood, or the smoke from the wood for curing tasty hams and bacon.

A further value of the great group of hickories with their attractive "shaggy" bark, is that this bark is excellent as a source of dye colors in the range of gold and brass.

Anyone who has been brought up in the country knows the joy of gathering these and other nuts in the fall and it could well be said that the hickories are one of America's finest trees.

Carya illinoensis—Pecan (South-central United States).
Almost everyone knows that one of the finest of all nuts to eat is of this native American tree; large, fast-growing, long-lived, and shapely, which, with a lot of natural and induced cross-breeding, has produced improved varieties over the years, including one sort called the hican (hickory and pecan).

As with those species mentioned above, there is also value as a dye plant, the hulls producing colors from brown to dark gray.

The name of pecan is from the Indian tongue where it was called a "pecaune."

Juglans californica—California walnut (Southern California).

Juglans cinerea—Butternut, white walnut, filnut, lemon nut. (New Brunswick to Arkansas)

Juglans hindsii—Smooth walnut (Central California).

Juglans major—Walnut (Colorado to Arizona).

Juglans nigra—Black walnut (Massachusetts to Florida to Texas).
It is hardly necessary to describe these generally large and fine trees, with variations being found in the species from various sections of the country.

As may be supposed with any of the nuts, these were much used by the Indians for food, the Narragansett Indians' name being *Wussoquat*, with the extracted oil being used for cooking. Beyond this and the modern uses for food, many values are found in all the walnuts and butternuts.

Medicinally an extraction of the bark is useful as a cathartic while the extracted oil is reputed as valuable for treatment of tape worms and fungus infections.

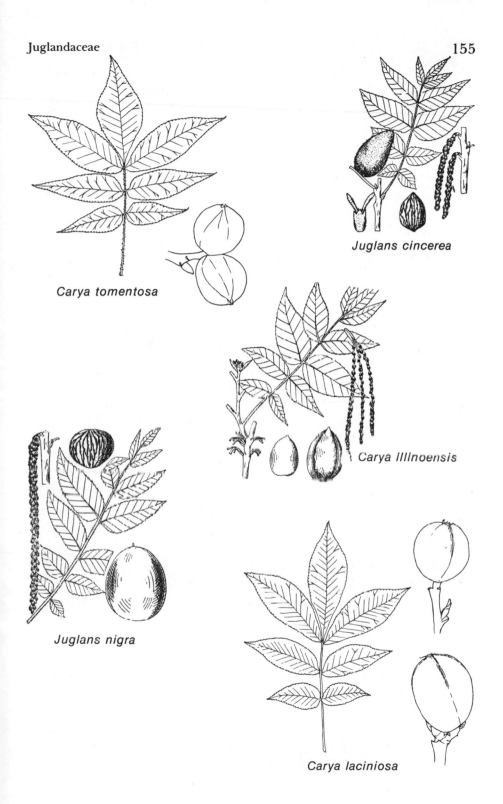

Carya tomentosa

Juglans cincerea

Carya Illinoensis

Juglans nigra

Carya laciniosa

As a dye plant, the Shakers found a way of making purple dye from the walnut tree, while present dying guides list the green hulls as producing good colors of tan and brown.

Before the stocks of these wild trees were depleted by the settlers, the fine wood of the Juglans genera was considered outstanding for cabinet work.

Today good candy may be made from the various kinds of walnuts, while one of the real delicacies of many country kitchens was the making of pickled (young and tender) walnuts.

One of the more modern findings about the walnut is the fact that it contains a depressant agent which has often been used illegally to immobilize fish in some parts of the country.

THE MINT FAMILY
LABIATAE

One of the most commonly useful plants of this book is the mint family which, because of the predominance of fragrant oils, has both culinary and medicinal uses. Some of these plants are native wild plants, some are from other countries, and many are a necessity for any herb section of the home garden. One characteristic that makes the plant always easy to place in the mint family is that the stems of the plants are square or squarish, with a cluster of flowers on a straight stem. If no other plant family interests the reader, a knowledge of this one is well worth a little study.

Cunila origanoides—Dittany, sweet horsemint, wild basil, stonemint.
  Widely spread from the East to Southwest, its aromatic properties have made it useful as a mild stimulant drug. One reputation is that it will kill rattlesnakes when held to their noses, but how one would do that, this author does not know.

Collinsonia canadensis—Horse or ox balm, citronella, hard-hack, knob-grass.
  The roots or the whole plant is recommended as a sedative and a tonic, and is variously used according to the section where found, which extends in most the United States east of the Rockies.

Dracocephalum parviflorum—Dragon-head.
  This plant is listed by some botanists as "Moldavica," this a

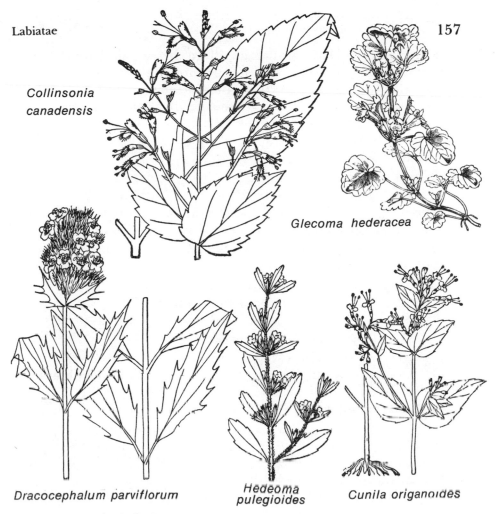

Collinsonia canadensis

Glecoma hederacea

Dracocephalum parviflorum

Hedeoma pulegioides

Cunila origanoides

botanical name in the West. In Arizona the Havasupai Indians make a nutritious flour from the seeds.

Glechoma hederacea (syn. *Nepeta glechoma*)—Ground ivy; gill-over-the-ground; ale hoof; catsfoot; creeping Charlie (or Jenny); and many others.

A weedy ground-hugging perennial vine with rather pretty purplish flowers. In olden days it was used to impart a bitter flavor to beer, hence the name "ale-hoof." The pungency of the crushed foliage is reputed to cure headaches. Gypsies are said to make an ointment of ground ivy combined with chickweed to use on cuts or sprains.

Hedeoma pulegioides—Mock pennyroyal, squaw mint, stinking balm, thickweed.

A widely spread weed which yields an oil known as oil of pen-

nyroyal, it is used as a stimulant tea. In the Appalachian region
it was formerly used for treating pneumonia.

It is worth noting here that common names mean much in
learning about plants, for here we note that "mock" means like
pennyroyal; squaw mint suggests it as one of the medicinal
plants of Indian tribes; while stinking balm indicates its smelly
nature.

Hyssopus officinalis—Hyssop.
In waste places on both the East and West Coasts plants of
hyssop will be found, an escapee from the Near East where, as
noted in early literature, it has been a plant used as an herb and
also as an aromatic stimulant, and at times a healing agent in
cuts and bruises.

Lamium amplexicaule—Hen-bit, dead nettle, white archangel.
A naturalized weed throughout the country, it is a plant which
may be boiled and eaten, but is otherwise not notably useful.

Lavendula spica—True lavender, spike.
Probably not often an escapee, most gardens will have a few
plants of the aromatic lavender, which is certainly valuable for
the ladies to use for keeping their linen sweet smelling. Any
medicinal values would come under the heading of "aromatic."

Leonurus cardiaca—Motherwort, lion's ear, throwwort.
Growing throughout all the country east of the Rockies, this wild
plant produces an herbal stimulant which has been used in
Europe for heart palpitations and asthma. One old saying about
it is that one can "Drink motherwort and live to be a source of
continuous astonishment and grief to waiting heirs."

Lycopus virginicus—Bugle weed, gypsy weed, purple archangel, wold-
      foot, wood betony, and other local names.
A plant from Asia, widely disseminated in the United States, it
has long been on the list of herbal remedies, noted as an astringent and sedative.

Marrubium vulgare—Horehound, houndsbane, marvel, marrub.
Another one of the wild plants widely spread, it has long been
known to have good uses as an expectorant, as a cough syrup,
or as an ingredient in cough-drops. Large doses puts it into the
class of laxatives. A healthful tea is made of it in the South and
for all purposes, the values are extracted from soft stems and
foliage.

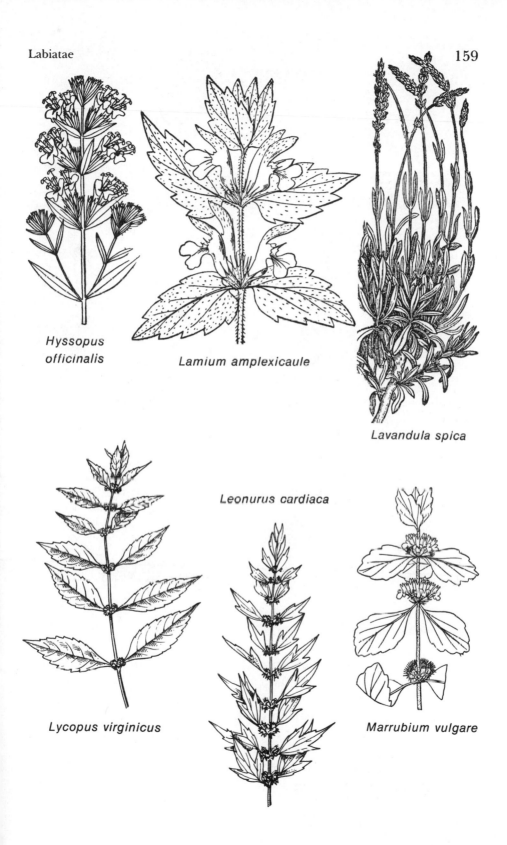

Hyssopus officinalis

Lamium amplexicaule

Lavandula spica

Leonurus cardiaca

Lycopus virginicus

Marrubium vulgare

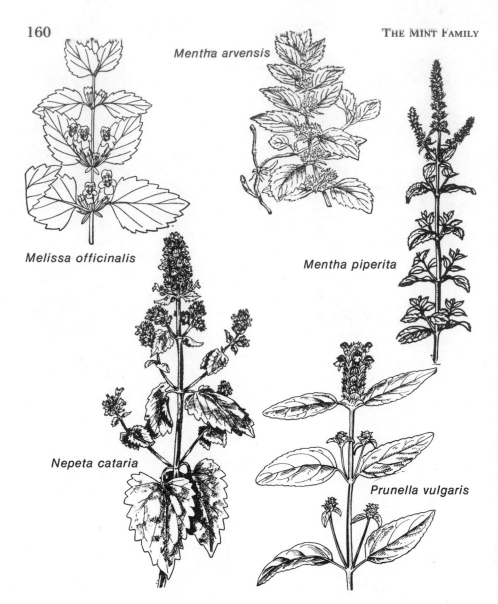

Mentha arvensis

Melissa officinalis

Mentha piperita

Nepeta cataria

Prunella vulgaris

Melissa officinalis—Garden or lemon balm, honey plant, dropsy plant,
    cureall, citronele.

A plant of Europe, widely spread, it has long been known for its
sweetness and possible medicinal values. The fragrant foliage
is of lemon, and leaves with flowers have been used to produce
a volatile oil used in perfumery and cosmetics.

When dried the foliage is excellent as a constituent of pot-
pourri, while, freshly infused with lemon and sugar, it makes a
pleasing summer drink.

Its medicinal values may be of question, but centuries ago it was a principal ingredient of Carmelite Water (with nutmeg, angelica, lemon and honey) and was highly regarded for head-aches and neuralgia. The noted seventeenth-century diarist, John Evelyn, wrote of it that "Balm is sovereign for the brain, strengthening the memory and powerfully chasing away melan-choly." Could one want anything better?

Mentha arvensis—Wild mint, field mint.

Widely distributed throughout the world, this is one of the mints strong with the oils for which the mints are all notable. From this species is extracted menthol used in many commercial ways.

Mentha piperita—Peppermint, curled mint, brandy mint.

All the mints escape easily from gardens, and always like to be near water, or on rich moist lands. Beyond the use as a flavoring for candy, everyone knows of the action of mint in relieving pains from the alimentary canal, thus claiming its medicinal name as an anti-spasmodic.

Mentha spicata—Spearmint, common or lamb mint, sage of Beth-lehem, Our Lady's mint.

This member of the mint genus is not as strong in oils as the ones noted above and the uses are largely culinary, for such pleasant uses as a flavoring for iced tea and mint-juleps.

Nepeta cataria—Catnip, catnep, catwort, catmint, field balm.

Another widely spread plant, the existence of which is often not known until discovered by the family cat, it is the catnep plant which seems to have been known for untold centuries, the word "cat" having been provided long ago as a species name. What-ever minor values it may have as a medicinal plant, it is mostly interesting for its action in sending cats into ecstasy. It is inter-esting in this connection to note that cats won't discover it unless the aroma is in the air, as with a broken leaf, giving rise to the saying that:

> If you set it, the cats will eat it,
> If you sow it, cats don't know it.

Whether or not rats dislike the plant (as is said) is a questionable point.

Prunella vulgaris—Heal-all, self-heal, sickle-heal, brown wort, blue curls, etc.

Doubtless this plant is not as great as all the "healing" names would suggest, but it was often used in the past for diarrhoea and as a throat gargle. A review of all the many writings about

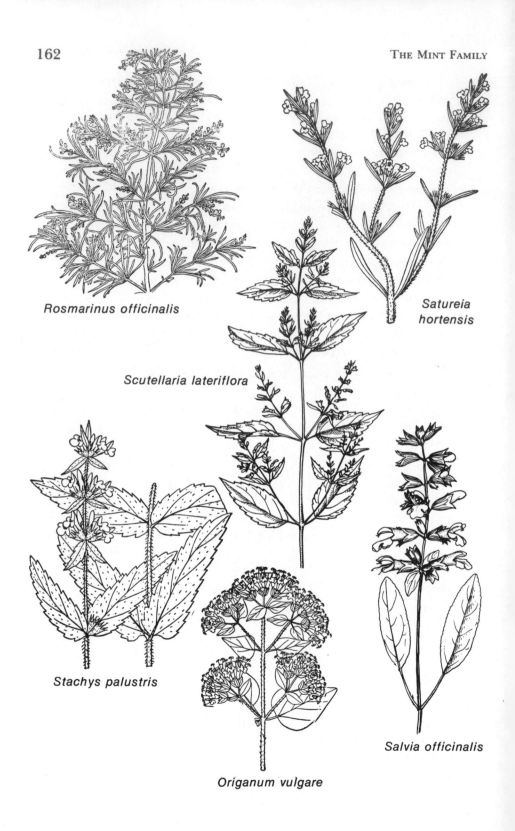

Rosmarinus officinalis

Satureia hortensis

Scutellaria lateriflora

Stachys palustris

Origanum vulgare

Salvia officinalis

prunella indicate that its values may have been largely psychological.

Rosmarinus officinalis—Rosemary, old-man.

Probably rarely found outside of gardens, it would be strange not to include rosemary in any list of useful plants, for no cook should think of cooking lamb without sprigs of rosemary to "kill" the greasy feeling of this meat. Whether wild or not, it is a plant for every garden.

Salvia columbariae—Chia.

A wild plant of California and to the south, the seeds were used by Mexicans and early settlers (after parching) for gruel and medicinally as a digestant. Seeds made into a poultice were used for gunshot wounds.

Salvia officinalis—Garden sage, scarlet sage, meadow sage.

This is the sage used by all cooks for flavoring meat and medicinally as sage tea—recommended for flatulent indigestion. Without further comment, readers should note the old saying that:

> He would live for aye
> Must eat sage in May.

Satureia douglasi—Yerba buena, Oregon tea.

This member of the mint family is found all along the Pacific Coast and has long been used as a stimulating digestant, known, as the Spanish name indicates, by the earliest settlers, as a good plant. It is a creeping plant with small white flowers. Another relative of this genera is found in *S. hortensis*, the garden savory.

Scutellaria lateriflora—Blue skullcap, mad-dog weed, blue pimpernel hoodwort, etc.

A widely-grown plant in wet places, it was once an "official" drug recommended for use for the nerves, sedative, etc. There are other "skullcap" plants, all with similar but somewhat questionable qualities.

Stachys palustris—Betony, hedge nettle, clown's woundwort, deadnettle, roughweed.

A plant introduced from Europe, but now widespread in the East and West, it grows about three feet tall with reddish-purple flowers. It has thousands of years of rated values behind it, but modern medicine finds little value in any use made of it. A good example of a plant with reputed values versus the many with known values.

THE LAUREL FAMILY

LAURACEAE

Lindera benzoin—Spice-bush, Benjamin-bush, feverbush, wild allspice.

From the Mideast to Midwest, one finds this shrub in moist
woods, the bark and twigs of which have been used medicinally
to treat dysentery, coughs, and colds. The twigs, leaves, and
fruit have been found to be a source of material for an aromatic
tea, while the dried berries are known as a substitute for allspice
for kitchen use. A nice spicy shrub to know.

Persea americana—Avocado, alligator pear.

A large tree-member of this family, which, while not exactly
from the United States area, nevertheless has spread from Mex-

Lindera benzoin   Sassafras albidum

ico and now is widely cultivated in the west as an excellent
producer of rich, healthful fruit. Housewives may easily grow a
nice house plant from the quickly germinated seeds.

Sassafras albidum—Sassafras.

Probably the first contribution of America to the drug counters of
the Old World, for the medicinal taste of the bark and roots gave
this plant (found along the East Coast from North to South) an
unwarranted reputation as a "cure everything" medicine. It is
still, in parts of our country, considered a "spring tonic."

Possibly the only authentic use made of it is as an ingredient
in the Louisiana Gumbo filé. It is said this use came from the fact
that the Indians of that area used simply the sassafras leaves
dried, powdered, and put through a sieve as part of a "soup"
mixture.

One other use of this interestingly foliaged tree with its hand-
like leaves is as a source of material for dyeing wool, the color
produced being a rose-tan or rose-brown, while used as a cotton
dye it gives a dark gray.

THE PEA FAMILY

LEGUMINOSAE

Acacia greggii—Texas mimosa.

Acacias are mostly foreign, but this species is native of Texas, and like other species, has "peas in pods" which are listed as edible.

Albizzia julibrissin—Silk tree.

This is not a native tree, but one found from Persia to Japan, and yet it is widely grown in this country as an ornamental and beautiful feathery tree, from Zone 7 southwards. The aromatic leaves are used by the Chinese as food. In Japan the tree is known as Nemu.

Amorpha **(various species)**—False indigo.

There are a number of species here, native of North America, and some of them, as indicated by the name, have been used as dyes.

Apios tuberosa—Indian potato, ground nut.

Found widely in the woods throughout the United States, this vine-like plant creeps on the ground and stores its food in tubers. Winslow, an historian, says that the Pilgrims in their first winter were forced to live on ground nuts. The nuts dug in the fall are edible uncooked, but the best way is to slice the unpeeled tubers and fry them like potatoes. Diabetics can use these as a medicinally safe substitute for ordinary potatoes.

Baptisia tinctoria—Wild indigo, indigo broom, horsefly weed, dyer's baptisia.

Regardless of possible uses as a source for indigo, the plant has

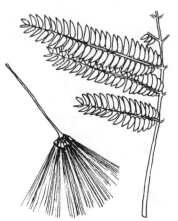

Albizzia julibrissin

Amorpha fruticosa

listed medicinal values and has been used in the cure of ulcers. It is poisonous in large quantities.

Cassia marilandica—Wild senna, Maryland cassia, locust plant. There are several species of Cassia found mostly in our southern states. *C. Caroliniana* is called the styptic weed, used as hinted by the name, for itches and inflammation; *C. occidentalis* is similarly called, for similar uses. The Maryland form of this brightly yellow-colored plant gives us the drug "senna" which is made from the dried leaves. This was a cathartic known to have been much used by the Indians, who also made poultices from the moist bruised roots and a decoction of the root for fevers.

Cercis **(various species)**—Redbud; Judas tree; June bud. The species *canadensis* is the eastern sort from New York to Florida. Beyond the spring beauty of the purplish-pink blooms, the astringent buds have been used in salads or have been administered in diarrhoea. The California species, *occidentalis*, also has flowers with a sharp acid flavor and has the same medicinal qualities as the above and is also used on the table, fried in butter. Some Indian tribes have used the pliable bark for weaving baskets.

Cytisus scoparius—Scotch broom, hayweed, broom tops. This is one of the plants of Europe, now naturalized in America and a plant of much beauty and interesting values. It is especially happy in dry, sandy, and salt-air areas and it has a good and seemingly great value as a plant for sloping ground. The yellow, tiny, pea-like flowers are beautiful and valuable as a source for a yellow dye. Its name of broom is easy to understand as the

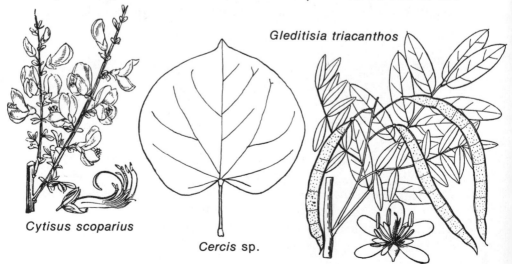

Gleditisia triacanthos

Cytisus scoparius

Cercis sp.

branches when dried easily make a simple broom when tied onto a handle. Medicinally there are many references to the use of the freshly-grown green tops (just before flowering) as a purgative and diuretic. In large quantities the fresh buds and pods should not be eaten, as they contain toxic alkaloids, but in some parts of the West the roasted seeds have been used as a coffee substitute. Altogether it is a good "imported" plant with many values.

Dalea terminalis—Pea bush, smokethorn.

This is a slow-growing herb of the Southwest with purple flowers and generally hairy growth. The Hopi Indians ate the sweet raw roots while the seeds were ground into flour.

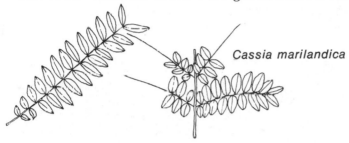

Cassia marilandica

Gleditsia triacanthos—Honey or sweet locust, black or thorn locust, yellow locust.

This tall-growing tree does not have many common uses for food or medicine, but the sweetness of the flowers is used by the bees for honey and the wood of large trees is especially valuable for posts to be buried in the ground, as they practically never rot.

Glycyrrhiza lepidota—Wild licorice.

From Missouri to the far West, this small shrub is the American counterpart of the European and cultivated licorice plant. The long fleshy roots contain flavorings, sweetness, and compounds used in medicine, candy, root beer, and other common items.

Hedysarum (various species)—Sweetvetch, sweetbroom, licorice root.

There are several species of this sweet vetch which inhabit only parts of the West, growing as low shrubs in dry ground. The roots are nourishing and edible, with *H. occidentale* having a mild licorice taste.

Hoffmanseggia densiflora—Hog potato, rushpea, Camote-de-raton.

An herbaceous perennial with yellow flowers growing from Arizona to California, the tuberous enlargements of the roots may be roasted and eaten.

Lathyrus maritimus—Beach pea.

This is known in some botanies as *L. japonicus*. Nature has given it many variable forms as to growth and size of pea. But it is a "beach" pea and is found on ocean beaches on both coasts. The young pods and seeds are sweet and can be eaten raw or made into soup. There are reports of the ripe peas being poisonous, but this seems to be probable only when they are eaten in quantity.

Medicago sativa—Alfalfa, purple medic, lucerne.

A European plant now naturalized and cultivated widely, this plant has well-known nutritional values and is much touted by the health food experts. The young tender leaves can be used as a part of a green salad.

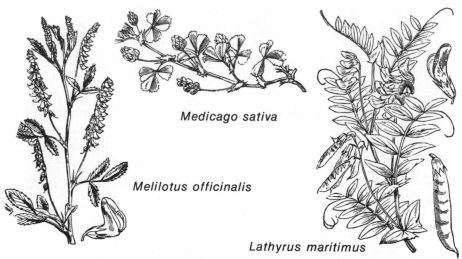

Medicago sativa

Melilotus officinalis

Lathyrus maritimus

Melilotus officinalis—Melilot, yellow sweet clover, sweet lucerne, king's clover, etc.

Of course everyone loves the clovers of various kinds, and they all are valuable as having something for the bees, which gives us healthful honey. Beyond this there are many, many claims made for the medicinal values of clover, but mostly the authorities say that "it is supposed" to do this or that. Perhaps worthy of note is that the drying clover contains a substance called coumarin which is the flavor of what we call vanilla, this also giving the lovely perfume of the drying clover plants.

Olneya tesota—Tesota, ironwood.

A plant of the far Southwest, a spiny tree with evergreen foliage, it has seeds which may be roasted and eaten. However, it is especially valued for the hardness of the wood, which may be used for tool handles, and in past times was used by the Indians for arrowheads.

Peteria scoparia—Camote-deMonte.
An herbaceous perennial of Texas and Arizona with an edible rootstock.

Phaseolus **(various species)**—Beans
It is hardly necessary to discuss the value of beans as a big part of American diet, but it may be of interest, that whereas so many edible plants have come to us from abroad, many of our beans are of American continental origin, such as the scarlet runner bean, the lima bean, the kidney bean, and others. One species, *P. acutifolius*, the tepary bean, is still found wild in the Southwest where it is used by local Indians.

Prosopis **(various species)**—Mesquite, screw bean, tornillo.
In the Southwest and down into Mexico, the mesquite is a common small spiny tree inhabiting vast waste areas. The pods have a natural sweetness, with the sweetness of *P. pubescens* exceeding that of *P. juliflora*. It is a centuries-old practice to grind them into a meal to make mush or cakes. Gum from the trees can be eaten as is, or made into candy. Some use of the bark has been made as a source of a black dye. One authority says that the ground meal produces what is perhaps "the most nutritious breadstuff in use among any people."

Psoralea esculenta—Indian breadfruit, scurvy pea, Indian turnip, prairie potato.
A plant of the western mountains, it is a low-growing perennial plant with an edible root which was considered as a special luxury to the Indians of that area. It can be boiled or roasted or dried and stored for winter use.

Robinia pseudo-acacia—Black locust, false acacia.
These trees grow to 80 feet with fragrant white flowers, and there are a number of varietal forms of this tree, according to the locale. Although they say that the flowers may be gathered and fried as food, there are other qualities of the tree which make it quite poisonous. It even has been reported that honey made from the flowers is dangerous. Again, as with other locusts, the wood is fine for fence posts, etc.

Tephrosia virginiana—Catgut; devil's shoestring; goat's rue; turkey, rabbit, or hoary pea.

A perennial growing to about two feet, with yellowish-white flowers, this is a plant which was used by the Indians for various complaints and as a fish poison. According to the U.S. Dispensatory, the roots are usable as a vermifuge or insecticide.

Trifolium pratense—Red clover, trefoil, sweet clover.

Almost everyone knows that the clovers secrete nectar, a source of a delicate-flavored honey. This same sweetness means that the dried flowers make (with other herbs) a good herbal tea, or since fresh plants are full of protein, they can be eaten if cooked.

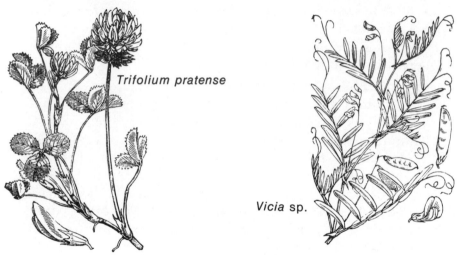

Trifolium pratense

Vicia sp.

Vicia (**various species**)—Vetch or wild pea, tare.

In this genera we find, formerly and now much cultivated in Europe, the faba or fava bean. In this country are a number of species which are native or have been naturalized. Some produce beans good when young and others produce forage crops or may be grown as "green manure" crops. This last quality comes from the fact that almost all the legumes produce nodules of nitrogen on their roots, leaving these in the soil when the plants die, as nitrogenous food for successive crops.

Wisteria (**several species and many varieties**)—Wisteria.

As either food or medicine, there is little to recommend the beautiful wisterias of China or Japan, but nothing is more lovely as a good landscape plant. The reason for its inclusion here is to note that the seeds which follow the flowers are extremely poisonous and should thus be kept away from children, for whom their large size and nice feel make an attractive toy.

THE BLADDERWORTS

LENTIBULARIACEAE

Utricularia inflata—Swollen bladderwort.
This plant is one which is found in wet spots near the coast from Delaware to Florida, and as the common name might indicate,

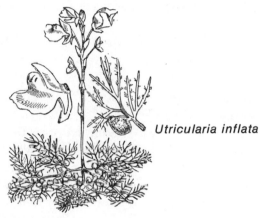

Utricularia inflata

it and other species of the genus all are reputed to have values as a diuretic.

THE LILY FAMILY

LILIACEAE

Aletris farinosa—Star grass, unicorn plant, colic root, ague grass, backache root, etc.
The above small samplings of the many names of this plant should show that this plant has long been held in esteem for its values. The roots and rhizomes are dug in the fall, dried and granulated, and then the useful element extracted with alcohol rather than water. In Appalachia, when mixed with brandy or whiskey, it is drunk as a treatment for rheumatism (ague). It is a widely spread plant found in mossy woods.

Allium (**various species**)—onions, leeks, garlics, chives, shallots, etc.
Who does not know the culinary uses of the various members

of the onion family? Chives are high in interest among herbal enthusiasts; leeks are a valuable and easily grown "second-crop" vegetable grown probably since the earliest times in Egypt; while the ordinary onion is used in countless ways.

But the disagreeable smelling garlic is not only necessary to certain choice kinds of cooking, but has long been used medicinally. People who eat garlic in quantity are known to be long-lived and considerable writing shows it to be an alleviant of high blood pressure. Other uses (and this goes for the garlics which are found in the wild) include uses as an antiseptic, beneficial in asthma, bronchitis, coughs and colds, and as a vermifuge. One authority rates it as a cure for poison ivy.

On the craft side, the skins and flesh of onions are used by dyers to get good burnt-orange, yellow-green, and deep orange.

Aloe vera—Healing aloe, savila.

This is not a true native American plant but in one way or another through gardening and escapes, and more lately through promotion, it has become a well-known, tropical-looking succulent plant which is quite happy growing on a household windowsill. All the claims made for it seem to be more than true and as a quick salve for a kitchen burn it is unbelievably effective. The mucilaginous juices of the leaves dry quickly, providing protection from the air, and again used in small cuts it is very effective, while for sunburn it is good if available, although now it is being offered as a manufactured salve. Get acquainted with this No. 1 healing household plant.

Asparagus officinalis—Asparagus, spear-grass.

Here again is a plant not native to America, but so widely spread by bird-dropped seeds that it is found all over in hedgerows and places where it can establish itself. It is hardly needed to tell about gathering the young spears for food, but beyond that, the shoots and the roots are rated as diuretics. Look for and use asparagus from the wild.

Brodiaea pulchella—Ookow.

Here is a plant of the northern West Coast which bears an Indian common name. It has a tall-stalked, violet-purple flower, and the deep-rooted bulbs were used by the Indians for eating, either raw, boiled, or roasted.

Calochortus (**various species**)—Mariposa lily, sego, butterfly lily, cat's ear.

Here is a plant with a small bulbous corm of which there are a

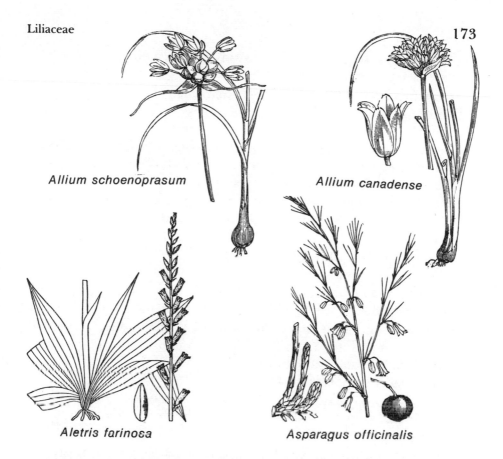

Allium schoenoprasum

Allium canadense

Aletris farinosa

Asparagus officinalis

number of species, almost all native of the Rocky Mountains and the far West. The little bulbs may be eaten raw, steamed, or roasted. It has long been used by the Indians as food and was an important food source for the Mormons when they first went west. Sparsely-leaved, variable flowers rise about a foot. Because of its beauty and value it is the state flower of Utah.

***Camassia* (various species)**—Quamash, camass, wild hyacinth.
Again, with the exception of the one eastern species (*C. esculenta*), this is a genera two feet in height, with starry, hyacinth-like flowers, growing on our Northwest Coast. The bulbs were a major vegetable crop of the Indians in that region. The flowers range from blues through white, thus distinguishing this plant from the "death camass" which has smallish yellow flowers.

***Chamaelirium luteum*—**Blazing star, fairywand, helonias, false unicorn, etc.
A shade-loving plant growing along the East Coast and to the Midwest, it produces spikes of white or greenish flowers on three foot stalks. Some common names contain the ending

"wort" indicating the use of the root-stock as a diuretic, diaphoretic, purgative, and tonic.

Chlorogalum pomeridianum—Amole, soap plant.
This bulbous plant, not unlike the camass in growth, has some
possible value for food but, as the name hints, it is known mostly
for its value as a soap or shampoo. For this the cleaned bulb is
crushed and then rubbed vigorously to produce a lather. Again,
the crushed green plant has values for stupifying fish in streams.
The flowers come on two to four foot stalks with white flowers
striped with purple. It grows in California and north into Oregon.

Convallaria majalis—Lily-of-the-valley.
There are a number of plants in this book which are not truly
"native" of which this widely-grown and much-naturalized and
favorite garden flower is certainly one. Medicinally it has values
for heart conditions not unlike that of digitalis, but, once so
used, it is no longer an "official drug." Against that value is the
fact that the same valuable property that is a medicine is in
quality a strong poison, and one finds the lily-of-the-valley listed
with poisonous plants.
    For readers interested in dye plants, the leaves here produce
greens and yellows.

Erythronium (**various species**) *E. Grandiflorum*—Yellow fawn lily.
A bulbous plant of the West, its leaves and green seed pods are
edible as a salad green.

E. americanum—Dog's tooth violet, adder leaf, yellow adder's
        tongue, etc.
The values of this eastern mountain plant are that "the herb is
an emetic emollient, and was used by the Indians for breath
complaints." An authority from the Rocky Mountains says the
bulbs can be eaten raw.

Fritillaria (**various species**)—Fritillary.
The garden forms of this flower come from the Near East, but
on our West Coast, there are a dozen or more species, some of
which are said to be edible. However, since some are poisonous,
one author says, "since these are all beautiful flowers, they
should be used as food only in an emergency."

Hemerocallis fulva—Day-lily, tawny day-lily.
This is one genera of plants in this book which seems to be
entirely a plant of the Far East, but one widely escaped through-

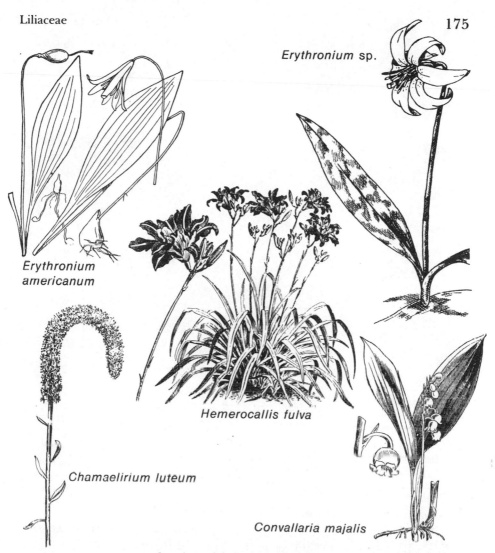

Erythronium sp.

Erythronium americanum

Hemerocallis fulva

Chamaelirium luteum

Convallaria majalis

out our country and quite widely regarded as a very edible plant. The tender shoots (as asparagus), the small egg-shaped tubers as a juicy nibble, or the buds to be cooked before opening are widely used. So extensive are the suggestions for day-lilies as food that one recipe at hand suggests the wilted flowers as a main ingredient in corned beef hash!

Lilium philadelphicum **var.** *andinum* (**syn.** *L. umbellatum*)—Western orange cup lily.

Lilium superbum—American Turk's cap lily, and other American forms.

There are in the world, a great number of what might be called the "true lilies" in that they all have a similar scaly bulb

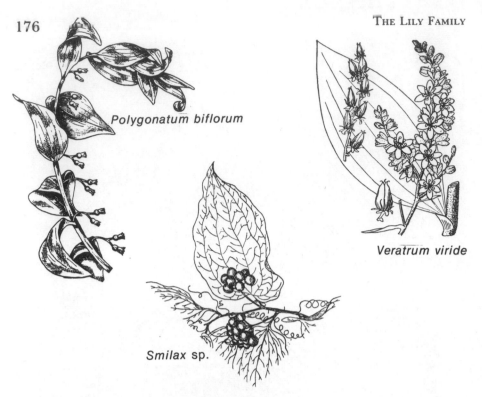

Polygonatum biflorum

Veratrum viride

Smilax sp.

and flower form and mostly are of great beauty and often fragrance. Seemingly most are edible and have been used for food in times of great need, such as by the Japanese during the war. Thoreau, writing of the Indians of Maine, tells of how they dug the lily bulbs in the fall and used them for food. Thus, if the need is greater than the desire to perpetuate beauty, eat your lilies.

Polygonatum (**various species**)—Solomon's seal, sealwort.
There are several species of the Polygonatums, some with large and others with smaller growth. One authority claims that the roots can be "macerated in water and used as food," but most values are medicinal, with the roots and rhizomes being listed as mildly astringent, diuretic, emetic, and tonic.

Smilacina (**various species**)—false Solomon's seals, false spikenard. This is a purely American genus and a review of the literature on uses would indicate that while edible under controlled preparation and with medicinal values much like Polygonatum (to which it is closely related) it is, whether found East or West, a plant which should be used with care.

Smilax (**various species**)—Greenbrier, smilax, catbrier, sarsaparilla. There are some ten species growing widely in the country and mostly the young shoots can be cooked and eaten. Medicinally most have qualities known as "alterative." One species has a mild sarsaparilla flavor and has been used as a substitute for same. The plant grows mostly as a coarse, branching, spiny vine, objectionable to hikers.

On the more useful side, the berries of a number of species are good as the source for dyes in colors of blue, violet, and purple.

Trillium erectum—Trillium, wake robin, birth-spot, etc.
Like so many other plants, there are two sides to the discussion of its values. Although this plant is not in any way an edible plant, there are many claims made for its medicinal use. The Indians used one species to aid parturition, and an herbal medicine was made of it by the Shakers in the eighteenth century, when they were the principal pharmaceutical manufacturers. It is worth some study before it is used.

Veratrum viride—White hellebore, Indian poke, devil's-bite, etc.
The beautiful, tall, white-flowered plant of swampish areas, it is a good plant to know, not for its usefulness, but as a deadly poison. It grows usually along with the edible marsh marigold, and skunk cabbage, but the eating of it could be truly fatal. Remember especially the vertically ribbed, lovely green leaves.

Xerophyllum tenax—Bear grass, Indian basket grass, pine lily, turkey beard.
This is a Western member of the lily family which has a head of white flowers on a plant with grass-like leaves. The roots have been used for food but, as one common name indicates, it was used by the Indians for making clothing and weaving baskets.

Yucca (**various species**)—Adam's needle, Spanish bayonet, Spanish dagger.
Here again the name indicates the appearance of the leaves of this interesting and beautiful member of the lily family. In one

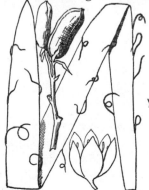

Yucca filamentosa

of many forms it grows in warm regions of the United States, except *Y. filamentosa* which is hardy through Zone 4.

The flower stalks of most species are best eaten when full grown but before the buds expand, by cooking the stalks in sections and removing the rind. The roots of yuccas produce a good lather when cut, mashed, and rubbed vigourously in water.

The fruits, called datiles in the Southwest, are liked by the Indians and are used fresh or dried. Cherokee Indians used a medicine from the roots for poultices and salves.

Zygadenus **(various species)—**Death-camas.

There is good and bad in every family of plants and here, with a pretty, perennial, white-flowered, grassy-growth plant, we have a plant with poison in every part of the plant. Found in browsing-fields where cattle roam, it has caused many yearly losses of livestock in the West. Some species grow in other parts of the country and the lesson of this plant is that one should not try eating any plant until it is identified as a truly safe and edible plant.

THE FLAX FAMILY

LINACEAE

*Linum usitatissimum***—**Flax: common, blue, prairie, wild.

A long-known and used wild plant of Europe, this miserable looking little plant gives us two very important products: the flax from which linen is made and linseed oil from the seeds. These plants have spread widely everywhere in this country. There are

Linum usitalissimum

a number of possible and minor medicinal uses, but mainly the value is in the oil which, boiled, is used in paint manufacture, or raw, is a valuable laxative, as well as an emollient and demulcent.

THE LOBELIA FAMILY

LOBELIACEAE

Lobelia inflata—Indian tobacco, bladder pod, asthma seed, puke-
    weed, eyebright, vomitwort, emetic herb, etc.

The names given above should be an indication of the possible values of the medicinal uses of this roadside weed of the eastern states. Actually it is a plant poisonous to animals and to man-kind, if the leaves and seed pods are chewed for some time, causing nausea and other effects. It has been used by the medical profession for treatment of asthma and bronchitis, but, as is true with so many plant drugs, it should be used under medical supervision.

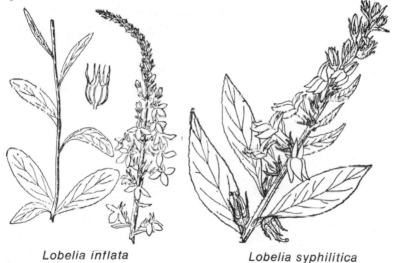

Lobelia inflata   Lobelia syphilitica

Lobelia syphilitica—Blue cardinal-flower, great lobelia.

Here is a plant with a name which places it of importance in curing the venereal disease syphilis, but unfortunately the spe-cific name was given many years ago when rumors went around that it had such a value—something now completely discounted. It has probably much the same values as the plant above, but is not listed among the present drug plants.

Somewhat as an editorial aside, it is much better for all to enjoy the wonderful species of lobelia which we call the cardinal flower, possibly one of our finest American wild flowers, though it is not "useful" except for beauty.

THE LOGANIAS FAMILY
LOGANIACEAE

Gelsemium sempervirens—Jasmine, jessamine, southern woodbine. The beautiful vines which grow in the wild in our southern states with yellow blooms seem a far cry from a shrubby member of this family which we call the buddleias, and yet they too belong

Gelsemium sempervirens

to this logan family and with small value, other than beauty. For this is a very dangerous poison plant, and while the very poisons, taken under medical supervision, may have values, it is best to put nothing but a danger sign here.

MISTLETOES
LORANTHACEAE

Phorodendron flavescens—American mistletoe, goldenbough. It should be understood that this parasitic plant found from New Jersey and to the south is not the same mistletoe which grew and achieved its reputation in Europe, but unfortunately it has the same efficacy in promoting New Year's osculations, for which it is chiefly useful. Medicinally it has had some uses, but the fact

Phoradendron flavescens

that the eating of berries is very dangerous rules out its use except for mythological purposes.

CLUBMOSSES

LYCOPODIACEAE

Lycopodium clavatum Club moss, vegetable sulphur, ground pine, plus such other interesting names as foxtail, lamb's tail, wolf's claw, hog's bed, snake moss, and stag's horn.

Here we have one of the widely spread families of plants which represent sort of a half-way point between lichens or mosses and flowering plants. While this and other species look like small pine seedlings or a moss, they are actually a plant which has no seeds, but spores. These spores applied to the hand will actually resist water and they have been used as a dusting powder to keep pills from sticking to each other.

Medicinally it has been used as a diuretic and one report tells of claims that it will produce sexual desire.

Lycopodium complanatum—Christmas club moss, trailing Christmas green, ground pine, ground cedar.

This plant is often gathered to use in making Christmas wreaths and roping (as the name indicates). This is a use of it that the reader can make. It is said also that it can be used to "improve bad wine."

Medicinally it has been thought to be of value as a diuretic, emetic, and in the treatment of diarrhoea, dropsy, scurvy, and other conditions.

In a modern practical use, the spore powder would be definitely useful as a dusting powder to prevent chafing in infants or for such adult problems as eczema and erysipelas.

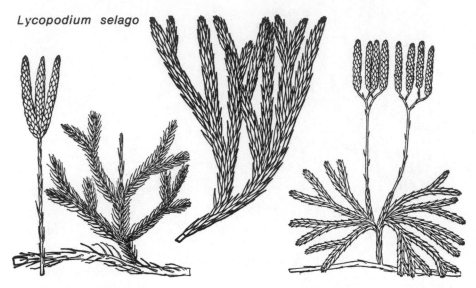

Lycopodium selago

Lycopodium clavatum   *Lycopodium complanatum*

Lycopodium selago—Fir club moss.

This is a species which is found mostly in mountain areas in the northern states and Canada, and has been used for killing vermin on animals. It is said to act medicinally as a narcotic and emetic. Like all the species, the spores are highly inflammable and have been used (in earlier times) in fireworks and for flashlights.

Beyond the above species there are other forms inhabiting special locations, but all with the low-growing, evergreen nature that is typical of the genus.

THE MAGNOLIAS

MAGNOLIACEAE

Liriodendron tulipifera—Tulip-tree, yellow poplar, cucumber tree, etc.

One of the truly tall straight trees of our east Coast, with its lovely tulip-like and often too-high-to-pick flowers, this member of the magnolia family gives a fine grainless white wood, useful to carpenters. But the common values to the nature lover are not too great as the only medicinal values are as a bitter tonic. Such uses go back to early times when doctors, drug stores, and TV suggestions were not as common as now. Another use for the bark would be as a source for a gold dye.

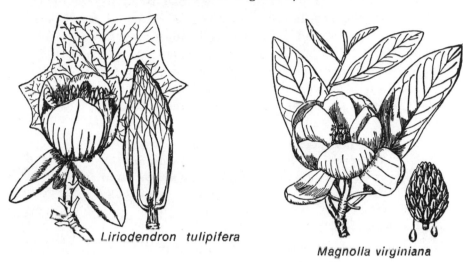

Liriodendron tulipifera

Magnolia virginiana

Magnolia (**various species**)—Magnolias, sweet bays, cucumber trees, etc.

Growing mostly in the middle South, there are a half dozen species of magnolia, all with more-or less huge white flowers, and evergreen leaves. Now to these have been added and hybridized a number of family members from the Orient. The spring beauty of magnolias is notable. Beyond this value as a landscape plant, they have little to offer.

THE MALLOWS

MALVACEAE

Althaea officinalis—Marshmallow, sweet weed, mortification root. When we eat a sweet marshmallow, do we wonder how it got its name? The answer is that the mucilaginous quality of the roots of this and other family members mostly native of Europe, yields a substance used in the best non-synthetic marshmallow paste.

The "officinalis" part of the name would indicate its long use in medicine as a demulcent and for conditions of the urinary system. It has also been used as an ingredient for coughs and bronchitis. Dried and cleaned roots have been recommended for teething babies.

Althaea rosea—Hollyhock.

Originally from China, the common garden hollyhock has medicinal values similar to the mallow discussed above, and it may be that the health values of any of the mallow family are beyond what is commonly recognized. But for the homeowner, the hollyhock in the garden is a chief ornament, especially with the introduction of the recent hybrids with long-lasting and colorful double flowers.

Of the total quality of this family, a poet, Abraham Cowley, says:

> The hollyhock distains the common size
> Of herbs, and like a tree does proudly rise;
> Proud she appears, but try her, and you'll find
> No plant more mild, or friendly to mankind.
> She gently all obstructions does unbind.

Gossypium herbaceum—Cotton.

Beyond the well-known uses of cotton as a fiber, there are medicinal values in cotton-seed oil, cotton for bandages, and in a preparation from the roots which is used as an emmenagogue and as an abortifacient. One authority claims that a preparation of cotton seed increases the milk of nursing mothers, and another that a decoction of the root will check hemorrhages.

Hibiscus esculentus—Okra, gumbo.

This garden plant introduced from Africa provides a mucilaginous seed pod which is liked as a vegetable throughout the South, while the flowers themselves are used as a dye. An Indian woman has sent the author a recipe for pickling okra which sounds tasty, using garlic, peppers, and dill as flavoring.

Malva neglecta—Mallow, cheese-weed.

This is a plant of the waste and desert places of the West, and one author allows that this species is the best of a number of species of Malva for flavor which may be cooked as a green, but the recommendation is that not too much be eaten at one time.

Malva parviflora—Mallow.

In discussing this and other species of mallows, Elmer D. Merrill, a very noted botanist, said that this plant is possibly the richest in vitamins and minerals of any plant ever analyzed in the

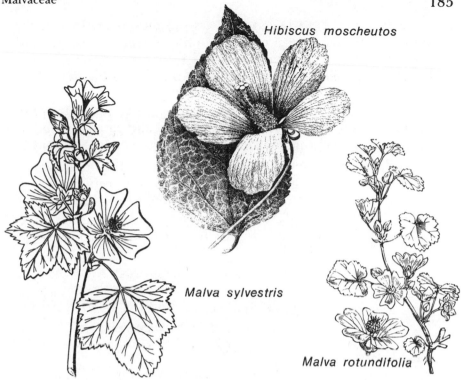

Hibiscus moscheutos

Malva sylvestris

Malva rotundifolia

nutritional laboratories of the world. In Manchuria, where it is grown, it is used as a major food crop.

Malva rotundifolia—Blue mallow, cheeses, fairy cheese, dwarf or low mallow, etc.

This and several other species, such as *M. sylvestris,* all have about the same mucilaginous qualities. Many of the Mallow species from around the world are widely naturalized in the United States. They have long been known for medicinal values, being mentioned thus by Theophrastes, Hippocrates, and Pliny. Readers should learn to know the values in *all* the mallows.

The truth is that those who would want to depend on natural medicines should learn to use infusions of the leaves of this and similar family members (one teaspoon of leaves to one cup of boiling water) using this infusion to loosen coughs and relieve sore throats, especially if honey is added to each dose. Its use tends to relieve irritations of the bowels, kidneys, and urinary organs. Again the fresh leaves, steeped in hot water, may be used as poultices on inflammations and bruises and also for taking away the pains and swelling of stings by bees and wasps.

THE MARTYNIAS
MARTYNIACEAE

Proboscidea jussieui—Proboscis-flower, unicorn plant, devil's claw, toenails, elephant's trunk.

This wild plant grows south from Delaware, and over into the Southwest, the pod-like fruit being boiled and eaten or used in pickling. (A synonomous name is that of *Martynia louisiana*.) It

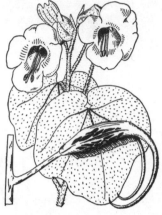

Proboscidea jussieui

is a low, widely-spreading, hairy, and sticky-leaved plant. The flowers are variable in color from white to red and the lower half of the flower is long, and becomes the beak or "proboscis"— from whence comes the name.

THE MELASTOMA FAMILY
MELASTOMATACEAE

Rhexia virginica—Meadow beauty, deer-grass, handsome Harry.
A plant of the low swampy lands from the East Coast to Louisi-

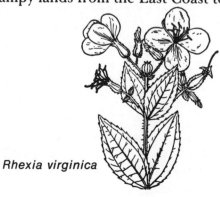

Rhexia virginica

ana, it has pretty purple flowers and leaves of a sweetish acid taste which may be eaten by man, but are an especial treat for the deer, from which fact comes the name.

THE MOONSEED FAMILY
MENISPERMACEAE

Menispermum canadense—Moonseed, Texas sarsaparilla, vine maple. This is a woody, twining, perennial vine common in the eastern United States of which a tincture of the fresh root has been used

Menispermum canadense

as a diuretic and stomachic, and sometimes as a substitute for sarsaparilla. But against this is the fact that the berries are poisonous and should never be used.

THE MULBERRY FAMILY
MORACEAE

Of the families of plants in this book, possibly none has such a variety of uses among its members as the mulberry family. Looking at the five genera discussed below, note that there is an hallucinogen, an excellent and healthful fruit, something essential to the making of beer, a noted hedge plant which gives a good dye, and a tree with edible fruit and leaves to feed the silk worms. Thus one can say that the family connections have little to do with uses.

Cannabis sativa—Marijuana, hemp.
That the name "hemp" is valid is shown by the fact that its fibres have long been used as a textile plant and are so grown and used in Mexico today. But it is more widely known as an hallucinogenic plant, providing the material of hashish when processed.
It has its home in central Asia and its "medicinal" use has

been known since the time of the Scythians and the Celts, and it is mentioned by Dioscorides, Galen, and other early writers. Its use was mentioned by a writer on America, as early as 1639.

Authorities are not entirely agreed as to the permanent damage done by smoking marijuana, but most agree that its use may lead to use of more dangerous substances, putting it into the category of tobacco and alcohol.

Ficus carica—Fig.

Except in northern states where it is not hardy, the fig is a common small tree providing an excellent and healthy fruit, beyond its uses as clothing for Adam. Medicinally the fruit is a mild laxative.

Humulus americanus—Hops.

This is a native species found in the Far West where it differs somewhat from the *H. lupulus,* the beer hop of commercial use. The bitter taste used in beer has made it important. The Apache Indians used the seeds and flowers for making bread and in fact the Indian name, translated, meant "to make bread with it."

Maclura pomifera—Osage-orange.

Because of the spiny growth of this plant, it has long been used as a tall, protective hedge plant. A native of the Middle West, it is hardy everywhere except our coldest zones. The large rough orange-like and valueless fruit give a name to the plant, while a good gold or yellow-tan dye can be extracted from the bark.

Morus rubra—Red mulberry or morus.

This is an East Coast native mulberry with soft, red, edible fruit which can be used to make a pleasing sweet drink. The fruit is mildly laxative.

From Texas to the West, there grows a shrub-tree called the Texas mulberry *(M. microphylla)* with similar fruit uses.

Morus alba—White mulberry, silkworm tree, Chinese mulberry.

Around a century ago, the idea was promoted that this country could be a great silk-producer, and trees of this species were imported from China to provide the foliage on which silkworms feed. On the Island of Martha's Vineyard, there are still large specimens of these trees, presumably planted at that time. The white fruit of this tree is usable (as of the red mulberry) but the mulberry is, possibly, the most undesirable tree to plant for fruit or beauty.

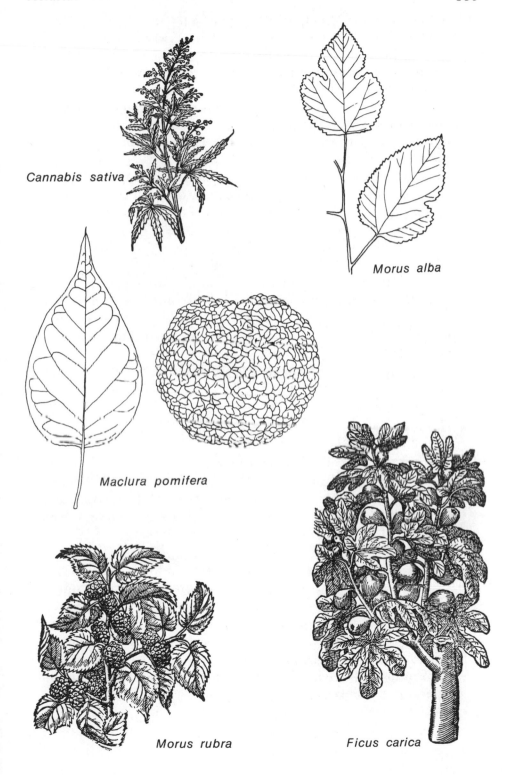

Cannabis sativa

Morus alba

Maclura pomifera

Morus rubra

Ficus carica

THE SWEET GALES

MYRICACEAE

Comptonia peregrina **var.** *asplenifolia*—Sweet fern, fern-bush, spleen-wort-bush, etc.

A characteristic of the members of this family is that they all have a pungent sweet smell coming from the oily, resinous "juices" of the plant. Growing widely in the East in poor, rocky, and sandy soils its low shrubby growth makes it a nice plant from which to snatch an aromatic handful of the fern-like foliage.

Medicinally it is said that a decoction of the leaves is a cure for diarrhaea. One old herbal interestingly tells that in the hometown of this author (Rhinebeck, New York) in 1781 an epidemic of "bloody flux" which "swept off the inhabitants daily" was cured by infusions of sweet fern.

But for the readers of this book, the best knowledge is that it is an old Indian-recommended cure for poison ivy, due, one assumed, from the oil in the leaves which dissolves the ivy-poisoning oil if the leaves are rubbed on soon after contact.

Myrica californica—Western bayberry.

A small tree or large shrub growing along the West Coast which belongs to this same family; found likewise on poor soil and with uses like that below.

Myrica cerifera **(syn.** *M. caroliniensis)*—Myrtle, wax myrtle, candle-berry, tallow shrub.

This is a shrub of up to 30 feet growing south from zone 7 to Texas and liking moist soils. The fruits (berries) are a main source of wax used in making candles. Medicinally the root bark is astringent and emetic, but it has also been ground and used as snuff. Old herbals make much of the values.

Myrica gale—Sweet gale, Dutch myrtle, meadow-fern.

A widely spread plant in North America, it is a low shrub grow-ing on moist peaty soils. Like all the *Myricas,* the astringent resins in the plant are useful for such conditions as the itch and eruptive diseases. Other uses noted by various authors include using the dried plant to drive away fleas, storing it with linen to protect from moths, using nutlets as spices, using the leaves as a seasoning with meat or as a tea-substitute, or in times before hops were used, as a flavoring for beer.

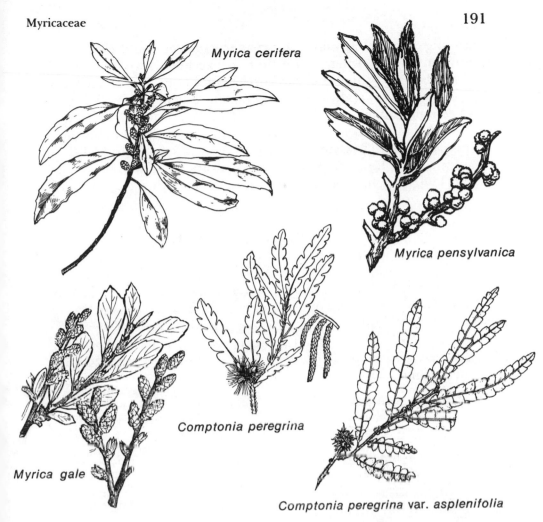

Myrica cerifera

Myrica pensylvanica

Comptonia peregrina

Myrica gale

Comptonia peregrina var. asplenifolia

Myrica pensylvanica (**syn.** *M. caroliniensis*)—Bayberry.

Here is a small shrub growing on sterile soil all along the East Coast and whatever minor medicinal values it might have are unimportant as related to the uses of the white wax which covers the plentiful seeds (nutlets). A culinary use is suggested for the leaves as a flavoring to take the place of bay leaves. It is also useful as a landscape shrub in coastal areas where the berries become an attraction for the myrtle warblers and many other species of birds.

Another use of the leaves would be as a source for a nice gray-green dye, while on Martha's Vineyard tons of the bay berries are gathered to be manufactured into waxing pads for ironing, something which any reader-gatherer could easily do for himself by sewing up a little thin bag filled with berries.

But basically the use of bayberry is in the making of the fragrant bayberry candles. There is no space here to give full instructions, but the author of *Bounty of the Wayside* tells in his book how his grandfather "melted green wax out of the gray berries by boiling them in water, and kept it in a pot on the back of the stove so that he could dip wicks into it any time he passed by, and hung the incipient candles on the dishcloth rack."

THE WATERLILY FAMILY
NYMPHAEACEAE

Brasenia schreberi—Water shield, water target.

This is a widely spread little water plant with small purple flowers, but with tuberous starchy roots which may be peeled, cooked, and eaten, or dried and ground into flour. One writer says that the "expanded leaves and lead stem may be eaten in salad, slime and all."

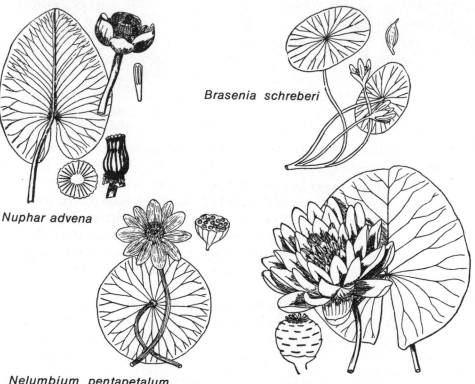

Brasenia schreberi

Nuphar advena

Nelumbium pentapetalum

Nymphaea odorata

Nelumbium pentapetalum—American water-lotus, water chinquipin, yellow nelumbo.

This relative of the famed lotus of the Nile is well-known for the edible quality of its seeds and is called chinquipin, because of some taste similarity to a "chinquipin chestnut."

Other values are found in the tubers, which were called the Indian potato of Iowa, for these tubers when dried and stored could be cooked with meat in winter. It has even been suggested that this lotus might some day be cultivated as a crop, much as the Chinese do their native species of lotus.

Nuphar advenum—Yellow pond lily, cow-lily, spatterdock.

This species is the most widely spread of the *Nuphars*, but in the West, to California, is found a similar species, *N. polysepalum*. Here again it is both roots and seeds which are edible. In the West they use the dry seeds to pop like popcorn, after which they may be eaten as is, or ground into meal.

Nymphaea odorata—Fragrant waterlily, pond-lily, bonnets, water cabbage.

This species is so beautiful and sweet and so widely spread that it has become the parent of many, many hybrids and selections, some with fancy names. But for the purpose of these notes, it has been valued for many years as a "folk medicine," although not anything found on the druggist's shelf.

Because of the mucilaginous nature of the roots, it has been recommended for bowel complaints, as a gargle for sore throats, a cure for baldness, and as a lotion for boils, sores, and ulcers.

As a sample of the kind of medicinal instructions provided about a century ago, *Good*'s *Family Flora* says (in part) about using waterlilies:

> In all cases a poultice (made from the roots) is an excellent sedative to relieve pain, and where there is a high state of inflammation, to reduce the swelling. The poultice may be prepared in the following manner:—To a teaspoon full of the fine powder, add a gill of boiling water, a teaspoon full of slippery elm, stir well together, then thicken with Indian meal, or, what is better, Boston crackers made fine . . .
>
> The proper time to gather the root of this plant is in the fall after the stalk is withered and the ponds are low.

Perhaps this is one plant that should be protected from too many "wildflower gatherers" as it is certainly one of America's great beauties.

THE SOUR GUMS

Nyssaceae

Nyssa sylvatica—Tupelo, pepperidge, sour gum, black gum, bettlebung.

A rather slow-growing tree which likes moist boggy situations.
It is not a tree of outstanding usefulness, though the attractive
foliage and intense early fall color makes it an interesting tree
to observe or plant. Its last listed name is a special one for
Martha's Vineyard, as a delightful clump of these trees is named
Bettlebung Corner. And here usefulness comes into the picture,

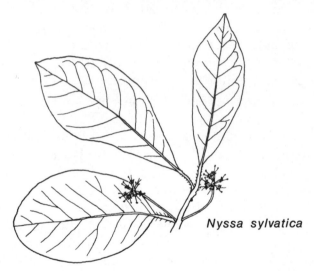

Nyssa sylvatica

for in the days of whaling, the very hard wood of the tree was
used to make "beetles" or mallets to drive in the bungs which
closed the barrels of whale-oil. The hard wood has also been
used elsewhere for tool handles, gun stocks, chopping bowls,
wheel hubs, flooring, and things of special need.

THE OLIVE FAMILY

Oleaceae

Chionanthus virginica—Fringe tree, flowering ash, graybeard tree,
snow-flowers.

From Pennsylvania down to Texas grows this odd-flowered,
tall-growing shrub member of the olive or ash-tree family, with

long panicles of white flowers which make it an interesting member of the family to plant as an ornamental shrub. The bark of the trunk and roots can be harvested in fall and used as a tonic, diuretic, and astringent. In Appalachia, where there is great dependence on plant remedies, a liquid of the boiled root bark is applied to skin irritations.

Fraxinus americana—White ash, cane ash, Biltmore ash.
The number of sorts of the ash tree are multifold, this one being of the East Coast, but others are spread throughout the country. Basically it is identified by the compound leaves and the flowers which spring from the leaf axils. The wood of the ash is very

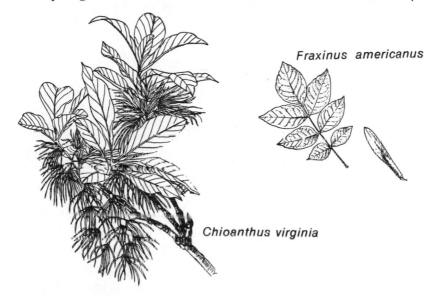

Fraxinus americanus

Chioanthus virginia

hard and is much used for furniture, athletic goods, basketry, etc.

Medicinally the inner bark of the tree has been used for centuries in Europe, and in colonial times in our country. This inner bark is rated as tonic, cathartic, diuretic, etc., while in the mid-South, the chewed bark is used for a poultice on sores, while one report says that a tea made from the buds is used for snakebite.

Interestingly enough, the ash was once a sacred tree in Britain, and in addition to the truly medicinal uses, it was said that the ruptures of young children could be cured by splitting a young ash and passing the naked ruptured child through the opening. The ash was then bound up and as the tree healed, so did the rupture of the child.

While there is much material on other species of ash, the conclusions are much the same as for that above.

Ligustrum vulgare—Common privet.

This is a European plant which is widely naturalized in the United States, as well as are a number of other species of privet, coming from China, Japan, or Russia. Here it is notable that the attractive (usually black) seeds of the privets are said to be quite poisonous, although there are records of medicine made from the leaves and flowers being used for ulcerated throats, etc.

Incidental to the discussion of privet comes the fact that some of the taller privets have flower heads hardly distinguishable from lilacs, leading to the comment that the old (and newer hybrid) lilacs are surely one of the finest of ornamental shrubs and a choice member of the olive family.

THE PRIMROSE FAMILY

ONAGRACEAE

Epilobium angustifolium—Fireweed, willow herb, Indian wicopy, purple fire top.

Here is a plant of wide-spread growth, equally noted as a food plant in the East and Far West. Its name of fireweed comes from the fact that it seems always to come up quickly in any spot where there has been a fire; it came up quickly in areas in Europe devastated by the fires of war, and even in the center of a city like London.

The young tender shoots can be cooked for greens or used for salads. While still in bud, flower stalks can be eaten raw or cooked, while the pith of stems is good in soups, or the dried leaves as a basis for tea.

Further, cotton from the seed pods makes an excellent tinder for campfires, while for those who expect medicinal values from any plant, the leaves and roots are demulcent, tonic and astringent.

It is surely a plant of great purple beauty and one of much use.

Jussiaea (various species)—Primrose-willow, yellow waterweed.

J. decurrens is found in the East, and *J. californica* in California as its name suggests. It is a yellow-flowered plant growing in bogs and marshes which is said to be an aid, as it grows, in purifying stagnant water, which is its usual home. Perhaps it is a plant the ecologists should look into.

Ludwigia alternanifolia—Rattle-box, seedbox.

This is a tall-growing perennial often used for ornamenting bog-gardens which, as a medicinal herb, has reputed values for diseases of the throat and lungs.

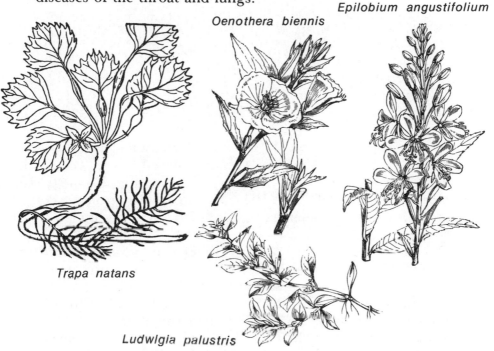

Epilobium angustifolia

Oenothera biennis

Trapa natans

Ludwigia palustris

Oenothera biennis—Evening primrose; King's cure-all; sundrops; scabish.

There are many species in this genera, and a number of them appear to be regional variations of the *biennis* form. It is a weedy growing, tallish biennial with bright yellow flowers. The young spring roots of it are cooked, while out in the Rockies, one writer tells of using the young leaves and shoots as salad.

The one name above should indicate great values medicinally, but it seems little recommended except for coughs and as a possible cure for skin eruptions.

Trapa natans—Water chestnut, water caltrop, Jesuit's water-nut.

This little floating water plant which has been introduced from Europe has mealy edible seeds in summer. Good to know about when found, and an excellent plant for aquaria.

THE FERN FAMILIES
OPHIOGLOSSACEAE—Adder's tongue ferns.

OSMUNDACEAE—The osmundas.

POLYPODIACEAE—Polypodys or common fern.

Considering that there are more than 10,000 listed species of these three fern families and others, and that the uses of a few of them are generally similar, the three families that are possibly most useful are here gathered together. Basically the nicest use of any of the ferns is in landscaping, wherein, in a shady spot in your garden, you can learn the beauty of ferns, as their gracefulness adds a soft touch to the yard.

Of least importance would be the ophioglossums, except as the non-fern-like leaf and the adder's tongue spore-bearing stalk is understandably the reason for the name. This genus is also of special interest to the scientific world, in that one of the species has the highest chromosome numbers reported for any living thing (2N— 1260 C.)

The second of these fern families are the osmundas, and here we have the useful royal fern, *Osmunda regalis,* of which the unfurling fronds are among those known as fiddleheads, which may be cooked and eaten, after first removing the rust-colored pieces of foliage. A widely spread fern, it has some listed values medicinally. Mrs. Grieve says that a decoction of the roots is of value in jaundice, while Culpepper gives quite different uses. Of interest here is the name "osmund" which is an old Saxon word for "domestic peace" which, in its beauty as a fern, it could well bring. Tanaka says that in Japan the white fibres of the young fronds are woven into clothes.

The third of these fern families is the one with the greatest number of possible uses, and these are polypodys.

Adiantum capillus-veneris—Maidenhair fern, Venus' hair, rock fern, duddergrass.

A widely spread fern growing in moist, shaded places and a plant used (dried fronds) as a tea substitute. In France a syrup for coughs and throat infections is made as a simple "tea," while another recipe adds licorice root and sugar. Another use given is as a hair tonic.

Dryopteris filix-mas—Male fern, sweet brake, basket fern, bear's paw, shield fern, wood fern.

This is a plant found growing everywhere in this country and beyond its beauty as a fern, it has a value as an anthelmintic, and taenicide (worm medicine). Certain properties found in the rhizome of this fern are definitely poisonous to intestinal worms, but, being a poison, the drug must be used with certain cautions —principally not to take a purgative after it, of castor oil.

It is interesting to note that in olden times the use of this fern was said to confer invisibility, possibly a fact known to Shakespeare, who in *Henry IV,* said:

> We have the receipt of fern seed; we walk invisible.

Pteridium aquilinum—Bracken fern, brake fern, pasture brake, fiddleheads (or necks).

Kinsey says of this fern that the "Brake is by all means the most widely known and generally the commonest of our ferns." And it is found from East to West, growing mostly in old fields, woods, and burned areas.

Here the tender unfolding fronds are used after rubbing off the fuzz, cooking until tender in salted water, and serving with butter. In the long-collected files of the author are recipes for preparing them in all sorts of ways. On the practical side, the shoots of the bracken are used by the dyeing enthusiasts to produce greenish-yellow and gray colors.

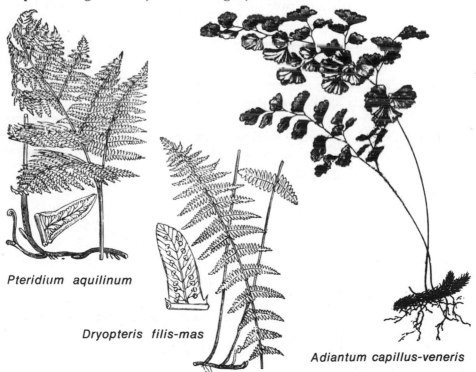

Pteridium aquilinum

Dryopteris filis-mas

Adiantum capillus-veneris

Matteuccia struthiopteris—Ostrich fern.

A fine vase-shaped fern, it grows in both the East and West, often to heights of six or more feet. If botanically interested, the reader may discover that its names are more numerous than its species, as generic names such as *Pteretis, Onoclea,* and *Struthiopteris* are used by various botanists. Botanical nomenclature is far from being fixed and immutable.

The unfurling fronds (called "croziers" after the Bishop's crozier) are used as with the bracken, and some writers recommend even using the young uncurled fronds, either boiling and serving with cream sauce, or as asparagus. Commercially, the croziers are often found in markets in the spring, as well as being offered as a canned green. In British Columbia, the heavy rootstocks are dug and roasted, while the big clumps can be dug in the fall, stored in the cellar, and the young greens used as they come up under warm cellar growth.

Of special interest to the author is the true beauty of the unfolding croziers, representing as they do, the same example of "dynamic symmetry" as the nautilus shells, the mathematics of both of which are supremely exemplified in the Greek Parthenon. In observing these lovely croziers learn how nature has given us forms and proportions from which all great art has come.

THE ORCHIDS
ORCHIDACEAE

With over 500 genera (variable types and classifications) and with each of these genera having multifold species to a total of 30,000,

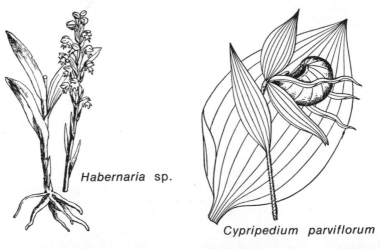

Habernaria sp.

Cypripedium parviflorum

and, beyond that, new and improved varieties and hybrids, the orchids are one of the largest of all known plant families. One species at least, the *Habenarias,* has a tuber-like root which is edible and a number of others have medicinal values known and used by the natives of a region, while others are definitely poisonous. But because of the feeling that the orchid is one of the most beautiful of all wild flowers and is not too common or rampant in reproduction, it would seem that unless in dire distress one should leave these flowers where their beauty can be admired by everyone.

THE BROOMRAPE FAMILY

OROBANCHACEAE

***Orobanche uniflora* (and various species)**—Cancer root, squaw root, broomrape, clap-wort, beech-drops.

With a variety of names suggesting major medicinal uses, it would be foolish to omit this plant from any list of useful plants,

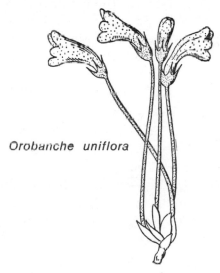

Orobanche uniflora

and yet Grieves *Herbal* says: "It is given internally in bowel affections, and is reputed to cure cancer, though this is doubtful." Obviously from its name it is one of the medicines of the herb-gathering Indian squaws and part of their shelf of medicinal plants.

THE WOOD SORRELS
OXALIDACEAE

Oxalis acetosella—Wood-sorrel, cuckoo bread, sour trefoil, shamrock, sour grass, oxalis.

Although one authority notes that, while this plant has been used to "remove cancerous growths from the lips," it is poisonous in large doses. But this and other species have been used as an acid little salad-bite, while there are recommendations to cook it up as one would apple sauce; make a pie of it with qualities like rhubarb, or use it (after cooking in granite-ware) as the basis of a good soup.

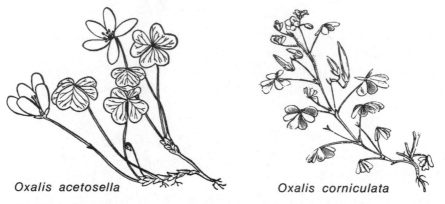

Oxalis acetosella   *Oxalis corniculata*

Oxalis (**related species to above**)—Redwood sorrel, procumbent sorrel, etc.

On the West Coast there is a species, *O. oregano* and more widely, *O. corniculata,* plus a number of others with variably-colored flowers and growths, but all more or less with the same common names and properties. As one author says: "The plants contain a high percentage of oxalic acid and should be eaten sparingly until one is accustomed to them." Another suggestion is to allow a "mass of them to ferment slightly to make a tasty dessert."

THE PALMS
PALMACEAE

Sabal palmetto—Cabbage palmetto, cabbage palm.

Of the more than 200 known genera of palms only some five percent are known in the United States. On the East Coast, southwards from North Carolina, grows the low-growing cabbage palm of which the buds have been eaten as salad, and the inner bark has been used for making pickles

Sabal palmetto

Washingtonia filifera—California fan palm.
Native of the extreme Southwest, this tall-growing palm tree produces, high up amidst hanging dead-foliage, bunches of berry-like black fruits which have thin, sweet, edible pulp around an edible seed, which may be eaten raw, or dried and ground into a meal or flour.

THE POPPIES

PAPAVERACEAE

Chelidonium majus—Celandine, tetterwort, wart-weed, felon-wort, wort-weed, swallow-wort.
A widely spread weed translated from its home in Eurasia, the values of this plant are shown in its names, and a dozen or more reputable herbal books all have comments on its usefulness, although none is in total agreement. The orange juice which drips out of the stems when broken is, if taken internally, vio-

lently purgative; but seemingly, because of its acrid quality, has long been used for skin diseases, especially warts, ringworm, herpes, and eczema. In Roman times it was used, apparently, for the removal of corneal opacities. In any case, celandine is one of the really old herbal medicines.

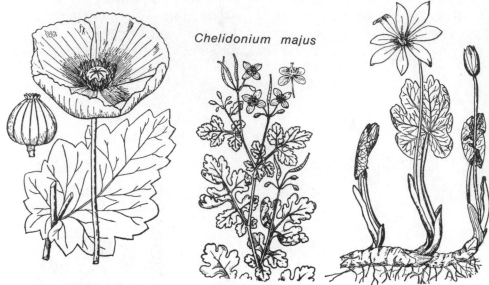

Chelidonium majus

Papaver somniferum

Sanguinaria canadensis

***Papaver somniferum*—**Opium poppy.
Here is a lovely member of the poppy family and one bright in the garden, but one of which no seed is sold in this country, for here is the poppy from Asia Minor which has given us opium, heroin, and other derivations, at once so valuable to the doctor and injurious to the addict. Like all family members, a juice is exuded from the seed-case which contains the sedative qualities, both useful and dangerous.

***Sanguinaria canadensis*—**Bloodroot; red, yellow, or white puccoon; tetterwort; coonroot; red root; sweet slumber; snakebite.
This is a lovely spring wildflower native to all the eastern states. Like other family members, an orange-red juice exudes from the stems or root giving its most common name. Like celandine, the juice may be purgative or mildly sedative, as with the opium poppy, and uses suggested are as for celandine. One suggestion is to use the dried powdered root as a sort of snuff to cure polyps in the nose.

THE PASSION FLOWERS

PASSIFLORACEAE

Passiflora incarnata—Maypop, passionflower, apricot vine.

This vining plant grows from Virginia to Missouri and south to Florida, and is but one of a number of species that are mostly from South America. Its name comes from signs and flower colors of Christ's passion noted by priests who first came to America. Regardless of the religious significance, the summer-

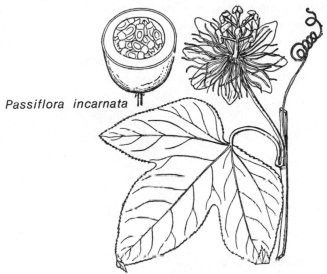

Passiflora incarnata

gathered dried flowers and fruit are pharmaceutically used as a "motor depressant in neuralgia and for insomnia, dysmenorrhoea and diarrhoea." It is reputed also as an aphrodisiac for elderly men, possibly because of the word "passion" found among its common names.

THE POKEWEEDS

PHYTOLACCACEAE

Phytolacca americana—Pokeweed, garget, pocan bush, cancer root, inkberry, jalap.

In the author's files there are almost more notes and scraps of information about pokeweed than any other of the 600 plants in this book. Actually it is a most curious plant in that the roots of the plant, and the crimson leaves and berries of autumn, are both highly poisonous, and yet the young asparagus-like shoots in the spring are a favorite spring green, often marketed. Of course this double nature is also true of something as common as rhubarb, but who eats rhubarb roots or foliage?

Actually the roots are prepared pharmaceutically and sold in the drug trade as an emetic and an "alterative" in chronic rheumatism.

A second important use of pokeweed is as a dye material, prepared from the berries in autumn, to make a very excellent red dye, or with variations in methods, a good salmon-orange. In this matter it is likely that the name has come from its use as a dye, for phyton is a greek-based word meaning plant, while lacca is a word for the color crimson-like.

Phytolacca americana

But the primary use is, as stated, for the young thick shoots appearing in spring, which are cut off at ground level when the shoots are six to eight inches long are parboiled for five minutes to remove a little bitter taste, and then cooked until tender in another water, make, with butter or sauce, a delicious treat.

It is an Eastern plant widely spread in spots which are often neglected, poor corners of hedgerows, and it seems to have a habit of seeding itself on newly bulldozed and often sterile ground.

This is one plant that every nature-user should get to know, and also of which to enjoy the fall-beauty, for no color is more beautiful and striking than the sun shining through the foliage as stems, leaves, and berries become crimson.

THE PINE FAMILY
PINACEAE

This family, which is basically known to nearly everyone is, however, a good example of the difficulties of the science of botany, as the reader will find that there may be some plants known as pines which are not found in the list below and others here which might be thought of as something else. But, following the writings of Liberty Hyde Bailey, the *Pines* with notable uses in this country are basically these:

Abies Fraseri—Balsam fir, double spruce, balsam spruce.
   This is one of the evergreens of the mid-Atlantic states which is used as a source for turpentine and of which the bark gives medicinal values of minor value.

Picea mariana (syn. *Abies mariana*)—Black spruce, double spruce.
   This is one of the common evergreens of the northern United States. By steeping the young shoots a flavor for spruce beer is made, while the resin becomes turpentine, and the wood is being used for making boxes. The cones are a source of a yellow-orange dye.

Pinus cembroides parryana—Parry pinyon pine, pinyon pine, nut pine.
   Here is a true pine with needles in bundles of three to four (sometimes five) which is a native of the Southwest. The excellently edible "nuts" are found in the fall inside the cone and actually in places the trees are being cut just to harvest the fine supply of nuts.
   Botanically, this tree is listed variously as *P. edulis, monophylla, and quadrifolia* or as just *P. cembra*. These variations are in part due to natural variations which sometimes make the pine appear as a large shrub or a giant tree.

Pinus palustris—Longleaf, fat, Georgia, hard, yellow, pitch, long-straw.
   This is a pine with needles three in a sheaf, which is so important

in the Southeast section of the country, with the many common names showing many uses. It is a great source of turpentine, tar, pitch, and rosin. This last item is well known to athletes and violinists, while therapeutically the pine tar has many uses, all beyond the great timber values of this tall-growing tree.

Pinus strobus—White pine, weymouth pine, Deal pine, soft pine, etc. This is the 200 foot growing pine tree with needles five in the sheath. It was a tree important in the development of the thirteen colonies when the giant trees were cut for masts for the British navy, and always since, it has been a source of an easily worked, soft, white wood.

Medicinally much use has been made of "white pine tar" in cough remedies, while in some areas rheumatism cures are reported from an extract from the cones. Euell Gibbons in one of his books devotes a chapter to many uses of pine bark, pine cones, and the pine "new growth" candles. One can look on this tree as a most important and useful American plant, and it is also the state tree of Maine, where it was first seen in 1605.

Pseudotsuga taxifolia (**syn.** *P. menziesii*)—Douglas fir. As the earlier mentioned pine trees are natives of the East, this is one of the great tall and economically valuable sources of timber in the Rockies and on the West Coast. Uses, other than for lumber, coming from the Indians, are for making fish harpoons and other implements, while the pliable roots are used in weaving baskets. The fresh needles may be steeped in hot water to make a refreshing tea, high in Vitamin C.

Thuya occidentalis—Arbor-vitae, white cedar, thuya, tree of life. This native American tree grows in the Northeast over to Wisconsin, and as against the tree pines, is distinguished by the flatness of the leaf-sprays, which, when young, are dried for medicinal purposes. A cedar-leaf oil is commercially distilled for perfuming soap and as an insect repellent, while for home uses, an infusion made from the leaves has values as a diuretic. In addition, strong decoctions have been used for fevers, coughs, and according to some, "may produce abortions." Further, leaves boiled in lard make a salve said to aid in rheumatic conditions. As a plant for use in the home landscape, a number of selected natural hybrid variations make for many fine ornamental evergreens.

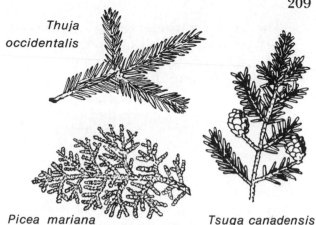

Pinus strobus

Thuja occidentalis

Picea mariana

Tsuga canadensis

Tsuga canadensis—Hemlock, hemlock spruce, hemlock fir.
The soft-foliaged and graceful hemlock tree grows widely in the eastern states in the cooler moister areas away from the sea. It has a number of natural variations; one especially valuable for landscape uses is a dwarf weeping form. The bark has a high tannin content, which makes it a strong astringent, and much use was made of it for various medicines in older days.

Tsuga heterophylla **and** *T. mertensiana*—Western or mountain hemlocks.
These members of the hemlock group are distinguishable as one of the great forest trees of Washington, Oregon, and California, and a source of lumber, while the bark is gathered for tanning. Western Indians made tea by steeping the fresh needles in hot water, while the inner bark was used in making a sort of not-too-palatable bread.

THE PLANTAINS

PLANTAGINACEAE

Plantago major **(and** *P. lanceolata*)—Common plantain, Englishman's foot, ribwort, black psyllium, psyllium seed, waybread, Indian wheat.
Here is a most common weed which has come westward, likely from Asia, and in the principal species has broad, prominently ribbed leaves with flowers and (later) seeds, growing on erect spikes. It is found on roadsides, lawns, fields, and woods and is not easy to eradicate.

That it is a long-known and much-used plant may well be shown by quoting a bit of poetry translated by a scholar who lived in China for decades. He tells us that the author was Shih Ching who lived in the 6th century B.C., and who wrote:

Gathering Plantain Seed
Pluck, pluck, the plantain spikes!
This is how we pluck them off!
Pluck, pluck, the plantain spikes!
In our hands we hold them firm!
Pluck, pluck, the plantain spikes!
This is how we crush them up!
Pluck, pluck, the plantain spikes!
Rub them thus to thresh them out!
Pluck, pluck, the plantain spikes!
In our aprons put the seeds!
Pluck, pluck, the plantain seeds!
With our girdles tie them tight!

Why would Chinese maidens be out plucking the seeds of plantains? Shakespeare suggests the reason why, in *Romeo and Juliet:*

Romeo: Your plantain sead is excellent for "that," Benvolio? For what, I pray?
Benvolio: For your broken shin.

In addition, one finds references to plantain in Chaucer and other English authors and seemingly complete agreement that this is a "wound plant," with much herbal reference to the fact that it is an excellent relief from stings and burns, itching and the like, while one less common species gives us the psyllium seed of the pharmacy.

Several reliable authorities on Indian practices, from both

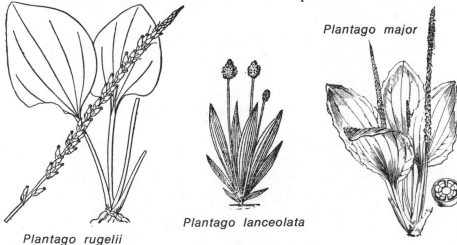

Plantago major

Plantago lanceolata

Plantago rugelii

East and West, used poultices of plantain for battle bruises and for drawing out snake poisons. For any such uses the whole plant is crushed, soaked, and bound to the sore spot. Other writers suggest that an ointment made from the leaves is good for sore eyes. The seed of one species, giving psyllium, is a reputable laxative.

In other non-medicinal uses the mucilaginous qualities have been used in hair lotions, while the leaves and roots are a source for a good green dye.

As a food plant its uses are minor, one author suggesting using the young leaves as a salad before the ribs get tough, or cooked as one would turnip greens, or mixed with dandelion or other greens, while a tea can be made from the dry leaves.

Plantain is thus a notable sample of how the commonest of wide-spread weeds can have many uses which can be known if one will but read and explore.

Plantago Rugelii—Pale plantain, white-man's foot, silk plant.
A widely spread plant, mostly in the Midwest, it has much the same values as species like the narrow-leaved plantain, *P. lanceolata, B. virginica, P. cordata,* and others.

THE MILKWORT FAMILY
POLYGALACEAE

Polygala senega—Seneca-snake-root, milkwort, mountain flax, rattlesnake root, polygala senega.
Throughout most of the eastern states in dry woods, one finds this weedy perennial which grows about two feet high with

Polygala senega

spikes of whitish or pinkish flowers. Its values are, as the word wort indicates, entirely medicinal. Investigating its use by the Seneca Indians (for snake bite) a doctor discovered other values for infusions of the root, and for a time, it became an accepted "official" drug for uses in chronic catarrh, croup, asthma, and lung disorders. Large doses of the root extract does, however, act as a strong cathartic and therefore it should be used carefully.

THE BUCKWHEAT FAMILY
POLYGONACEAE

Eriogonum **(various species)**—Wild buckwheat, desert trumpet.
In this rather large genus which is found widely in the Southwest and West, one finds annuals, perennials, herbs, and shrubs. The stems of many of the species are known to be edible and may be eaten cooked or raw.

Fagopyrum esculentum—Buckwheat.
A grain from Asia which sometimes may be found in the wild, giving a nutritious food which, however, if eaten too heartily, may cause dermatitis. A somewhat unlikely use may be noted, wherein the stalks are used by dyers for a good blue color.

Oxyria digyna—Alpine sorrel, mountain sorrel, scurvy grass.
A plant largely found in the high elevations of the West, it grows close to the ground and has green to crimson flowers in panicled racemes. Like other sorrels, it can be eaten raw or boiled. Among various Indian tribes, it was chopped up with watercress and allowed to ferment, to provide a sort of sauerkraut.

Polygonum aviculare—Knot-grass, goose-grass, bindweed, hog-weed, etc.
This is just one of a number of *Polygonums* which grow very widely and are persistent weeds, the worst of which seems to be the so-called Japanese bamboo, *P. cuspidatum* which is almost completely ineradicable.
One author says that "a decoction of the plant mixed with oak bark has been used as a substitute for quinine." The seeds of this species have been used whole, or may be ground as flour, as it is suggested by a writer from the West. Species such as *P. bistort-*

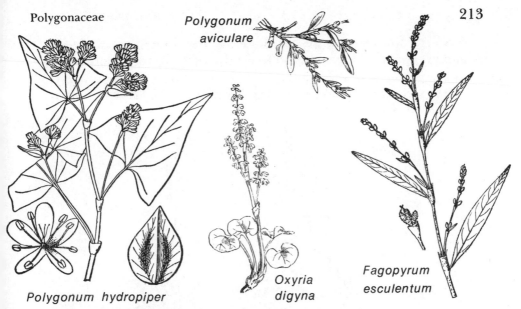

Polygonaceae

Polygonum aviculare

Polygonum hydropiper

Oxyria digyna

Fagopyrum esculentum

oides and *P. vivparum* have starchy roots which are edible when roasted.

Polygonum hydropiper —Water pepper, smartweed, biting knotweed, biting tongue, etc.

The leaves of this plant are acrid, pungent, and antiseptic, as the names would indicate, and various authorities give various medicinal uses. It has been used as a diuretic and in uterine disorders. In Europe it is used as a hemostatic drug to control internal and hemorrhoidal bleeding. This species is partly identifiable by its 18 inches height with reddish stems, and lanceolate leaves. The stalks give dyers a yellow-gold color.

Rheum rhaponticum —Garden rhubarb, pie plant.

It may seem odd to include this garden "vegetable" among wild plants, and yet often one finds rhubarb growing where old gardens have been, or where it may have been spread by birds. This is just to point out that however good rhubarb is, it should be known that the roots and the green foliage of the stems are highly poisonous, and should never be cooked.

Rumex acetosa —Sheep sorrel, cuckoo bread, field, wood, or red sorrel.

Another naturalized plant from Asia which, with its arrow-like leaves is well known as a good little plant for soups and sauces. Among the voluminous notes accumulated for writing this book, the references as to how to prepare and use sorrel are numerous. The mild sour taste has made it "the little vinegar plant" and every nature lover should make use of it as a real "gourmet" item.

Beyond edible qualities the stalks and leaves are used for a gray-blue dye.

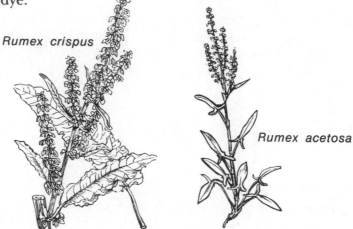

Rumex crispus

Rumex acetosa

Rumex crispus—Curly dock, narrow-leaved dock, garden patience. This was the first wild plant known for its use in place of spinach that this author came in contact with in childhood. Here, as with sorrel, there are pages of reference material, all extolling the use of dock for such things as:

1. It is rich in Vitamin A. A ten-minute cooking of the young leaves gives a delicious vegetable.

2. The seeds of the tall stem may be ground and made into cakes or gruel.

3. This species is listed by the Department of Agriculture as an important medicinal plant. The root, collected in late summer, split and dried, has values for curing skin infections, itches, etc. More simply, the freshly-gathered leaves, washed and crushed, are laid on sores as a healing agent.

4. The roots have been used, especially by the Indians, as a yellow dye.

5. Garden club flower-arrangers often find the rich brown colored stalk a fine artistic bit to point up a notable autumn bouquet.

Here, then, is a very, very common weed, found everywhere, which has values one should not neglect.

THE PICKEREL WEEDS

PONTEDERIACEAE

Pontederia cordata—Pickerel weed.

This plant which grows on the wet margins of streams and ponds is well known to all who roam the wild. Not so well known is the fact that the starchy fruit (seeds) of pickerel weed can be picked and eaten as a grain or that, indeed, one may cook the whole plant. Beyond all this is the fact that when in bloom the flowers are a lovely blue.

Escaped from Asia to parts of our Southwest is another family member, *Monochoria vaginalis* which in its homeland is gathered as a whole plant and sold in the markets.

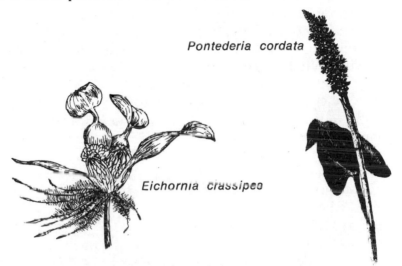

Pontederia cordata

Eichornia crassipes

Eichornia crassipes—Water hyacinth.

Here is another family member with delightfully beautiful blue flowers. Writers from sections where it grows say that at the young foliage and buds may be cooked and eaten. But for those southern regions in our country where the plant has taken hold in rivers and streams, this fast-growing "hyacinth" has become one of the most serious intrusive weeds that has ever been known in America.

THE PURSLANE FAMILY

PORTULACACEAE

Calandrinia (**various species**)—Red maids, rose calandrina.

This fleshy annual plant is found widely through the Pacific states and Arizona, and all of the species have dark round seeds which may be eaten raw or ground into meal.

Claytonia (**various species**)—Spring beauty, claytonia.

Some species of this plant grow in the Far West and others are in the East. A plant of no great importance, one writer from the Rocky Mountain area suggests that the roots may be boiled about 25 minutes and peeled, and are somewhat like potatoes.

Lewisisa rediviva—Bitterroot.

A plant of the Rockies, north and west from Colorado, it is the state flower of Montana, and the use of the bulbous roots as food was introduced to the Lewis and Clark Expedition by the Indians. A tiny white-flowered perennial, the roots are gathered in spring, cooked until the bitter root slips off, and then the white starchy "tuber" is used as food.

Montia perfoliata—Miner's lettuce, spring beauty, winter purslane.

A plant related to claytonia, it is annual with succulent leaves growing about six inches tall, found mostly west from the Cascade Mountains. It is recommended by many as an excellent salad plant, its common name coming from its popular use among the gold miners of California.

Portulaca oleracea—Purlane, pussley.

Here is one of the commonest of all weeds, and one found most often as a "garden pest." A plant which has worked itself from India west, throughout the world, the ground-covering plant with its succulent reddish-purple stems and small fattish leaves is far more edible than generally realized. The whole plant may

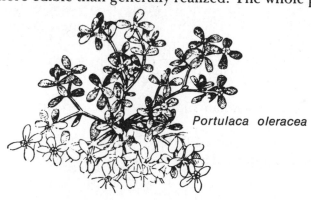

Portulaca oleracea

be boiled and eaten, or used fresh as a salad. Its juices are good to thicken soup, while the larger stems can be used as pickles. And, unlike so many "wild" plants, it grows continuously all season. Here one might well say—"harvest the weeds."

THE PRIMROSE FAMILY
PRIMULACEAE

Anagallis arvensis—Scarlet pimpernel, red chickweed, poor man's weatherglass.

A naturalized plant from Asia, this red-flowered annual plant grows widely here and there, near civilization. While it has been

Anagallis arvensis

used medicinally for a few conditions, the poisonous qualities in it, which are fatal to dogs and horses, make its use questionable, even though some side effects are reputedly aphrodisiac.

THE WINTERGREEN FAMILY
PYROLACEAE

Chimaphila umbellata—Pipsissewa, bitter wintergreen, prince's pine, ground holly, rheumatism weed, waxflower, etc.

This is a tiny (ten inch high) evergreen plant that grows in the forests very widely in our country. The first name comes to us from the Indians, who made much use of the plant. One student of the Pequot tribes writes that some Indians used it steeped, for blisters, while others used the dried leaves as an astringent and tonic, or for rheumatism. It has also been used to give its pleasing taste to root beer.

Monotropa uniflora—Indian pipe, pinesap, ice-plant, ghost-flower, corpse-plant.

Actually, this is a plant of little value, but one that should be found of much botanical interest. It is saprophytic (lives on dead plant life) and looks quite unlike any other plant, as there is no green chlorophyll in the growth or flowers, and it appears sort of ghost-like in the dense woods where it grows. It is said to be edible, raw or cooked.

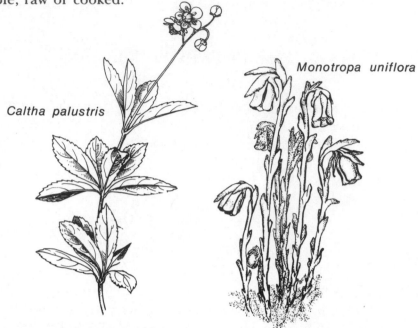

Monotropa uniflora

Caltha palustris

***Pyrola rotundifolia*—False** wintergreen, round-leaved pyrola, shin leaf, etc.

This is not, it should be noted, the true wintergreen which is *Gaultheria* (q.v.) but again it is a plant like the other family members, which loves the deep woods. In addition to this species there are others spread in many parts of the country, with the nomenclature of the species as widely divergent as the plant. All forms are listed as having values as astringents and diuretics.

THE BUTTERCUP FAMILY
RANUNCULACEAE

If this book were one written about ornamental plants, it would contain many of the names on the list below, for here we have such fine garden plants as the larkspurs, anemones, clematis, peonies, columbines, and a host of other fine flowers. Some of these plants offer other values—some medicinally valuable and others containing poisons which are useful in controlled situations.

Actaea (**various species**)—Baneberry, black cohosh, snakeberry, necklace berry.

A low shrubby perennial, *A. alba* grows from East to West—*A. rubra* with red berries in the East and *A. arguta* in the West and all with pretty berries which are highly poisonous. Beware of this pretty plant of the moist shady spots.

Caltha palustris—Marsh-marigold, cowslip, meadow bright, colt's foot.

Here again is a plant with various species found in different parts of the country. For the West, *C. leptosepala* grows from Canada to New Mexico, and *C. Palustris* grows in the East where the young leaves and flower buds are gathered in spring as a pot-herb. One recipe calls for cooking the shoots anywhere from ten to 60 minutes. In parts of the South the flower-buds are pickled as a substitute for capers. Everywhere the bright yellow flowers found in moist and boggy situations are a sign of spring.

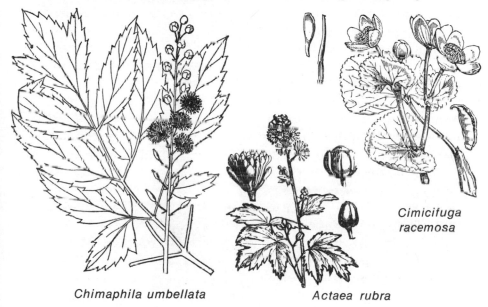

Cimicifuga racemosa

Chimaphila umbellata

Actaea rubra

Cimicifuga racemosa—Cohosh, black snakeroot, papoose root, bugbane, etc.

A perennial plant of the open woods, this close relative of *Actaea* is a favored eight foot growing background plant for flower borders. As a medicine it is said (as a name indicates) to be of value for snakebites, while the extractions from the roots and rhizomes are listed as valuable as a sedative, and antispasmodic and especially for minor rheumatism.

It is of interest to note that the generic name of *Cimicifuga*,
means "cim" a bug and "fugo" to drive away, indicating known
uses when the name was applied long ago.

There is evidence to indicate that this was one of the basic
remedies in the Indian "medicine cabinet."

Clematis virginiana—Virgin's bower, white clematis.

Everyone knows that *Clematis* is a fine-flowered vine and this
particular species is a native of eastern woods. There are some
125 or more known species of *Clematis* in all parts of the world
and many of them have been hybridized into the lovely vines of
our gardens. This native one (among others) has been used
medicinally for itches and eruptions on the skin, which, if used
too much, it will also cause.

Coptis groenlandica (syn. *C. trifolia*)—Gold-thread, mouthroot, yellow
root, canker-root.

The name here would suggest that this little perennial growing
in swampy areas in northeastern America would be a dye-plant
giving yellow or gold colors, and this indeed it does. Two
medicinal qualities are well known—first, that a decoction made
in conjunction with golden-seal has been found to destroy the
appetite for intoxicating liquors, and secondly, used as a tincture it is valuable for ulcerations of the mouth. A New York State
mother has written me that it is very valuable for "baby's sore
mouth." A good little plant to know about.

Hepatica acutiloba—Liverleaf, liverwort, sharp-lobed or heart liverleaf, spring beauty.

This and the species *H. americana* grow widely as a low, small-
flowered perennial in rich woods in all of the eastern United
States. It has been described as an "innocent herb," as infusions
may be taken freely without much fear of overdosage. Medicinally it is listed as a tonic, mild astringent, and diuretic. Variations in the genera have given rise to a similar plant known as
H. americana, growing a little lower, with flowers white to rose.

Hydrastis canadensis—Golden seal, orange-root, Indian turmeric, eye
balm, jaundice root, ground raspberry, Ohio curcuma, etc.

A low-growing, small-flowered perennial plant of rich woods, it
grows from East to the Midwest. Our knowledge of its medicinal
values came from the Cherokee Indians. The roots are the part
used, either as a source for a yellow dye, or in reputable medical
practice as an alterative and bitter tonic. One recent writer says

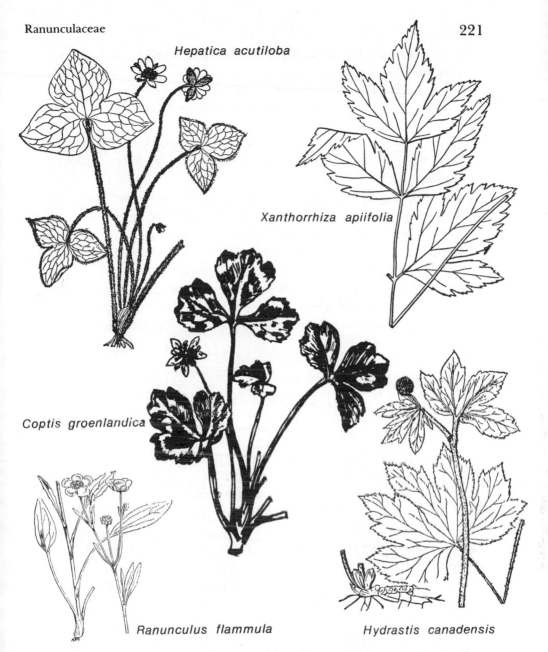

Hepatica acutiloba

Xanthorrhiza apiifolia

Coptis groenlandica

Ranunculus flammula

Hydrastis canadensis

that it may be given alone or with other medicines, and that it promotes digestion, acts as a general stimulant, and that in convalescence it is highly beneficial.

Ranunculus (various species)—Buttercups, spearwort, crowfoot. Widely spread throughout the world and in the United States, there are some fifty species of buttercups, a lovely yellow flowered plant which it is hardly necessary to describe. Actually it is included here only because it is quite poisonous, taken in any form. Early settlers, however, pickled the young flowers, while some western Indians parched the seeds and ground them into flour, as well as using the roots for yellow dye. Mostly one should enjoy their flowers and especially the blooms of some of the near-eastern species, which are grown as a fine florists' flower.

Xanthoriza simplicissima (syn. *X. apiifolia*)—Yellowroot.

An evergreen native of the damp woods and stream banks in the East, this is a plant which has little medicinal value although it has been listed as a tonic plant, or again as a source for the dye which comes from the truly "yellow-roots." But to this author this is one of the best of all low, foreground-facing shrubs for planting in a shady place. Once established, it needs little care and keeps down other growth. Consider this a prime landscape plant.

THE ROSE FAMILY
ROSACEAE

Of all the families in this book, that of the roses is probably the one known under one name for the longest time, and the one having the most useful family members as well as those considered the most beautiful. There is good evidence that roses were a favorite garden flower of the Egyptians and Persians, possibly having come there from China. References are made to the beauty of roses by Homer (800 B.C.) and their use in the gardens of the Romans is known. Virgil, whose *Georgics* give us authentic details of garden and farm life in Italy, mentions the "rose-gardens of twice-blooming Paestum (a city)."

Going beyond the flowering roses to the purposes of this book, Virgil suggests one could cure "sick bees" with a mixture of dried rose leaves and (oak) galls while the Roman Pliny wrote about the use of rose oil and petals for medicine.

But beyond the beauty and values of the flowering rose, the botanists have found that there are many plants which fit into the characteristics which make up the rose family. Thus *Rosaceae* has more useful family members than any other group in this book, providing not only one of our most popular fruits, but a number of plants for medicinal use, as dye plants, and a host of plants for ornamental landscape use.

Agrimonia gryposepala—Agrimony, cocklebur, sticklewort.

Pliny, who wrote his natural history book in the time of Christ, coined the name for this plant, which even then was known as medicinal, but is something today which we might call a "simple," as it has never been in our pharmacopoeia. Yet recommendations have told of the curing of "gravel stone," while most writers credit infusions of agrimony (with honey) as valuable for sore and husky throats.

The tiny brush-like yellow flowers with some mild fragrance make a distinctive, if not beautiful plant, growing widely all through the eastern United States and on the West Coast.

For readers interested in plant dyes, the leaves and stalks provide a color which one might call a "yellow-tan" gold.

Agrimonia eupatoria

Alchemilla vulgaris

Alchemilla (**various species**)—Parsley-piert, lady's mantle.

This is a tiny weed, sometimes a problem, which has come mostly from Europe where much legend is associated with it, because the leaf-shapes were imagined as a "mantle" suitable for the Virgin. Medicinally, due to its tannin content, it has been recommended as an astringent and styptic, but much of its interest lies in the gathering of legend, some of which may have come from the generic name *Alchemilla*, which came via the Arabic tongue. There is so much of interest in the names and history of plants.

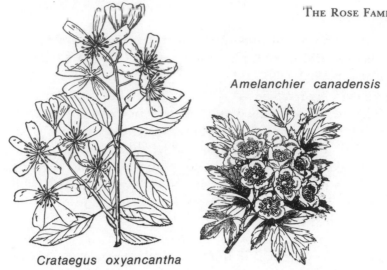

Amelanchier canadensis

Crataegus oxyancantha

Amelanchier (**various species**)—Service berry, sarvis, shadbush, June
    berries, Indian pear.
The variances in this plant are found in the several species, some
of which are found in the East and others in the West, with
specific names of *A. alnifolia, canadensis, laevis,* and *vulgaris.*
Sometimes a large shrub or a feathery tree, the mass of bloom
in the early spring coming, as it used to do, when the shad ran
up the rivers—it is surely the most beautiful native announce-
ment of spring.
    Later on, the tiny "apples" or berries arrive which ripen
through the summer and were, when dried, part of the "pemmican" which the Indians used in winter to liven their diets of meat
and vegetables.
    Today, the berries can be used for excellent pies, or may be
stewed, frozen, or canned. Meanwhile, if they do not grow wild
in your area, nursery plants may be grown to give you a lovely
early shrub with later food values.

Cercocarpus ledifolius—Mountain mahogany.
A narrowly distributed evergreen tree of 30 to 40 feet, it is found
on the West Coast to Arizona. A beautiful red dye is obtained
from the bark and roots. Additionally, the scraped bark makes
a flavorful addition to what is called Mormon tea, a form of
Ephedra.

Cowania mexicana—Cliffrose, quinine bush.
An evergreen man-sized shrub which is found in the Southwest
down to Mexico, it has large white flowers with lovely grey bark

and reddish twigs. The hard wood has been used by the Hopi Indians for making arrows, while the braided bark has been made into clothing, sandals, and rope. A mild tea is made from the leaves while a stronger tea has emetic qualities.

Crataegus **(various species)**—Hawthorn, thornapple, red haws, black haws, cockspur thorns, etc.

In America there are hundreds of species of haws, growing in the East, West, North, and South. All species produce edible berries, but some produce fleshier fruit than others. The berries are edible raw, or may be used for jams or jellies—this was another one of the ingredients of the "pemmican" of western Indians. Typical of the hawthorns are the varieties of "thorns" of various sizes and shapes, all with very tough wood, making the branches hard to break.

Filipendula ulmaria—Queen-of-the-meadow, meadowsweet.

Once classed with the *Spiraea* genera, and formerly called *S. ulmaria*, this is a naturalized plant found widely as a tall-growing herbaceous plant and fine for flower border backgrounds. It is included here, since the plant tops are used for giving a yellowish-green dye.

Fragaria **(various species)**—Strawberries.

Who does not know the tastiness of wild strawberries, some species of which grow in the East, some throughout the West, while some grow widely in China and Europe. One writer tells that the "western Indians prepared tea from the (astrin-

Fragaria sp.

gent) green leaves," while the fruit, medicinally, has been prescribed as an old-time gout remedy. The pleasure of well-ripened wild strawberries found on a sunny bank should be the experience of everyone. Roger Williams, the founder of Rhode Island, said that "this berry is the wonder of all the fruits growing naturally in these parts."

Geum rivale—Avens, chocolate root, purple or water avens, cureall.
This is a three-foot herb with purple flowers found growing in
bogs or wet meadows all over the United States, except for the
West Coast area. The roots have a powerful astringent action,
making it of special value in dysentery, a fact that was known and
used by the Indians very widely. The root makes a chocolate
colored drink of supposed tonic values.

Gillenia trifoliata—Indian physic, bowman's root, false ipecac, Indian
hippo.
A branching herb found in the eastern states, it has stalks of
white flowers about three feet tall and is found growing in moist
rich soil. The bark of the root is a mild and efficient emetic, with
actions that are similar to ipecac.

Heteromeles arbutifolia—Toyon or Christmas berry.
A thirty foot evergreen shrub of California, it is used there for
holiday decorations because of its bright red berries. These
fruits are edible raw, toasted, steamed, or boiled, or they may
be used for making cider.

Holodiscus discolor—Rock spirea, mountainspray, cream or foam
bush.
A spreading, much branched tall shrub found on the West
Coast, this plant has white flowers, followed by small one-
seeded fruits which were eaten raw or cooked by many western
Indians.

Malus sylvestris—The apple.
Botanically there is confusion about the correct scientific name
of this plant, but surely there is not any confusion about the
meaning of the common name of apple, nor perhaps should
much space be given to its values. Surely everyone knows that
"an apple a day keeps the doctor away." A few years ago in
Michigan, where the apple is the state tree, 1300 students ran
a three-year test on apple-eating with results showing many less
respiratory infections, less tension-caused illnesses and general
sickness. The presence of ascorbic acid in apples was credited,
as well as a naturally occurring tranquilizer.

The place of apples in cookery is well known and to this may
be added the healing qualities of the seeds and skins found in
the pectin substance common to all apples. Also an apple before
bedtime is recommended for its effect on the gums. Cider is
known as a healthful drink and in countries where it is much

used, conditions such as kidney stone or calculus are unknown.

Although the apple as sold to the consumer is a product of orchards, nature-lovers should remember that the fruit of seedling wild apples is equally of value, as are also the smallish apples from wild or planted ornamental crab apples *(M. ioensis)*.

All of the books on dye-plants tell of the use of apple bark for producing good shades of yellow.

One wonders if Eve tempted Adam by feeding him an apple to cure his troubles, rather than just to display of its (and her) beauty.

Osmaronia cerasiformis—Oso berry, Indian plum.

A shrub belonging to the rose family, it is found on the West Coast with rather poorly-flavored fruit, although the fruit is edible raw or cooked.

Malus sylvestris

Potenilla anserina

Potentilla anserina—Silverweed, cinquefoil, goose-grass, goose tansy, five-finger.

A weed spread everywhere in the country, but coming from Eurasia, it is a low-growing, powdery-leafed plant with yellow flowers, as are many other *Potentillas*. In Gaelic it is known as "the seventh bread," as the roots when boiled or roasted are said to taste like parsnips.

Medicinally the top of the plant, gathered in June, then dried, is used in infusions for cases of difficult menstruation and in diarrhoea. Containing much tannin, it is also used for piles or for other conditions where an astringent is indicated. Taken with honey it is a good gargle for sore throat. Or strongly distilled, it is said to take away freckles or cure sunburn.

Prunus (various species of stone fruits).

Within the rose family itself, there are possibly more genera of useful plants than in any other family in this book. So also within this one genera, the *Prunus*, there are more species (and horticultural varieties) than with any other such classification. One standard reference book in listing *Prunus* describes nearly 100 species, a great many of which are native, to a greater or less extent, to all parts of our country.

From that number a few have been selected for mention as being very common or notable in their uses. As is surely realized by every reader of this book, the uses of cherries (of whatever kind) are commonly for fresh fruit or for making jams and jellies, usually of the improved cultivated kinds (often not as sharply tasty as the wild ones); in a few cases for medicines; and/or again the bark or roots are used for variously colored dyes.

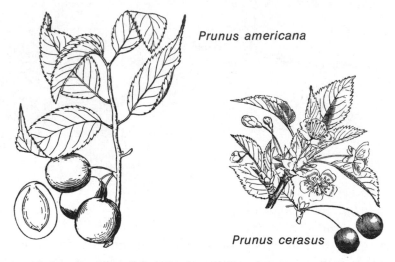

Prunus americana

Prunus cerasus

Beyond the purely wild or improved native sorts there are in common use such plants as the apricot, coming from China, the Japanese plums, the almond from western Asia, and the sloe from Europe. In the case of the apricot, there is presently interest in claims of possible cures of certain forms of cancer from the extract of the seeds. Some of the species worth noting are:

P. AMERICANA—River plum, wild plum. This is a tree growing to some 30 feet with usable fruit, prevalent in the eastern United States.

P. ANGUSTIFOLIA—Chickasaw plum. This is a small tree or bush found south and west from Delaware to Mississippi.

P. AVIUM—Sweet cherry, mazzard cherry. Although this is not a native, it has escaped and been improved. It is hard-fleshed and a fine sweet cherry.

P. BESSEYI—Sand cherry. The sand cherry is a bushy plant growing in the Midwest with black edible fruit.

P. CERASUS—Sour cherry. Again this is a plant from Asia, but much planted and naturalized with various names.

P. DOMESTICA—Common plum. Another import from Eurasia, a selection of this species is the famed Damson plum.

P. GRACILIS—Oklahoma plum. Found in Oklahoma and Texas, this is a tall shrub plant with usable fruit.

P. HORTULANA—Hortulan plum. A parent of a number of cultivated plums, the Hortulan plum is native of mid-central states.

P. ILICIFOLIA—Islay plum. A native of California, it is a tall evergreen tree with dark red fruits.

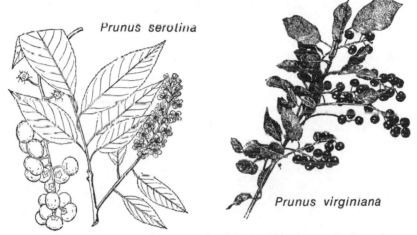

Prunus serotina

Prunus virginiana

P. LYONII—Islands cherry. Likely a variation of the above plant, it is found on coastal California islands.

P. PERSICA—Peach. A native of China, the peach has multiple variations.

P. PUMILA—Sand cherry. With variations, it is found as a dwarf or prostrate plant in moist locations in various parts of the Northeast.

P. MARITIMA—Beach plum. Along the East Coast to Virginia this often large-fruited bush gives tasty fruits for preserving and for commerce with tourists.

P. PENSYLVANICA—Wild red cherry. A northern cherry extending to Colorado, it has small red fruits.

P. SEROTINA—Wild black cherry, rum cherry. The fruits in the fall of this rather tall tree are wonderful for beautiful colored, tasty jelly, while a careful use of extracts of the bark has made it a part of excellent cough syrups.

P. SUBCORDATA—Pacific plum, Sierra plum. A small tree or large shrub found in California and Oregon, it has slightly acid fruits, especially good when they are juicy.

P. VIRGINIANA—Chokecherry. In some variety of species, this plant is found from East to West, and again is a small tree or large shrub, with drooping racemes of fruit which ripen in September. The small berries are flavorful and fine for jelly. As with *P. serotina,* it should be noted that the bark, the hard seeds, and the leaves contain cyanide and are poisonous for man or beast, but this same condition makes for use in effective cough remedies. These, with other fruits (among those above), the Indians ate raw or made into cakes after mashing the fruit, including the pits, and then (after leaching out the hydrocyanic acid with water) drying them for winter use separately or as a part of pemmican.

The juice of both the rum and the chokecherry makes possibly the most beautiful of all jellies, while the spicy flavor of the juice when boiled up with sugar, and used in equal parts with brandy, makes a tasty cordial which will bring guests to your home.

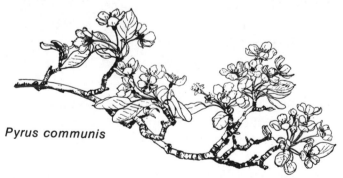

Pyrus communis

Pyrus communis—Pear.

Pears are a common home orchard fruit and everyone knows the goodness of its fruit, but there is a "useful" value in the pear tree in that the leaves are used by dyers to produce a good yellow-tan color.

***Rosa* (various species)**—Roses: native, introduced, or garden roses. Beyond the values of roses for landscape use, for the flower garden, or for your enjoyment in the wild, the great value from the standpoint of food or medicinal use is found in the fruits, seed cases, or what is more generally known as rose hips. For in these hips one finds a concentration of the vitamin essential for general good health and freedom from colds—Vitamin C. It is commonly known that this vitamin is found in oranges, but one claim being made is that, weight for weight, rose hips contain 40 times the Vitamin C of oranges, the fruit commonly accepted for its value.

As the fruit remains on the rose bushes all winter with values intact, it is a good emergency food, and even better is the fact that the "hippy" roses are found everywhere.

Coming to us from Japan is perhaps the rose with the largest hips, *Rosa rugosa,* found now not only naturally wild along

Rosa rugosa

beaches, where it is happy, but widely planted because of its fine foliage and flowers.

But there are other species which have additional values:

R. CAROLINA—A pasture rose from Canada to Texas.

R. GALLICA—Originally from Europe, it is used for rose oil for perfume.

R. MULTIFLORA (plus many minor species, wild or escaped from cultivation)—Recommended for protective fencing and the parent and/or root stock of many garden roses. It is invasive in small home landscapes.

In considering the values of the high content of Vitamin C found in rose hips, every gardener with rose bushes, or a forager in the wild, should do everything possible to gather and use rose-hips of whatever kind of bush they come from. The restorative virtues of these "apples of the rose" is no recent discovery but goes back hundreds of years. A lady attending one of the author's lectures a short time ago said that in England and Scandinavia during World War II many children might not have survived, except for the Vitamin C from the hips of the wild roses. The noted Linus Pauling has said in print and on television that he and his family take massive doses of Vitamin C tablets all to the maintenance of their health at an advanced age.

Some ways in which the reader might use rose hips would be these:

Rose Hip Jelly

1 quart clean rose hips
5 tart apples unpeeled
1 lemon and 1 teaspoon of cloves.
Cook altogether until tender, crush, and strain in jelly bag. Add 1 cup sugar to each cup of liquid. Boil until it jellies and put in jars. Tasty and healthful. With a similar mixture of ground and cleaned hips, a nice jam can be made.

Rose Hip Soup

5 cups of hips with seeds removed
4 1/2 ounces blanched almonds
4 drops vanilla
2 tablespoons flour
1 cup red wine
Pepper and salt to taste.
Grind hips and almonds in meat chopper, then cook ingredients together with five cups water for about five minutes. Add wine, boil five minutes more, chill, and then serve cold with whipped cream.

Rubus (**various species**)—Blackberry, blackcap, black raspberry, brambleberry, cloudberry, dewberry, loganberry, raspberry, salmonberry, thimbleberry, wineberry, etc.

As these members of the *Rubus* genera are widely spread over the United States, it is hardly necessary to distinguish and picture all the various kinds of what is perhaps the best known wild fruit. Nor is it possible, within the present limits, to list the various specific names, as in this family one standard botany lists 200 distinguishable species of *Rubus*, and when it comes down to just the blackberries, not even the best botanists are all agreed on nomenclature.

For those interested in useful plants, it is probably well known that beside the good fruit qualities, the blackberries, used either as fruit or as medicine prepared from the root-bark, are highly valuable in cases of diarrhoea, and every family should have such a medicine on hand for intestinal upsets.

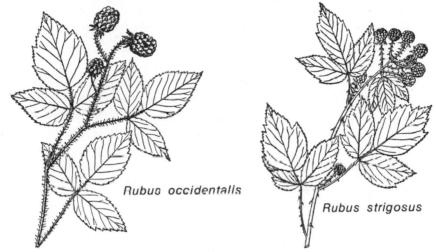

Rubus occidentalis

Rubus strigosus

Readers interested in dyeing will find that the young green shoots produce a color ranging from dark gray to almost black.

It is also worthy of note that the Indians in various sections of the country used the tender young shoots either raw or cooked, while off in another area comes the suggestion that the large young leaves of some species "make a fairly good toilet-paper substitute."

Sanquisorba (**various species**)—Burnet.
There are species of this wild plant, well known to people with herbal interests, found in both the East and the West. The young leaves are used in making salads and it is an herbaceous plant having flowers of variable color, on long, naked stalks.

Spiraea (**various species**)—Spiraea, hardhack, steeple-bush, etc.
In this genera are a number of very good plants much used in home landscaping, but for this survey one would mention only, *S. tomentosa* which grows from New England south and west.

Here one finds astringent medicinal qualities, as is true in great degree with the *Rubus*.

Sorbus (**various species**)—Mountain ash, rowan, service tree, etc. This is a small tree with fern-like compound leaves and attractive white flower heads, followed by clusters of bright red berries. The species *S. americana* is found in the eastern United States. While not quite as beautiful as the European mountain ash *(S. aucuparia)*, its berries have been used to treat scurvy and as a vermifuge. Some Indian tribes also used it for heart disease.

THE BUCKTHORN FAMILY

RHAMNACEAE

Ceanothus americanus—New Jersey tea, wild snowball, red-root. One of the most noteworthy of wild plants in colonial days, and one with much connection with the American Revolution, the New Jersey tea comes from a low shrub with downy leaves and

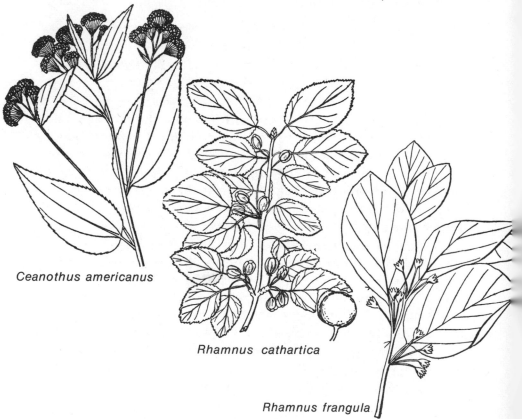

Ceanothus americanus

Rhamnus cathartica

Rhamnus frangula

white flowers, growing widely in the eastern states. After British tea was dumped in Boston Harbor, various substitutes were tried, principally the dried leaves of this plant. The knowledge of this was most likely taken from the Indians, since many tribes were using it for sundry medicinal purposes, none of them now acceptable.

Throughout the West there are a number of other species commonly called wild lilac, buckbrush, and soapbloom. This latter name comes from the fact that the fresh flowers of some species make an excellent lather when crushed and rubbed in water, making the skin soft and faintly fragrant.

Other species have provided a dye material from the roots, giving a cinnamon color to wool.

Rhamnus cathartica—Buckthorn, Indian cherry.

The common name will indicate the medicinal value of the berries of this tall shrub, which is often used in landscaping and which, while it is not a native American, is widely an escape.

As is true with other fruits of this genera, they are laxative and purgative, and should be used with care.

Rhamnus frangula—Black-alder, berry-alder, arrow-wood, bird cherry.

This is another imported shrub, now widely naturalized, as the new plants are distributed by birds. Growing about ten feet tall, it is a nice shrub with olive-green leaves and attractive fruit.

In this species the medicinal qualities are taken only from dried and seasoned bark, for extractions from the new bark may cause violent pains. Medicinally, it is, as above, a cathartic and purgative.

Rhamnus purschiana—Cascara sagrada, brittle wood, polecat tree, coffee berry.

In this case one finds this 20 foot native tree of the West Coast, along with a related species, *R. californica,* as another source of laxative medicine. Here again the bark is taken from this tree and dried well over a long period, and provides what one writer calls—"the most gentle and best laxative known." It is said that in the West, old-timers recommended using daily a little dried bark soaked in water overnight as a basic tonic. Today, one can buy this cascara in the local store and partake of one of the good American wild medicines.

The bark is also used for dyeing, when it is called chittam

wood, giving colors ranging from dark yellow-tan to browns, tans, and grey.

Interestingly the name Cascara sagrada was given the plant by the early Spanish missionaries (translated as the sacred bark) from the respect which they found the medicine had among the Indians.

THE MADDER FAMILY

RUBIACEAE

Cephalanthus occidentalis—Button-bush, honey balls, button-willow. One of the interesting water-edge shrubs of wide distribution, this plant is excellent to use for a landscape planting in a wet situation.

Like so many other natives it has long been valued for various medicinal purposes—one recipe calling for boiling the root and mixing with honey for "lung diseases."

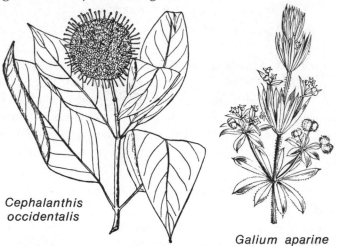

Cephalanthis
occidentalis

Galium aparine

Galium aparine—Cleavers, goosegrass, bedstraw, cheese rennet herb, etc.
This is another very widely spread herb for which a number of uses are suggested, although none of them is of great account. A list would include using: the roots for a yellow or yellow-red dye; the seeds roasted and ground as a substitute for coffee— a not surprising fact, as true coffee belongs to the same family. The dried plant is used as a tea substitute in some countries, and medicinally this species has been officially listed as an anti-scor-

butic. As the name indicates, it has found a purpose as a rennet to curdle milk for cheese-making and is said to import a sweet flavor to cheese.

Galium verum—Common cleavers, poor robin, gravel grass, Our
        Lady's Bedstraw.

Much the same thing may be said about this similar family member as for *G. aparine.* One pretty story about it is that one common name has been Our Lady's Bedstraw, a name coming from the fact that the plant gives out a pleasing fragrance when dried, and in some countries has been used as a stuffing for mattresses. It is interesting here to note the great number of plants which, in popular mythology, bear the name or connection with the Virgin.

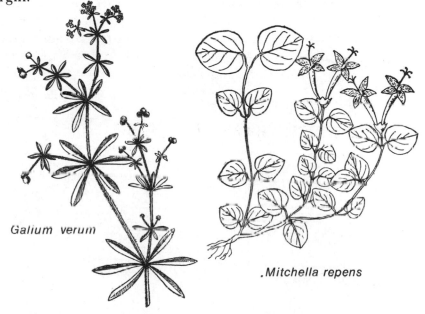

Galium verum

.Mitchella repens

Mitchella repens—Partridgeberry, checkerberry, squaw vine, winter
        clover, running box.

Throughout the East and down to Texas, one will find the checkerberry in moist deciduous woods. Anyone who roams the wild is apt to know this nice creeping, perennial and evergreen vine with its bright red berries. It is often gathered for use in little terraria in the home. Medicinally it was known to the Indians, as the name squaw vine indicates. It was used by them to ease parturition, being administered as a decoction of the dried plant in the last month of pregnancy.

THE RUE FAMILY
RUTACEAE

Possibly the most important fruit in the United States is the orange, which is not only the basis of economy in two states, but medicinally offers easily-obtained Vitamin C, as well as attractive food and drink. It is not, however, a "wild" plant in the sense of this book and hence will be only "noted."

Other members of the rue family include:

***Ptelea baldwinii*—Hoptree.**

This particular species is the form of the hoptree found in the Southwest, and is a small tree with growth similar to the species listed below. As in the East, the fruits of this plant have been used as a substitute for hops in brewing, and also they may be ground, mixed with yeast, and used to make quite a good bread.

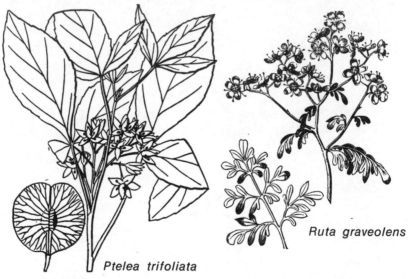

Ruta graveolens

Ptelea trifoliata

***Ptelea trifoliata*—Wafer-ash, hoptree, stinking ash, swamp dogwood, wing seed.**

The name stinking ash is applied here for, even as orange blossoms are overpowering when smelled closeup, the aroma of the flowers here is lovely only at a distance.

It is a shrub of the eastern United States, about ten feet tall with white flowers, followed by the little "wafers" or seeds which are the "hops substitute." Infusions of the bark are rated as soothing to the mucous membranes and as promoting appetite.

Ruta graveolens—Rue, herb-of-grace.

Here is a plant from the herb garden, grown for unknown centuries, and mentioned in the Bible and in much literature. A dwarfish, bluish-foliaged plant, it actually has small value today except where bitterness is needed in salads, etc. In the past, it has had a reputation for restoring dim vision and for tonic and sedative qualities. The second name above tells of how it was used in ancient times, in exorcisms by the early Church, while its strong odor was thought to be a protection against pestilence, and was used as a "bouquet" by judges on the bench, against possible infections. One curious tradition is that cuttings of it will only root well if stolen from another's garden, a fact which the author, as a life-long cutting-snitcher, knows about many other plants, as well.

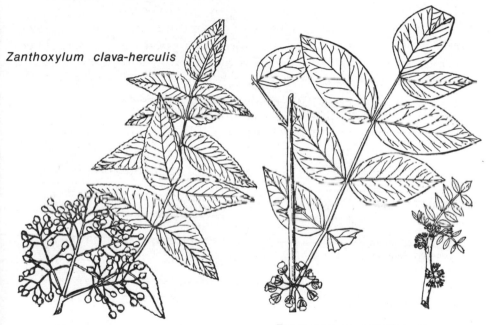

Zanthoxylum clava-herculis

Zanthoxylum americanum

Zanthoxylum americanum—Prickly ash, pellitory bark, toothache bush, yellow wood.

A large shrub growing throughout the Northeast, it is found on river banks and in rich woods. Here the bark of the stem is taken in spring and fall and prepared for use as a sudorific, tonic, or antispasmodic. The red fruits in the fall, which are aromatic, have been used as a flavoring.

Zanthoxylum clava-herculis—Hercules club, toothache tree, wild
     orange, prickly ash.
    A plant similar to *Z. americanum* but growing south from Virginia
to Florida and Texas, its values are much as other species, except that it seems to have more reputation as a cure for tooth-
ache, using extracts of the bark, leaves, and fruit.

THE WILLOW FAMILY

SALICACEAE

Within this family there are two genera, the poplars and the willows,
and many species of both, plus many natural hybrids. Not even the
expert botanists are able or willing to know all the "children" by
name. Of willows in this country there are said to be at least 150 kinds
identified, some of which have come from abroad, as have a few
poplars. Of this later genera not too much good can be said. The
economic uses of certain species provide pulp for paper manufacture; the buds of another provide qualities used in cough syrups,
while the leaves of some are used by dyeing enthusiasts to get a good
lime-yellow color. On the negative side, poplars are not good trees
to unthinkingly plant in the home landscape as the branches are
brittle, while the roots quickly inhabit drain pipes and clog them.
Species which are fairly well known and have some possible value are
these:

Populus balsamifera—Balsam-poplar, tacamahac, Carolina poplar.
    This grows in the northern and eastern part of the United States
    and has all of the above useful qualities plus an overabundance
    of root-invasiveness. A tree not to be planted in the home land-
    scape.

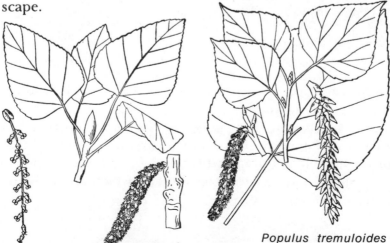

Populus tremuloides

Populus balsamifera

Populus candicans—Balm-of-Gilead, balm-buds.

Beyond many negative values, the dried winter buds of this tree produce a resin said to be very useful in healing wounds and internally a stimulating expectorant in the treatment of bronchitis.

Populus fremontii—Cottonwood, Fremont cottonwood.

A tall tree of California and Arizona found, as are most of the willow family, growing along streams or other wet places, and providing catkins in spring, which may be eaten raw or boiled in stews. The inner bark of this and other members of the family are said to have been eaten as emergency food by western Indians.

Populus tremuloides—Quaking aspen, white poplar, quiver leaf.

This American tree which is found, like so many others in this family, mostly in the cooler northern states, has always been interesting because of the quivering qualities of its leaves. Beyond this quality which has made it the subject of some mythology, it has in extracts of the bark about the same characteristics as the salicylic acid which is found in the willows, discussed below. One herbalist writer suggests that the extract of the bark is a substitute for quinine and that "for all cases of debility, indigestion, faintness, hysteria, etc." it may be freely given.

All of this is perhaps suggested in the lines from Sir Walter Scott where he says:

> Oh, woman! in our hours of ease
> Uncertain, coy, and hard to please,
> And variable as the shade
> By the light quivering aspen made,
> When pain or sickness rends the brow,
> A ministering angel thou.

The second of the two genera of the willow family is the willows themselves, the genus, *Salix,* and here there are many more qualities of usefulness than with the poplars. Probably first in the usefulness of willows by the populace at large is (or was) the medical use of the salicylates for the cure of pain and fever, a synthetic material now well known as aspirin. Approximately 150 years ago salicylic acid was isolated and found to be the reason why the Indians here knew the values of chewing willow bark, and the substance was named, as will be noted, from the name of *Salix.* When later synthesized it was named aspirin, after somewhat similar values known also to be in the spirea plant.

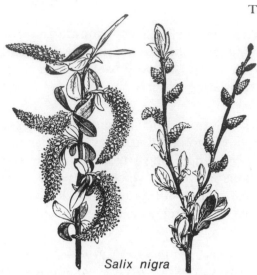

Salix nigra

But beyond this original and important substance, in the willows the genus has many other values, somewhat varying between the 150 species in this country. The Romans used willow wood as shields, and for centuries the young growth has provided material for wooden thongs, for basket-work, or for willow work furniture, in which circumstances the material from special species was known as *osier*. One American species, *S. nigra*, is grown in our Midsouth area for lumber. Other uses from special sorts are for artificial limbs, canes, cricket bats, and polo balls. Willow wood charcoal was once used in making gunpowder, or more latterly for artists' crayons. And what boy does not know of making whistles out of willow twigs, or using the flexible branches as fishing poles? The dyeing fraternity has found that the bark and leaves give a good rose-tan or yellow color. At one time the dried leaves were used to adulterate tea. Consequently, one could go on and on when discussing the values of willows, the only adverse comment being that, as with poplars, the roots can easily clog drainage systems and that their growth is sometimes over rapid. And yet for great variety of growth and graceful beauty many willows are lovely in the landscape, and especially the weeping willow which can provide a spot of relaxation, as we note in Psalm 137 where it says:

> By the rivers of Babylon, there we sat down, yea, we
> wept, when we remembered Zion . . . We hanged
> our harps upon the willows in the midst thereof.

Several species of willows to be noted are these:

Salix alba—White willow.

This is one of the European forms which has spread itself in many parts of our country. It is a tall tree with narrow leaves and flowers as catkins. In addition to the medicinal values above, a tea made of the dried leaves has been used in Appalachia to break up fevers.

Salix nigra—Black willow, pussy willow, swamp willow.
The bark of this species is used as noted above and the roots have been used in decoctions to purify the blood and for fever. The catkins are said to be an aphrodisiac.

THE SAXIFRAGE FAMILY
SAXIFRAGACEAE

Many plant families in this book represent an assemblage which is mostly found as trees, as herbaceous materials, annuals, or plants quite alike, but in this saxifrage family one finds an assortment of types of plants including some good shrubs such as the mock oranges, the deutzias, the hydrangeas; perennials such as the astilbes, heucheras, and bergenias; and some house plants such as the so-called strawberry geranium. Edible sorts are well known like currants and gooseberries, while some have moderately valuable medicinal properties.

Heuchera americana—Alum-root, American sanicle, cliff-weed, ground-maple.
This perennial herb grows in the East and to the Far West. Unimportant is the stalked flower head rising from basal leaves, but good to know is that campers who may contract diarrhoea may dig and eat the raw roots of this plant and effect a prompt cure. There are several other species of similar nature having the same basic properties.

Hydrangea arborescens—Smooth hydrangea, seven-barks.
This plant, often used as an ornamental, grows widely in all the eastern United States and is recognized by the large oval leaves and white or greenish flower heads. The roots and rhizomes have been used as a diuretic, cathartic, and tonic, with some reputation for values in preventing kidney stones.

Peltiphyllum peltatum—Umbrella plant, Indian rhubarb, great shield-leaf.
A native of the Northwest, this coarsely leaved perennial is

found along streams, and was most likely used by the Indians. The fleshy leafstalks may be peeled and eaten as is, or in salad. They may also be cooked, but this destroys some of the flavor.

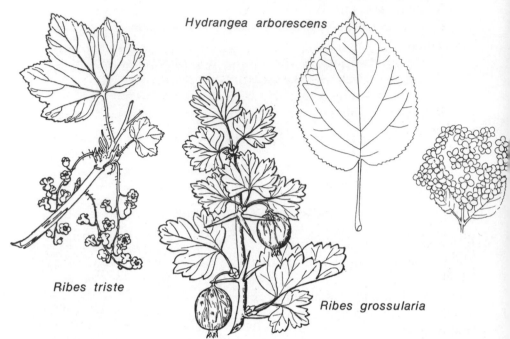

Hydrangea arborescens

Ribes triste

Ribes grossularia

Ribes (various species)—Currants, gooseberries.

In this genera there are many, many species extant in the nation, some wild, some cultivated, and some natural or produced hybrids. Most readers will certainly know the values of the fruits used raw, dried, or cooked, and certainly we know they were much used by the Indians in making pemmican, while some are mildly medicinal for stomach complaints.

The negative aspect of the genera is that a number of species are the host to the white pine blister rust, with prohibitions against growing them, where this lovely pine grows. The native black currant, *R. americanum,* makes a tasty jam, but because of its being a host to the disease, it and the even better European black currant, *R. nigrum,* are under prohibitions for planting. These latter black currants are especially valuable for providing, with extraction of the juice, a wonderful alleviant to a sore throat, while an infusion of the leaves is cleansing and diuretic —all to say nothing of the delicious nature of black currant wine. If permitted to be grown in the reader's part of the country, this is one of the best of all fruit plants for the garden.

Among other more common species and their home area are these:

R. AUREUM—The Midwest and West.

R. CEREUM—The West Coast.

R. GROSSULARIA—The cultivated gooseberry imported from Europe.

R. ODORATUM—South Dakota down to Texas.

R. ROTUNDIFOLIUM—Massachusetts to North Carolina.

R. SATIVUM—The common red currant brought from Europe.

R. TRISTE—The native red currant found across the northern United States.

THE FIGWORT FAMILY

SCROPHULARIACEAE

In some ways this family brings together a strangely assorted lot of plants, many of them truly native wild plants, and others, wildings which have given us choice garden subjects. The evident reason for being in this family is that with tiny or large flowers, all of them have tubular blooms such as everyone knows in the common foxglove or snapdragon.

Castilleja (various species)—Indian paintbrush, painted cup.
Mostly found in dry open ground in the West, this plant with red-flowered stalks is a conspicuous flower of the area and the flowers are rated in most species as edible when picked raw and fresh.

Chelone glabra—Balmony, snake-head, turtle-head, fishmouth.
A widely spread plant in this country, its common names suggest the appearance of individual flowers. It grows in moist lowlands and was used medicinally by the Indians. Present recommendations are that the leaves are used for reducing inflammations and as a remedy for worms, and for general tonic purposes.

Digitalis purpurea—Foxglove, thimbles, fairy fingers.
Although not a native plant, it has widely escaped throughout our country, and probably the name of *Digitalis* is the best known of all medicinal plants, especially for use in various cardiac difficulties, the value of which was first made known to the medical profession by a housewife in Britain. But as such a medicine, it should be taken only under medical supervision, as a little too much ceases to be beneficial and is very poisonous.

Gratiola officinalis—Hedge-hyssop.

This is a plant of ditches and muddy spots throughout the United States which, while poisonous to cattle, has been used as a strong cathartic, diuretic, and emetic.

Linaria vulgaris—Toad-flax, butter and eggs.

A common and widely known little yellow-flowered weed with flowers similar to snapdragons. It is recommended to be used for jaundice (in tincture) and externally for hemorrhoids. One correspondent of the author's reports that a salve made from toad-flax has been found of value in curing poison ivy in his family.

Pedicularis canadensis—Wood-betony, lousewort.

One species of this small-growing, purplish-flowered herb grows widely in all the East, while other forms are found in the West. It was used by the Indians to cure rattlesnake bites and as a magic charm, although to sheep eating it, it is poisonous.

Scrophularia marilandica—Figwort, healall, pilewort, scrophula plant, etc.

This one plant, bearing the above generic name, has many, many common appellations according to locality. It is a tall growing perennial found in the East to the Mississippi (other species in the West). The many names of "wort" indicate long-known medicinal values, which include such uses as diuretic, diaphoretic, tonic, and especially reducing hemorrhoids.

Verbascum thapsus—Mullein, verbascum, flannel plant, candlewick, lungwort, as well as some 25 other common names.

Too often in this book, great values are placed on plants not outstanding in beauty, but the lovely gray foliage of this plant in winter and spring, plus the six foot spikes of long-blooming yellow flowers in summer, make this one of the finest of our widespread wildflowers.

Its uses are many, it being noted that the Greeks and Romans dipped the great stalks in oils and used them as candles, while in Wisconsin, young girls wishing to have pink cheeks at dances, would rub their faces with the "fur" of the young leaves. In Appalachia, a tea made of the leaves is used for colds, while in New Mexico the dried leaves are smoked as a treatment for asthma. Among the Navajos it is also smoked for the alleviation of "mild mental disturbances." One correspondent writes that fresh leaves wrapped around a bleeding finger make a fine emer-

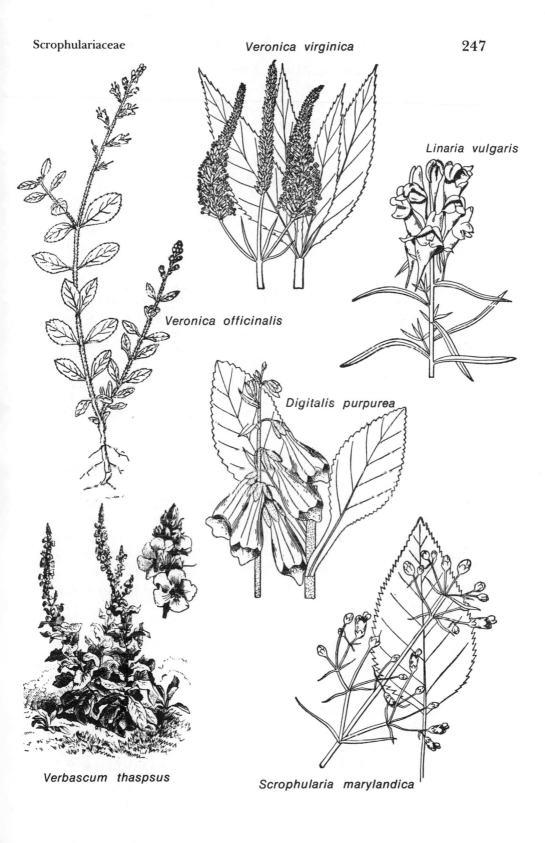

Veronica virginica

Linaria vulgaris

Veronica officinalis

Digitalis purpurea

Verbascum thaspsus

Scrophularia marylandica

gency bandage. As a dye plant it gives material for a good yellow color.

Verbascum is thus one of the very good plants of this book to admire, as well as to use.

Veronica (**various species**)—Speedwell, culver's root, physic root, brooklime.

Veronicas are an herbaceous plant with blue flowers, of which some species are found in the East and others in the West, usually in moist places. Various names suggest medicinal uses, and it has been used for scurvy, as a cathartic and emetic, but care should be taken against overuse of any extracts from the roots. One writer in the West says that the leaves and stems may be eaten in salad.

Closely related to the Veronicas and bearing the same common names, is *Veronicastrum virginicum,* a seven-foot-growing herb found from Vermont to Texas and with similar medicinal uses.

THE NIGHTSHADE FAMILY
SOLANACEAE

Next to corn, this truly American family, with its deadly-sounding name, has offered to the world not only some very poisonous plants, but a list of valuable vegetables without which the world would be much poorer. It is, to the author, the true American family, especially in those genera coming from South America, such as the potato, the tomato, red peppers, and egg plant. And who could forget the family's contribution to our flower gardens in the form of the petunias, schizanthus, browallias, and others? Or in the world-wide trade and use of tobacco?

In presenting below the native states of the plants which are found in the wild, any reader who disagrees with nomenclature should remember the comment of the author of *Hortus* when he says that the genus of *Solanum* in this family "is difficult to botanists."

Capsicum frutescens—Red pepper.

Here is a native American plant, of the warm areas of our country, and one which with hybridization appears in many different varieties. The culinary uses of these hot peppers are known to everyone, while medicinally a fluid extract of the berries is listed as a sedative for cases of epilepsy.

Chamaesaracha coronopus—No common name.

This is a wild plant of Arizona of which the berries were used either raw or cooked by the Navajo and Hopi Indians.

Datura stramonium—Jimson weed, Jamestown weed, datura, stramonium, apple of Peru, thorn apple, stinkweed, devil's trumpet, angel's trumpet.

A very widely spread, ill-scented weed, it grows to four feet, producing a thick capsule of seeds. Like other members of the family it contains hyoscymine, atropine, and other powerful drugs. It is extremely poisonous because of this, and is used professionally as an antispasmodic, antiasthmatic, and sedative. In Appalachia, poultices made of the leaves have been used to treat wounds and kill pains while in the Southwest it has been used as an hallucinogenic. Other species of Europe and South America have similar properties, it being said that the delphic oracle used the plant to produce visions and prophecies. But, in general, one should beware of this poisonous plant and its cousins.

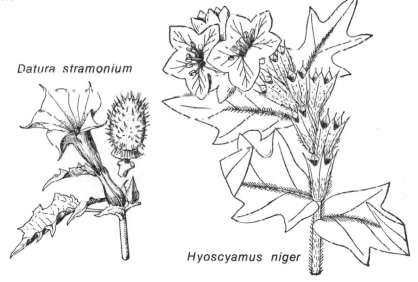

Datura stramonium

Hyoscyamus niger

Hyoscyamus niger—Henbane, stinking nightshade, poison tobacco.

Again a barnyard plant of which the name of "bane" should indicate its danger, as the drugs from this are not unlike those of *Datura*. It is found across the country to Montana.

Lycium pallidum—Wolf berry, desert thorn, squaw berry, tomatillo.

These are shrubby, spiny plants, often vining, as is the commonly cultivated matrimony vine from Europe. This species grows from Utah to Mexico. The scarlet berries have been used for sauce, but are not as hot as other members of the "pepper" group.

Lycopersicon esculentum—Tomato.

Little need be said of the culinary values of the common tomato and while it may not seem to be a wild plant, it does easily seed itself in and out of gardens.

Nicotiana tabacum—Tobacco.

Little need be said about the sedative values of tobacco or of the world-wide use made of the dried leaves of this and other species of the genus. It is perhaps interesting that while the truly poisonous qualities of other members of the *Solanaceae* family are fully known, it is only in recent years that the cumulative effects of tobacco have made smoking a "deadly" habit.

Physalis (**various species**)—Ground cherry, husk tomato, tomatillo, strawberry tomato.

There are a number of species of this plant, some growing well in the North and others in warm climatic zones. The berries are often covered by a husk and mostly they are good to eat when fully ripe, and especially when made into preserves and pies.

Solanum dulcamara

Solanum (**various species**)—Potato, egg plant, etc.

There are a great number of species of this genus which bears the family name, some of which are edible and others which are noxious or just plain bad weeds. Principally to be noted here is that all the *Solanums,* like other genera here, have poisonous properties including the common potato, which is so basic to our diet. If potatoes are left exposed to the sun for a time after being dug, and become green in appearance, their use should be avoided, just as no one should have a diet of the raw skins of potato, which is where the alkaloid poison resides.

Worthy of special note in this genus is the common woody vine of Europe, much naturalized here, called the climbing or bitter nightshade, *Solanum dulcamara,* of which the scarlet berries are poisonous.

This plant varies from that of *Solanum nigrum,* widely known as the black-berried nightshade, of which some cultivated forms are known as the garden huckleberry or wonderberry and where the poison is found in the unripe berries, but not as bad as in the red-berried form.

Solanum carolinense—Horse nettle, bull nettle, apple of Sodom, nightshade.

This plant grows wild in the dry fields and pine barrens from southern Canada to Illinois and down to Texas and the uses of the plant are much as others in the family. The ripe fruit is reputed to be diuretic; the root is sedative to the central nervous system and has had uses in asthma, bronchitis, etc.

Solanum fendleri—Wild potato.

Growing in open pine forests of New Mexico and Arizona, this, like *S. jamesii* of the Rocky Mountain area, has small tubers which may be cooked as our cultivated potato, but everyone should remember that the *Solanums* contain the active poison called solanine which suggests that all should be cooked before eating.

BOG MOSS

SPHAGNALES

Sphagnum symbololium—Sphagnum moss.

However much this lowly and bog-loving moss which is found growing almost everywhere, may be outside the generally-flowering plants of this book, no discussion of useful plants could ignore the values of sphagnum. Certainly we know that it is the deeply-buried lower dead parts of sphagnum which give us the useful peat moss which, when wet, is so retentive of moisture in the garden.

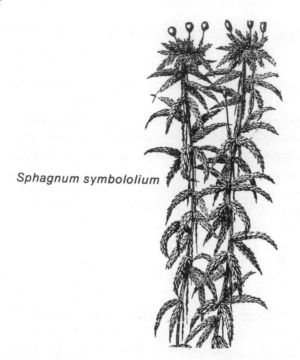

Sphagnum symbololium

But the top living growth of sphagnum is also useful in many ways and should be collected and used by every gardener or householder. For garden use this moss, partly dried and ground up, is ideal for a growth medium for rare seeds, as the chemistry of it resists the growth of fine algae and diseases which might affect seedlings. Other garden uses as a medium which retains up to 20 times its own weight in water will suggest themselves.

In the household, the use of this moss to absorb blood in emergency situations should be recognized because the acids in the moss contain healing qualities and possibly some iodine. During the last war it was used for dressings in England, and it is known that the Indian mothers used it for diaper material and very likely for wounds. Certainly for sanitary napkins it would have great values and at times has been used in their manufacture. This plant rates high on the list of useful plants.

THE BUR-REED FAMILY

SPARGANIACEAE

Sparganium androcladum, S. americanum, **and** *S. eurycarpum*—Bur-reed.

Aquatic plants found in shallow waters or on muddy shores, there are a number of species quite alike in appearance except for the variable seed-heads. The bulbous base of the stem, and the tubers of the rhizome, are edible when cooked.

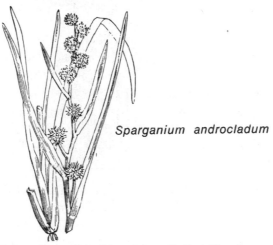

Sparganium androcladum

Members of this genus are found in all the Northern hemisphere and this was one of the medicinal plants of the "founder" of medicine, Dioscorides, who, 50 years before Christ, claimed the root and seed of the bur-reed drunk in wine would help cure snake bites.

THE LINDEN FAMILY

TILIACEAE

Tilia americana—Basswood, American linden, whitewood, lime.

In the Northeast quadrant of our country grow the attractively barked, giant basswood trees, the wood of which has value for making wooden ware, and the inner bark for roping and mats, while the bees find honey in the flowers. There are some records of the medicinal uses of the bark. Of special note here is the fact that the flowers of a much-planted European species of the *Tilia*

(*T. cordata*) which is known there as the lime or linden, is the source, using the dried fresh flowers, of a slightly sedative and pleasing linden tea or, in France, what is more commonly known as "tilleul."

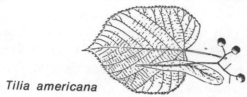

Tilia americana

In making cordage of the bark as did many of the Indian tribes, the inner bark, found in various layers, is pulled apart and separated into long threads by running the fingernails between the fibers. Light twine can then be made by taking two of these thin strands and twisting them together in one direction between the palm of the hand and the thigh. At the end cut one strand shorter than the other and add on by more twisting of additional threads. This can be continued until it is of considerable length and then these strands can be further combined with others to make cord of desired strength.

THE CATTAILS

TYPHACEAE

Typha angustifolia **and** *T. latifolia*—Cattails, flags, reed mace.
The cattail grows, as is known to every nature-lover, in the edges of swamps and shallow waters, in every part of our country. Euell Gibbons, a well-known nature writer, says of the cattail that it rates as "the supermarket of the swamps."*

One writer on the Rocky Mountain flora says that both the broad and narrow-leaved cattails are perhaps the "most famous of all edible plants of the Northern hemisphere" to which one might add the word "useful"—for not only are the roots used for food, but the young shoots and even the pollen have value, and beyond this the dried stalks are excellent for weaving rush seats or the down for tinder and for garment insulation.

Detailed uses are these:

1. The tender cores of the young plants are excellent for green salad or for cooking an asparagus-like vegetable.

2. When the pollen spike is partly developed it may be boiled and eaten like corn-on-the-cob.

3. Later when the pollen is ripe, it can be shaken off and added to wheat flour, being very high in protein.

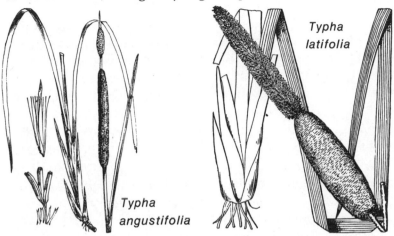

Typha latifolia

Typha angustifolia

4. In early summer, when the young white shoots appear, they can be eaten.

5. The rootstock can be dug, dried, peeled, pounded, and a nutritious flour sifted out.

6. The down from developed heads is excellent material for stuffing garments and as a filler for life preservers.

7. The dried stalks were much used by Indians for making mats and bags.

8. The twisted cattail leaves are the prime material for making rush seats, which are most comfortable and long-lasting.

9. The young flower stalks in summer are ideal for adding to bold bouquets, and when dried, they are useful for long-lasting arrangements.

10. Medicinally, the down was used by Indians, mixed with animal fat, for a healing poultice for cuts, bruises, and burns.

Altogether, not only one of the most useful plants of this book but in addition, cattails have a certain bold beauty that place them at the top of most lists.

THE ELM FAMILY

ULMACEAE

***Celtis* (various species)**—Hackberry, sugar-berry, bastard elm.
A tallish tree with several species, it is found mostly in more northern sections of the country. The leaves are similar to the common elm in shape, but the little flowers are followed by small orange, red, or yellow fruit which is sweetish and is edible raw. From the far West comes a report that among some Indians the fruit was dried and ground up, the pit and all being made into flour.

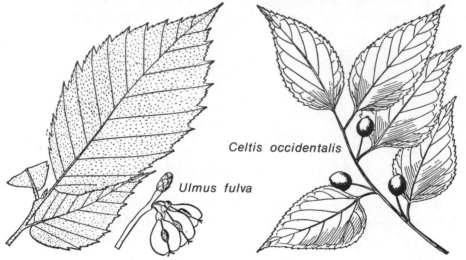

Celtis occidentalis

Ulmus fulva

***Ulmus fulva*—**Slippery, moose, or red elm.
In the East, from north to south, grows this smallish elm tree, not too unlike the American elm, whose future as a tree is so uncertain at present. The tree has rough, gray, and fragrant bark and the inner bark is mucilaginous, from whence comes the common name of slippery elm. This substance has long been used, most commonly for treating colds and bronchial affections and for plasters, as well as a laxative. Its values were well known to the Indian squaws who also used it as a tea for some months in advance, to ease child-birth pains.

THE PARSLEY FAMILY

UMBELLIFERAE

Aegopodium podograria variegata—Gout weed, bishops-weed.

Here is a green and white variegated-leaf plant (and also a plain green one) which has become naturalized in the United States, and a real invading pest it can become, however nice as a pretty ground cover. One author says that the young leaves are eaten in Sweden and Switzerland in the spring as a fresh green.

It so happens that this is about the first Latin name which this author learned, and all readers are invited to pronounce the name out loud and note the poetic lilt to the threesome of words.

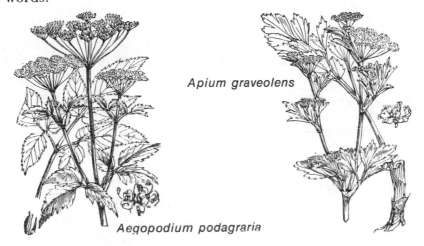

Apium graveolens

Aegopodium podagraria

Aethusa cynapium—Fool's parsley.

A slender plant much resembling parsley, it is found growing in waste places in many spots in Canada and the United States. Like a number of members of this family it is poisonous (see *Conium* below) and, however similar it is to parsley, should not be used as a substitute.

Apium graveolens—Celery, smallage, marsh parsley.

In the wild form our common and improved celery has a wide habitat in the world, including, it is reported, existence in California. Mentioned as a possible medicinal plant back in Greek times, it has come to be a common (and not poisonous) vegetable of our markets. The seed which is used as a condiment, has often been recommended as a cure for rheumatism and it has also been mixed with linseed for making poultices.

Angelica atropurpurea—Angelica, Alexanders, masterwort.

The plant of the name angelica which is commonly known to herbalists is a plant of Europe, but this one, which grows and looks like a huge five foot plant of celery, although having some slight use medicinally, is still among those plants which are slightly poisonous.

It may be of interest in this connection to note that decoctions of the European species of angelica are part of the flavoring of such drinks as vermouth and chartreuse, and sometimes an addition to the flavoring of gin which is usually produced from juniper berries.

Carum carvi—Caraway.

This is a European plant which has become naturalized in many places and likely most readers know of the pleasant taste of caraway seeds which additionally are said to be a mild stomachic.

Another species, *A. gairdneri,* is native on the West Coast where it is called squaw-root, but what the squaws used it for is not known.

Cicuta maculata—Water-hemlock, snakeweed, cowbane, musquash-root, children's bane.

One need only to read the names of this plant of the swamps of the East Coast to take warning of its poisonous nature. Any part of the plant is dangerous to ingest, but especially the roots.

Conium maculatum—Poison hemlock.

Again a plant with much the same fern-like leaves of various members of the parsley family, this is a European plant naturalized in this country. One method of identification is by the six-foot height to which it grows and the purplish blotches on the stems. This is the plant used to make the potion which killed Socrates some 2400 years ago and is very, very dangerous. Learn to recognize it.

Cryptotaenia canadensis—Honewort, wild chervil.

A plant of the rich woods from North to South, it grows about two feet tall. The tops are used as a green and it was first reported as valuable by the discerning Swedish explorer of America, Peter Kalm. It is deemed a most important vegetable crop in Japan where the young leaves are eaten boiled and the roots fried.

Cymopterus purpurescens—Gamote, camote.

This is a plant of our Southwest and one often found in Mexico, where the root is said to be much sweeter than parsnip. It is a

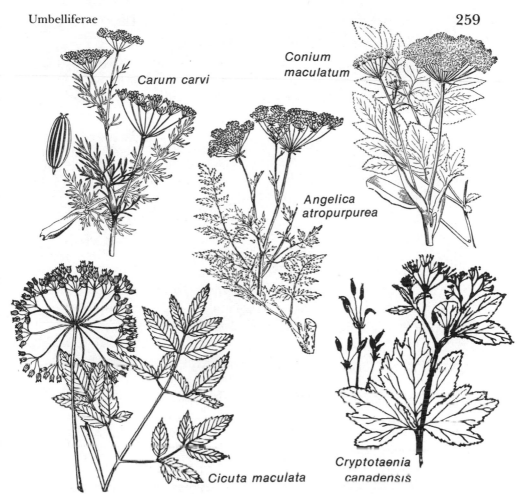

Carum carvi

Conium maculatum

Angelica atropurpurea

Cicuta maculata

Cryptotaenia canadensis

small, stemless perennial rising from a slender taproot.

Daucus carota—Queen Anne's lace, wild carrot.

Probably one of the most beautiful and decoratively useful weeds of the wide-open fields everywhere are the lacy white heads of Queen Anne's lace and from this wild form has come, over the years, the essential vegetable—the common carrot.

Eryngium aquaticum—Button snakeroot, rattlesnake master.

This interesting plant of the eastern United States grows in wet soils with white or pale blue flower-heads. As suggested by the name, it has been used as a possible cure for snakebites with other suggested values. Certain Indian tribes used a drink made from the plant as an emetic at festivals, as part of their rituals.

Heracleum lanatum—Cow parsnip, masterwort, mouthwort, hogweed; cow cabbage.

This is one of the largest-growing perennial herbs, found in wet

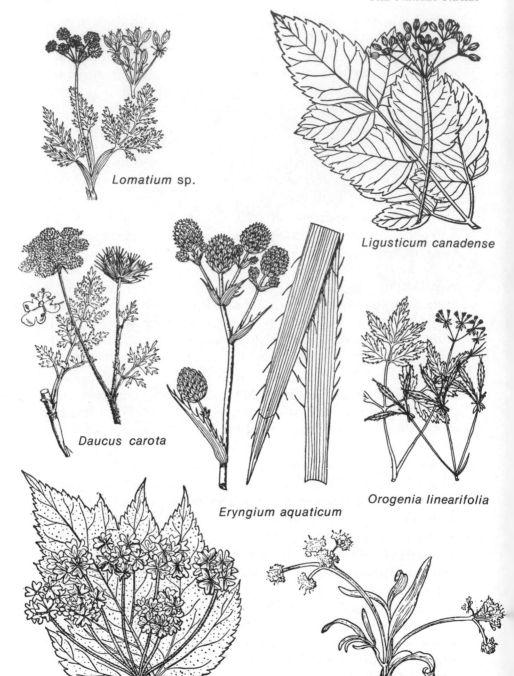

Lomatium sp.

Ligusticum canadense

Daucus carota

Eryngium aquaticum

Orogenia linearifolia

Heracleum lanatum

Osmorhiza longistylis

spots in much of North America. Growing up to eight feet in height, it is bold in effect and is often planted in "wild gardens" for its appearance. The young growth is said to be edible and with an aromatic and sweetish flavor, and is noted as one of the food plants of Indians. The strongly flavored basal part of the plants was used also by them as a substitute for salt.

Ligusticum canadense—Nondo, American savage, angelica, white root.

A plant of the rich woods from Pennsylvania to Kentucky, it has umbels of white flowers, and the seeds which follow were used by Indians as a cough remedy. Another species is *L. filicinum.*

Lomatium (various species)—Biscuitroot.

A genera of some six species of perennial herbs with thickened roots, all are found growing in arid dry grounds of the West. All of the species have edible roots, but tea can be made from the leaves, stems, and flowers. The roots are edible in a raw state or they may be dried and ground into flour. The tiny seeds also can be eaten raw or roasted. It is reported that Indians and early settlers made "cakes" of this flour, which, when dried and become hard, were hung on saddle bags as emergency food.

Orogenia linearifolia—Turkey pea, Indian potato, snowdrops.

This is a tiny plant of the Rocky Mountain area which grows only about three inches tall, with foliage coming directly from the root system. These roots are rubber-like and make a palatable food either fried, baked, or boiled.

Osmorhiza longistylis—Sweet Cicily, anise root.

A native of much of eastern United States it is one of the familiar plants to herb gardeners and medicinally is known for its aromatic and stomachic qualities.

Petroselinum crispum—Parsley.

It is perhaps not in order to include here a strictly garden resident, but parsley is such a common plant and so long cultivated that a word should be said about its value as a medicinal-food plant and its history. It was first mentioned by Greek writers. It has a connection with death due to the fact that the leaves of the second year (it is a biennial) are poisonous, as are so many other members of the family, which bears its common name.

It used to be said that parsley seed was slow to germinate because the seeds "must visit the nether regions three times, to

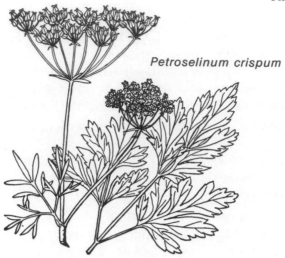

Petroselinum crispum

obtain permission to grow in the earth." Not true, but it is a fact that seed will not germinate unless it is truly fresh.

Medicinally (in addition to its value as a graceful adornment to many dishes on the table) it is known as a good diuretic, and especially as a kidney stimulant if combined with juniper berries or onions.

THE NETTLES

URTICACEAE

Urtica dioica—Nettle, stinging nettle.

Although the nettles are European plants, they are widely spread through the United States and many people suppose, because of the stings from the tiny "poisonous" spines on the leaves, that they are poisonous, and a plant to be uprooted. And yet the nettles have been used from ancient times for all sorts of purposes: cooked as food, a source of fiber for weaving, a source of dye and in some areas a source of home remedies.

Nettles are a tall-growing perennial, which grow in sun or shade, in poor or rich ground. On the food level one writer allows that it is the most nutritious and tasty of any plant food, rich in vitamins A and C and in protein, and is to be cooked like spinach. Another recommendation is to use it as a substitute for rennet in milk, or after the whole plant is dried, use the leaves for tea. For a good yellow dye the roots are boiled.

Urtica dioica

To list all the medicinal uses which are suggested for nettles would take too much space, but one authority says that nettle seeds are "accepted medicine for the cure of tuberculosis" or an infusion of the seeds for goiter. Another method of use, recommended for rheumatism, would work on the theory of "counter-irritation," wherein bundles of fresh nettles are used as whips to beat rheumatism sufferers on the part affected, the pain of the nettles (and possibly the acid injections) covering up, if not curing, the suffering.

Dian Buchman in her book on beauty treatments with herbs says that nettle juice is considered particularly effective for dandruff. She suggests a strong infusion of four tablespoons of nettle leaves to a pint of water, boiled for several hours. Add to this a quarter of a cup each of cider vinegar and eau de cologne, and massage nightly.

Thus it is that one finds that a disreputable weed may actually be close to the top of a list of useful plants.

THE VALERIAN FAMILY

VALERIANACEAE

Valerian edulis—Edible valerian, tobacco root.

With the exception of California, this plant is a wide spread wild plant, a perennial about two feet high. It is related to the species *V. officinalis*, the European garden valerian, which is a medicinal plant cultivated for use as a calmative in nervousness and hysteria.

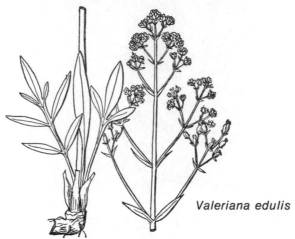

Valeriana edulis

As indicated by the name, *V. edulis* is edible in that the rather ill-smelling roots are rendered palatable by long steaming. It can be eaten as is, made into soup, or dried and ground into bread flour. These plants were an important food source to a number of western Indian groups.

Referring to the ill-smelling roots, it is said that valerian acts upon cats much as does catnip, and in fact, also on rats. It is said that the secret of the Pied Piper of Hamelin was the roots of valerian which he carried in his pocket.

THE VERVAIN FAMILY

VERBENACEAE

Verbena hastata—Blue verbena or vervain, iron weed, simpler's joy, wild hyssop.

A tall-growing perennial with violet-blue flowers, this plant is found very widely in this country. Although with a bitter quality, it was roasted and ground into flour by California Indians. There are some records of medicinal uses, but no strong claims are made for it.

An exploration of the story of vervain does, however, lead us down some ancient avenues and provides an explanation for belief in the efficacy of the plant in herbal medicine. As with so many of our customs, one starts with the Romans, who gave us the name verbena, which to them meant any one of a number of plants used in sacrifices, purgation, supplications, and the

Verbena hastata

like. Finally the name was attached to one particular plant, and the virtues ascribed to verbena by the Romans were passed along through the centuries, until in the Middle Ages, it was said to have been a plant which, growing on the Mount of Calvary, staunched the wounds of the Saviour. The transferral of virtues from pagan to Christian (like our Christmas celebrations) was not unusual and it early became one of the holy herbs associated with St. John. A writer in 1608, John White, wrote that when vervain was picked it was to be crossed with the hand, blessed with a charm or a suitable verse, and then worn about the neck against "blasts."

Again in Roman times we find Pliny saying that "if the dining chamber be sprinkled in water in which the herb verbena has been steeped, the guests will be merrier." Such a story led to a belief in its efficacy as a cure against the plague, and actually one finds it described, as with other herbs, as a remedy for almost anything. It even had supernatural powers and several Welsh names have meanings such as "devil's hate" and "enchantment herb." An ancient couplet goes:

> Vervain and Dill
> Hinders witches from their will.

It is the exploration of stories such as this which often reveals the none-too-scientific basis for the medical reputation of many plants. And yet one does find this species of verbena noted in Youngken's pharmacognosy book, indicating that the constituent of the plant is "a bitter glucoside, verhenalin," and that hot infusions of the dried plant are employed as a diaphoretic, tonic, and expectorant.

THE VIOLETS

VIOLACEAE

Viola **(various species)**—Violets of many specific and varietal names. The second book published by the author, back in 1926, was on the cultivation of violets, and there is more to write about in this family than just on the usefulness of violet plants and flowers.

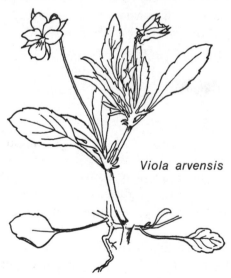

Viola arvensis

Years ago, I supplied shipments of violet flowers for experimental use as a cancer cure, but there is nothing likely in such a use, as the suggestion came from a centuries-old supposed cure of some royal person. Going back in time even further, the

Roman, Pliny, recommended a garland of violets as a cure for a hangover headache, a further doubtful value.

One herbal writer of repute, Fernie, points out that the acrid principle in juices from the violet plant provides material of value in the treatment of boils, empetigo, ulcers, and other eruptions. Other writers basically concur with his findings, and it might be worth a trial.

Another more common use for violet flowers is in crystallizing them as an adornment to ice cream and the like, while, reduced to a syrup, the flowers provide a coloring agent for candy.

One writer from our Northwest suggests using the leaves and buds in salads, perhaps cooked up as a pot-herb, or used to thicken soups. Actually the leaves of violets are a rich source of Vitamin C, perhaps indicating why preparations of violets have been used since medieval times to treat a variety of illnesses.

GRAPES

Vitaceae

Vitis (**various species**)—Grapes: native, hybridized, and imported. It could well be said that this final family of a long list of useful plants should perhaps have been the first family to have been explored, for, long before Columbus, about the year A.D. 1006, Viking explorers found some bunches of grapes in America and gave the country the name of Vinland, just as, only 600 years later, the English explorer Gosnold found great fields of wild grapes on this author's home island and named it Martha's Vineyard.

Some years later, a wild seedling was named Concord, and from this and other findings have come a whole race of grapes, some, like the variety Niagara, just as good for wine as ancient European sorts, but also of great importance in providing disease-free root systems used everywhere around the world.

It is well known that the fine wild grapes of a number of species found variably from East to West were valued by the Indians, not only for luscious fruit to be eaten and juiced, but as medicine. Dr. Sidney Riggs, a local Indian authority, tells of how, for instance, the leaves were bound on the head for headaches. From the modern medical viewpoint, the values of grapes are listed as antiscorbutic and refrigerant, while more popularly the "sugar energy" of fresh grape juice is much advertised.

This sweetness of all grapes is easily converted to alcohol for the production of wine, which is well known to "gladden the heart," as is recommended in the Bible when Paul says: Drink no longer water, but use a little wine for thy stomach's sake.

A further use of products of the vine is the culinary custom introduced to Americans from the Near East, wherein the cooking of meat is done in rolled-up grape leaves—either freshly gathered, dried, or preserved through salting.

Vitis labrusca

One final use of the grapes is for providing a good violet color for dyeing woolens.

Among the more common of the grape species in this country would be these:

V. AESTIVALIS: Summer grape—from New England to Kansas.

V. ARIZONICA: Canyon grape—Texas to California.

V. CANDICANS: Mustang grape—Arkansas to Texas.

V. CINEREA: Sweet winter grape—Texas north to Illinois.

V. LABRUSCA: Fox grape—New England to Georgia.

V. RIPARIA: Riverbank grape—Maine to Texas.

V. ROTUNDIFOLIA: Muscadine—Delaware south to Mexico.

V. VINIFERA: Wine grape—Largely in California.

V. VULPINA: Frost grape—Pennsylvania to Florida and west.

LICHENS

It is not possible here to extend a discussion of a group of plants such as lichens very far, for the number of various species of lichens is limitless. One authority says that there are 16,000 known kinds of lichens, and an examination of them is a subject not too appealing to either botanist or gardener. It may be worth noting here that these curious flowerless plants are extremely interesting, in that any one form of a lichen combines within the odd shape and color, and is actually a composite organism consisting of a fungus living symbiotically with an algae. In this organism takes place complicated chemical reactions, so much so that this chemical and the acids thus formed result in the extremely slow disintegration of rocks on which the lichens often grow, thus changing, through the millenia, rocks into soil.

Disregarding all the colorful beauty of many lichen-covered stone walls and woodsy scenes, the values of lichens for those using this book would be primarily for dyeing, something for which they are much used in northern countries throughout the world. Some forty or fifty kinds give dyes of lovely soft color, such as seen in the Harris tweeds, with the bright moss-like lichens on stones giving better colors than others. Some species provide forage for deer and other animals in northern climes, or at times emergency food for humans. There is some considerable evidence to indicate that the "manna" of the Bible was a form of lichen, which is still eaten by some desert tribes, and which, when blown loose from its mountain habitat, will roll into the valleys just as the Bible story indicates.

In the United States about the only generally edible form would be *Cetraria* or Iceland moss which contains a large amount of starchy matter called lichenin which is soluble in boiling water and which gelatinizes on cooling. Eating this is said to improve appetite and digestion.

Cetraria islandica

Nature-lovers will find much of interest in watching for, and studying this interesting family which, as said, falls between the primitive alga and the fungus. Photography of beautiful specimens could be rewarding, and the uses of some forms for such things as Christmas table decorations could provide "conversation pieces."

More and more is being learned of the medicinal values of various lichens as scientists follow up the values of such things as penicillium. One writer says that there is in some lichens "characteristic activity in antibiotic tests with suitable bacteria" and in time we may find qualities in lichens not now known. Among knowing "country folk" the Iceland moss (*Cetraria*) is said to improve digestion and appetite, relieve coughing, and to be of some value in catarrh and bronchitis.

Cladonia sp.

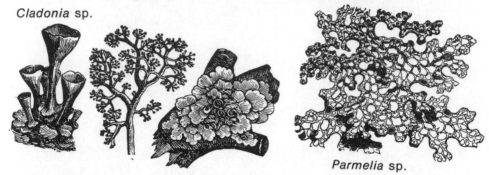

Parmelia sp.

Among the more ordinary of the lichens which have been given common names one finds:

ROCK TRIPE—*Alectoria*
REINDEER MOSS—*Cladonia*
BEARD LICHEN—*Usnea*
SULPHUR LICHEN—*Parmelia*
ICELAND MOSS—*Cetraria*
TREE LUNGWORT—*Sticta*

Those readers who might wish to read further on this subject are directed to a pamphlet published by the Smithsonian Institution called *Economic Uses of Lichens* by George Llano (No. 4040–1951).

EDIBLE FUNGI

In speaking of "edible fungi" it would be better perhaps to talk of "mushrooms," and to classify all other fungi under "toadstools." This is a sort of popular classification which came into being when the French gourmets introduced "champignons" into England, where, for untold centuries, anything of the nature and habits of a fungus was called by a derisive folkloric name of toadstool. Not that the common use of tasty and completely edible mushrooms is still as popular among English speaking people as it is with most of the eastern Europeans. There are still countless Americans who think that *any* plant which grows as a wild mushroom is automatically something poisonous. In addition there is the heritage of belief that, although it "grows," it still does not appear green, as are the flowering plants of the world.

Unfortunately there is not room in this discussion to tell about a special group of fungi called the hallucinogens, which when eaten cause hallucinations and mystic sights. They have been used for possibly many millenia for religious observances, and were known in ancient literature as the "soma." Such uses have been confirmed as being practiced today in Mexico by R. Gordon Wasson, while a noted writer, John Allegro, has suggested in his book, *The Sacred Mushroom,* that the story of Christ was invented by a Jewish sect to cover up their use of hallucinogenic mushrooms. In many early societies the very likely connection which the ordinarily umbrella-shaped mushroom has with an object perpetuated in many religious depictions as the phallus, again brings out the importance of fungi as more than just something to eat. Much has been written on these phases of the use of fungi, some of it extremely well researched and doubtlessly authentic, and some of it based upon linguistic variations, whose correctness is doubted by many.

However, the concern here is mostly with mushrooms as a gustatory addition to the dinner table—and even here the notice must be minor. For the truth is that in addition to some 55,000 species of microscopic fungal organisms (such as penicillium) there are classified an estimated 30,000 species of the larger fungi which are, in the English language, known commonly as mushrooms. Probably the reader has not noticed so many, but one authority claims that within a radius of 20 miles of almost any spot in the United States there could be found, in the course of a year, as many as 1,000 kinds or more.

Thus it is that the author of this book would recommend that every reader interest himself in this great family and learn that there are many more edible forms than the fine commercially-grown ones found in the supermarket. Of the best to use from the wild are the large puffballs found in late summer; the little ink-caps found on tree stumps; the interestingly tree-shaped morels, and a number of others.

In the course of such study one would learn easily to identify the few bad members of the fungus family such as the deadly *Amanita,* and certain others less potent but quite inedible. One would refer to some of those books listed in the bibliography.

As hinted earlier, there are a number (a minimal number) which are indeed poisonous and even death-dealing, such as the *Amanita.* How does one acquire the proper knowledge? First of all, one can eat only those kinds sold in the markets fresh or canned, or buy the dried ones which likely may have come from Europe. Secondly, one can learn to identify the easily recognizable eatable kinds, and here it seems to be a good thing to learn by being told by a friend who has eaten them, which kinds are safe and at hand. Thirdly, one should do a little studying to learn the typical forms of the bad kinds, especially of the *Amanita,* of which more below.

And one must come to know also that many of the very best edible kinds are not necessarily in the stalked, round-capped shape which says "mushroom" so commonly. The Boletus, the puffballs, the coral fungi, and bracket type are all quite different in habit and many of them good.

For the beginner botanist it is well to note that (of some 3,000 species which grow in the United States) these are "flowerless" plants which grow from tiny spores, largely underground or in old dead plant growth. To fruit and produce seeds (spores) they throw up fruiting bodies which are called mushrooms, toadstools, or what have you. They are always without green leaves, although not necessarily white or colorless, for some of the most interesting and beautiful forms are in reds, browns, or gray.

Picking out now a few of the common and most edible of the mushrooms, a few words about recognizing, picking, and eating them are needed. Of special interest here is the fact, as noted, that we in America are basically afraid of eating mushrooms, whereas in Russia and related countries, they are looked on with great respect and highly prized as choice eating.

Amanita muscaria—Fly amanita, fly agaric, deadly amanita, fly killer. This species and several similar ones are found in both the East and West, and all contain poisonous principles, some more deadly than others. Basically to be noticed is the bulbous nature of the bottom of the stem and a "skirt" which grows just above the ground. It is the basic similarity of this mushroom to the edible ones which makes it important that gatherers of mushrooms learn carefully to differentiate the good from the bad.

Agaricus campestris—The field mushroom.

This particular species is actually the cultivated one, but a native form is *A. arvensis,* plus some other species, which while not poisonous, are not notable as food material. One interesting species grows as a "fairy ring" and invades lawns (to their detriment), but makes a good addition to the table.

In gathering any of the *Agaricus* group, the cap or top of the mushroom should be white or pinkish with a texture like a kid glove with the "gills" underneath pinkish (best) or white. The stem should be white and solid with a ring or frill near the top.

Agaricus campestris

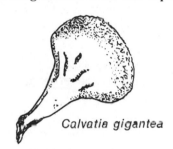

Calvatia gigantea

Calvatia gigantea—Puffball, giant puffball.

It should be noted that this species and the following one are both called puffball and are quite similar except in size. When this puffball appears in late summer just after a warm rain, it should be gathered when big and still hard and white inside, and then sliced and fried in butter.

It is interesting that the values of this puffball were well known to our Indians, for, beyond use as food, the dried spores of a developed puffball were known as an excellent styptic or haemostat, and it is so also known in Japan. Correspondents have told the author of the value of these spores to stop nose bleeds, while a century ago, before electric flash bulbs, the "powder" was used as a photographic flash powder.

A further item of interest is that some research has been done on the chemical principle in these puffballs as a possible source of a cure for certain kinds of cancer.

From all the above the puffballs should be more highly regarded than just as a "football" for children to kick around when found.

Coprinus micaceus—Inky mushroom, glistening coprinus, ink-cap.
This is the quite tiny mushroom which grows up from the roots
of a dead elm (of which there are many around these days) and
old stumps of other trees. There is another species again commonly known as the inkcap, *(C. stramentarius)* which will be found
on old manure heaps, on rubbish, or rich fields. These are
delightful to use when just up and whitish in color, but even then
when cooked they will make a blackish stew. One author suggests they are best when baked, and that by adding dried bread
crumbs, the juice will be absorbed and make the dish more tasty.

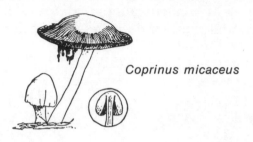

Coprinus micaceus

Lycoperdon cyathiforme—Puffball and smoke balls; devil's snuffbox.
This is the other genus of mushrooms which grows about base-
ball size in fields and on lawns and of this there are several other
species such as *L. pyriforme* and *L. gemmatum* which grow on
rotted wood and, with the last one, smallish on lawns. These all
have the millions of tiny spores which, when dried, are so good
for stopping blood flow. The powder smoked carefully has also
been used as a narcotic to stupefy bees when taking honey.

Finally and in a comment from a reader of *Using Wayside Plants,*
comes the statistic that with any large puffball it has been estimated that inside it when dried, there may be "7,500 billion
spores and that if each of these grew into a similar ball down to
the second generation, a fungus colony of 800 times the size of
the earth would be formed." So, watch out, Earth, here come the
puffballs!

Morchella **(various species)**—Morel.
This is one of the most interesting appearing of mushrooms,
looking somewhat like a sponge growing on a stick. By those
who are specialists in the field, this is considered the most tasty
of mushrooms. They are not too commonly found and they
grow in rich woods or in orchards and usually in half-shade.

The stem is inseparable from the top and they may be stuffed and baked or cooked and served with butter with the juice used as a sauce. If you find them, use them.

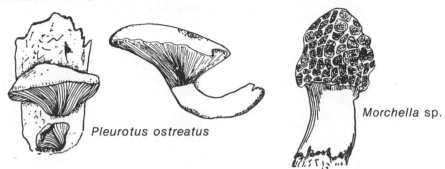

Pleurotus ostreatus

Morchella sp.

Pleurotus ostreatus—Oyster mushroom.

One writer has called this fungi "devourers of the forest" for they grow only on dead trees—especially elms, poplars, aspens, and cottonwoods. There are actually several species quite alike. They grow as sort of a bracket and if taken when they are fresh, firm, and pale, these "oysters" of the woods are quite edible, though not as tender as others above. They are to be soaked briefly in salt water, drained on towels, dipped in egg batter, and fried in butter.

Here have been discussed just a few of the more common and more usable species, but it must be observed that with the 3,000 species known in this country, there are a great number which are non-poisonous and edible, if not tasty. This is the job of the specialist, but everyone loving the outdoors should attempt to know the best usable mushrooms as well as the poisonous, for the benefit of himself and his friends.

And, now, in conclusion, a bit of poetry from a friend, a noted mycologist, George S. Coffin, who in a "six-liner" called "Cooking Mushrooms," says this:

> Cook your mushrooms the slow heat way,
>   Don't overcook, the chefs all say.
> I could all day quote recipe
>   Easiest way, butter sauté.
> Cook gill sides up, then turn in pan.
>   Cook up a fungus, eat well among us.
>   *and finally*
> Of the mushrooms which you know not,
>   Put them never in your pot.

Check your pickings with an expert
For if you heed not this alert,
And take a wild chance on a fungus
You'll soon be missing from among us.

THE SEAWEEDS
ALGAE

In the world of plants there are a vast number of plants which are grouped together as algae, but for the purpose of this assessment we are discussing those which are commonly called seaweeds. It must be understood that they are not "weeds" in the common sense of that term (a plant of no value), since the great number of genera of algae are highly useful.

Again in considering the seaweeds it is quite impossible to explore all the many uses of these plants of the ocean waters. The author can only simply suggest that all interested in useful plants (and especially the countless thousands who live along the many miles of United States coastline) should take time to explore what can be done with the flora of the marine floor. Indeed, though not within the scope of this book, one could explore the possible future uses of common green *fresh-water* algae which may well, in future times, be a main source of food. The scum of green algae has been used as food by primitive people in Africa and among the Aztecs of Mexico, and now eminent scientists are exploring how "flour" of great nutritional value can be made from these simple plant forms. Our American Indians knew something of such values also, in that where they lived in coastal areas they ate the sea lettuce *(Ulva lactuca)* which was a green seaweed, where it formed not only a condiment or seasoning, but also was an important source of salt in their diet.

Such knowledge of algae was widespread, going back to the earliest medical practices of the Chinese (possibly 5,000 years ago) when seaweeds were used for the treatment of goiter (iodine treatment), with some species being used for bronchitis, abscesses, intestinal troubles, etc. Nor can one ignore the known values placed on various seaweeds by Egyptians, Greeks, and Romans and other peoples where, indeed, one species of *Fucus* was a source of face-paint for the ladies.

Thus it is that all interested in "natural foods" and plant uses and who live near the sea should explore intensively the many values of sea plants. Beyond the commonly known uses for puddings (see *Using Wayside Plants*), Irish moss is used industrially in ice cream, cheese pies, jellies, and candy, as well as in the packaging of meat and fish. When shopping one will often note the term of alginate, alginic acid, or carrageenin as part of the contents. Or one can go to such seaside cities as Boston and find in the markets the dried seaweed known as dulse, while those who like to eat Japanese food will find seaweeds as part of choice menus. Actually, the production of the extraction from seaweeds called "alginate" is a big business on the West Coast with huge harvesting machines used to gather the kelp of that region, which is the largest size of any in the world.

Thinking of pure medicinal values of seaweed, we know that from such products found in the ocean come iodine, laxatives, and cough syrups, while exploration is presently going on for possible use of seaweeds as antibiotics and anti-bacterial agents. Carrageenin is a possible source of growth stimulant for connective tissue and other kinds of algae are used as anti-blood-clotting agents.

In the industrial field, experiments are going on to make artificial silks and wools from seaweeds—it is used for sizings, in printing inks, and somewhat for dyes. Some species are being looked at as a source of fuel when dried, and certainly all gardeners who live by the sea know the value of seaweeds as a mulch or for assistance in composting.

One could go on to note the industrial production of alginate in Scotland; the extensive harvesting of Irish moss in Scituate, Massachusetts, and other less than major enterprises all over the world. With the supply of world food sources for the expanding population, and especially of fish, decreasing, countries such as the United States and Russia are cooperating in research. Many natural products are found to be better than those from the chemical laboratory, and great things are looked for from the world of seaweeds.

Considering all the facts about the values of the "vegetables from the sea," an article in the magazine *Good Food* (February 1974) notes that:

> The characteristic of sea vegetables that probably fascinates scientists and food economists most of all is the potential size of the harvest. Sea plants can grow both taller and closer together than land vegetables, and for those reasons alone the yield per acre might be far bigger than anything a land farmer can hope for. . . . Sea minerals are rich in

minerals and trace elements and are also good sources of
vitamins. . . .

For readers wishing to explore this subject more carefully, attention is directed to an exhaustive bibliography on seaweeds and their
uses issued by the Nova Scotia Research Foundation in Halifax, N.S.,
Canada, and to a more recent work by Dr. Tore Leving. Or for an
intensely interesting history and complete story of useful algae, the
reader is directed to pages 401–460 of the 1941 Report of the Smithsonian Institution.

Just a few among the kinds of seaweed plants mentioned in that
essay and presently of value are these:

CHONDRUS CRISPUS—Irish moss.

PORPHYRA—Laver.

RHODYMENIA PALMATA—Dulse.

GIGARTINA STELLATA—With values similar to *Chondrus.*

FUCUS VESICULOSUS—Bladderwrack.

ASCOPHYLLIOUS NODOSUM—Another form similar to bladderwrack.
This species and the one above *(Fucus)* are both principal sources of
the economically important alginate.

MACROCYSTIS PYRIFERA—Giant kelp.

For the ordinary nature-lover, some of the uses of seaweed may be
out-of-range, but just as a sample of what the seashore hunter can do
with any Irish moss found in beachcombing, here is a recipe from
a Boston paper, which is similar to the one used in my home.

Sea-Moss Pudding

*After gathering the sea-moss, it is washed thoroughly until the
sand is out, then spread out and dried. Then to one quart of
milk a piece of the dried moss (about the size of a golf ball) is
added, along with three tablespoons of sugar and a pinch of
salt. Cook together for a half hour in a double boiler, strain,
and allow to cool, adding vanilla for flavor when half solid.
Other flavorings can, of course, be added as desired.*

Further suggestions are that when still warm, the "pudding" can
be taken as a drink good for raspy throats or, as one book has it, "for
the lungs." Again, the extracted gelatinous material can be a fine
kitchen remedy for burns and bruises, or as a hand lotion.

Index

Plants are indexed under both common and botanical names.
Page numbers in italics refer to illustrations.